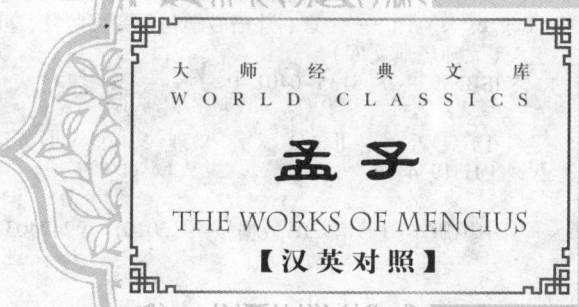

大 师 经 典 文 库
WORLD CLASSICS

孟 子
THE WORKS OF MENCIUS
【汉英对照】

○ 孟子 著

○ [英] James Legge 译

外语教学与研究出版社
FOREIGN LANGUAGE TEACHING AND RESEARCH PRESS
北京 BEIJING

图书在版编目(CIP)数据

孟子 = The Works of Mencius: 汉英对照/(战国)孟轲著;(英)理雅各 (Legge, J.)译. — 北京: 外语教学与研究出版社, 2010.12
(大师经典文库)
ISBN 978-7-5135-0401-0

Ⅰ.①孟… Ⅱ.①孟… ②理… Ⅲ.①英语—汉语—对照读物
Ⅳ.①H319.4:B

中国版本图书馆 CIP 数据核字 (2010) 第 247403 号

出 版 人: 于春迟
责任编辑: 周 晶
封面设计: 牛茜茜
出版发行: 外语教学与研究出版社
社 址: 北京市西三环北路 19 号 (100089)
网 址: http://www.fltrp.com
印 刷: 北京市鑫霸印务有限公司
开 本: 850×1168 1/32
印 张: 9.25
版 次: 2011 年 1 月第 1 版 2011 年 1 月第 1 次印刷
书 号: ISBN 978-7-5135-0401-0
定 价: 19.90 元
* * *
购书咨询: (010)88819929 电子邮箱: club@fltrp.com
如有印刷、装订质量问题, 请与出版社联系
联系电话: (010)61207896 电子邮箱: zhijian@fltrp.com
制售盗版必究 举报查实奖励
版权保护办公室举报电话: (010)88817519
物料号: 204010001

目 录
CONTENTS

1 　　卷一　　　梁惠王章句上
　　　　BOOK I　　King Hui of Liang　Part I

20 　卷二　　　梁惠王章句下
　　　　BOOK II　　King Hui of Liang　Part II

44 　卷三　　　公孙丑章句上
　　　　BOOK III　　Gongsun Chou　Part I

65 　卷四　　　公孙丑章句下
　　　　BOOK IV　　Gongsun Chou　Part II

85 　卷五　　　滕文公章句上
　　　　BOOK V　　Teng Wen Gong　Part I

105 　卷六　　　滕文公章句下
　　　　BOOK VI　　Teng Wen Gong　Part II

125 　卷七　　　离娄章句上
　　　　BOOK VII　　Li Lou　Part I

146   卷八   离娄章句下
       BOOK VIII   Li Lou   Part II

166   卷九   万章章句上
       BOOK IX   Wan Zhang   Part I

186   卷十   万章章句下
       BOOK X   Wan Zhang   Part II

206   卷十一   告子章句上
       BOOK XI   Gao Zi   Part I

226   卷十二   告子章句下
       BOOK XII   Gao Zi   Part II

247   卷十三   尽心章句上
       BOOK XIII   Jin Xin   Part I

270   卷十四   尽心章句下
       BOOK XIV   Jin Xin   Part II

卷一　梁惠王章句上

BOOK I　KING HUI OF LIANG　PART I

1.1　孟子见梁惠王。王曰："叟！不远千里而来，亦将有以利吾国乎？"孟子对曰："王何必曰利？亦有仁义而已矣。王曰：'何以利吾国？'大夫曰：'何以利吾家？'士庶人曰：'何以利吾身？'上下交征利而国危矣。万乘之国，弑其君者，必千乘之家；千乘之国，弑其君者，必百乘之家。万取千焉，千取百焉，不为不多矣。苟为后义而先利，不夺不餍。未有仁而遗其亲者也，未有义而后其君者也。王亦曰仁义而已矣，何必曰利？"

1.1　Mencius *went to* see King Hui of Liang. The king said, "Venerable sir, since you have not counted it far to come here, a distance of a thousand *li*, may I presume that you are likewise provided with counsels to profit my kingdom?" Mencius replied, "Why must Your Majesty use that word 'profit'? What I am 'likewise' provided with, are counsels to benevolence and righteousness, and these are my only topics. If Your Majesty say, 'What is to be done to profit my kingdom?' the great officers will say, 'What is to be done to profit our families?' and the inferior officers and the common people will say, 'What is to be done to profit our persons?' Superiors and inferiors will try to snatch this profit the one from the other, and the kingdom will be endangered. In the kingdom of ten thousand chariots, the murderer of his sovereign shall be *the chief of* a family of a thousand chariots. In the kingdom of a thousand chariots, the murderer of his prince shall be *the chief of* a family of a hundred chariots. To have a thousand in ten thousand, and a hundred in a thousand, cannot be said not to be a large allotment, but if righteousness be put last, and profit be put first, they will not be satisfied without snatching *all*. There never has been a man trained to benevolence who neglected his parents. There never has been a man trained to righteousness who made his sovereign an after consideration. Let Your Majesty also talk about benevolence and righteousness, and these shall be the only themes. Why must you use that word 'profit'?"

1.2　孟子见梁惠王。王立于沼上，顾鸿雁麋鹿，曰："贤者亦乐此乎？"孟子对曰："贤者而后乐此，不贤者虽有此，不乐也。《诗》云：'经始灵台，经之营之，庶民攻之，不日成之。经始勿亟，庶民子来。王在灵圃，麀鹿攸伏，麀鹿濯濯，白鸟鹤鹤。王在灵沼，於牣鱼跃。'文王以民力为台为沼，而民欢乐之，谓其台曰灵台，谓其沼曰灵沼，乐其有麋鹿鱼鳖。古之人与民偕乐，故能乐也。《汤誓》曰：'时日害丧，予及女偕亡！'民欲与之偕亡，虽有台池鸟兽，岂能独乐哉？"

1.2 Mencius, *another day*, saw King Hui of Liang. The king *went and* stood *with him* by a pond, and, looking round at the large geese and deer, said, "Do wise and good *princes* also find pleasure in these things?" Mencius replied: "Being wise and good, they have pleasure in these things. If they are not wise and good, though they have these things, they do not find pleasure. It is said in the *Book of Poetry*, 'He measured out and commenced his spirit-tower; he measured it out and planned it. The people addressed themselves to it, and in less than a day completed it. When he measured and began it, *he said to them* — Be not so earnest. But the multitudes came as if they had been his children. The king was in his spirit-park; the does reposed about, the does so sleek and fat; and the white birds shone glistening. The king was by his spirit-pond; how full was it of fishes leaping about!' King Wen used the strength of the people to make his tower and his pond, and yet the people rejoiced to do the work, calling the tower 'the spirit-tower', calling the pond 'the spirit-pond', and rejoicing that he had his large deer, his fishes, and turtles. The ancients caused the people to have pleasure as well as themselves, and therefore they could enjoy it. In the *Declaration of Tang* it is said, 'O sun, when wilt thou expire? We will die together with thee.' The people wished *for Jie's death*, though they should die with him. Although he had towers, ponds, birds, and animals, how could he have pleasure alone?"

1.3 梁惠王曰："寡人之于国也，尽心焉耳矣。河内凶，则移其民于河东，移其粟于河内。河东凶亦然。察邻国之政，无如寡人之用心者。邻国之民不加少，寡人之民不加多，何也？"
孟子对曰："王好战，请以战喻。填然鼓之，兵刃既接，弃甲曳兵而走。或百步而后止，或五十步而后止。以五十步笑百步，则何如？"曰："不可；直不百步耳，是亦走也。"曰："王如知此，则无望民之多于邻国也。不违农时，谷不可胜食也；数罟不入洿池，鱼鳖不可胜食也；斧斤以时入山林，材木不可胜用也。谷与鱼鳖不可胜食，材木不可胜用，是使民养生丧死无憾也。养生丧死无憾，王道之始也。五亩之宅，树之以桑，五十者可以衣帛矣。鸡豚狗彘之畜，无失其时，七十者可以食肉矣。百亩之田，勿夺其时，数口之家可以无饥矣。谨庠序之教，申之以孝悌之义，颁白者不负戴于道路矣。七十者衣帛食肉，黎民不饥不寒，然而不王者，未之有也。狗彘食人食而不知检，涂有饿莩而不知发；人死，则曰：'非我也，岁也。'是何异于刺人而杀之，曰，'非我也，兵也。'王无罪岁，斯天下之民至焉。"

1.3   King Hui of Liang said, "Small as my virtue is, in the government of my kingdom, I do indeed exert my mind to the utmost. If the year be bad on the inside of the river, I remove *as many of* the people *as I can* to the east of the river, and convey grain to the country in the inside. When the year is bad on the east of the river, I act on the same plan. On examining the government of the neighboring kingdoms, I do not find that there is any prince who employs his mind as I do. And yet the people of the neighboring kingdoms do not decrease, nor do my people increase. How is this?" Mencius replied, "Your Majesty is fond of war, — let me take an illustration from war. — *The soldiers move forward to* the sound of the drums; and after their weapons have been crossed, *on one side* they throw away their coats of mail, trail their arms behind them, and run. Some run a hundred paces and stop, some run fifty paces and stop. What would you think if those who run fifty paces were to laugh at those who run a hundred paces?" The king said, "They may not do so. They only did not run a hundred paces, but they also ran away." Mencius replied, "Since Your Majesty knows this, you need not hope that your people will become more numerous than those of the neighboring kingdoms. If the seasons of husbandry be not interfered with, the grain will be more than can be eaten. If close nets are not allowed to enter the pools and ponds, the fishes and turtles will be more than can be consumed. If the axes and bills enter the hills and forests *only* at the proper time, the wood will be more than can be used. When the grain and fish and turtles are more than can be eaten, and there is more wood than can be used, this enables the people to nourish their living and bury their dead, without any feeling against any. This condition, in which the people nourish their living and bury their dead without any feeling against any, is the first step of Royal Government. Let mulberry trees be planted about the homesteads with their five *mu*, and persons of fifty years may be clothed with silk. In keeping fowls, pigs, dogs, and swine, let not their times of *breeding* be neglected, and persons of seventy years may eat flesh. Let there not be taken away the time that is proper for the cultivation of the farm with its hundred *mu*, and the family of several mouths that is supported by it shall not suffer from hunger. Let careful attention be paid to education in schools, inculcating in it especially the filial and fraternal duties, and grey-haired men will not be seen upon the roads, carrying burdens on their backs or on their heads. It never has been that the ruler of a state, where such results were seen, — persons of seventy wearing silk and eating flesh, and the black-haired people suffering neither from hunger nor cold, — did not attain to the Imperial dignity. Your dogs and swine eat the food of men, and you do not know to make any restrictive arrangements. There are people dying from famine on the roads, and you do not know to issue the *stores of your granaries* for them. When people die, you say, 'It is not owing to me; it is owing to the year.' In what does this differ from stabbing a man and killing him, and then saying — 'It was not I; it was the weapon.' Let Your Majesty cease to lay the blame on the year, and instantly from all the empire the people will come to you."

1.4　梁惠王曰:"寡人愿安承教。"孟子对曰:"杀人以梃与刃,有以异乎?"曰:"无以异也。""以刃与政,有以异乎?"曰:"无以异也。"曰:"庖有肥肉,厩有肥马,民有饥色,野有饿莩,此率兽而食人也。兽相食,且人恶之;为民父母,行政,不免于率兽而食人,恶在其为民父母也?仲尼曰:'始作俑者,其无后乎!'为其象人而用之也。如之何其使斯民饥而死也?"

1.4　King Hui of Liang said: "I wish quietly to receive your instructions." Mencius replied, "Is there any difference between killing a man with a stick and with a sword?" *The king* said: "There is no difference." "Is there any difference between doing it with a sword and with *the style of* government?" The king's reply was: "There is no difference." *Mencius* said: "In your kitchen there is fat meat; in your stables there are fat horses. *But* your people have the look of hunger, and on the wilds there are those who have died of famine. This is leading on beasts to devour men. Beasts devour one another, and men hate them *for doing so*. When *a prince*, being the parent of his people, administers his government so as to be chargeable with leading on beasts to devour men, where is that parental relation to the people? Zhongni said: 'Was he not without posterity who first made wooden images *to bury with the dead*?' *So he said*, because that man made the semblances of men, and used them *for that purpose*. — What shall be thought of him who causes his people to die of hunger?"

1.5　梁惠王曰："晋国，天下莫强焉，叟之所知也。及寡人之身，东败于齐，长子死焉；西丧地于秦七百里；南辱于楚。寡人耻之，愿比死者壹洒之，如之何则可？"孟子对曰："地方百里而可以王。王如施仁政于民，省刑罚，薄税敛，深耕易耨；壮者以暇日修其孝悌忠信，入以事其父兄，出以事其长上，可使制梃以挞秦楚之坚甲利兵矣。彼夺其民时，使不得耕耨以养其父母。父母冻饿，兄弟妻子离散。彼陷溺其民，王往而征之，夫谁与王敌？故曰：'仁者无敌。'王请勿疑！"

1.5　King Hui of Liang said: "There was not in the empire a stronger state than Jin, as you, venerable sir, know. But since it descended to me, on the east we have been defeated by Qi, and then my eldest son perished; on the west we have lost seven hundred *li* of territory to Qin; and on the south we have sustained disgrace at the hands of Chu. I have brought shame on my departed predecessors, and wish on their account to wipe it away, once for all. What course is to be pursued to accomplish this?" Mencius replied: "With a territory which is only a hundred *li* square, it is possible to attain the Imperial dignity. If Your Majesty will *indeed* dispense a benevolent government to the people, being sparing in the use of punishments and fines, and making the taxes and levies light, so causing that the fields shall be ploughed deep, and the weeding of them be carefully attended to, and that the strong-bodied, during their days of leisure, shall cultivate their filial piety, fraternal respectfulness, sincerity, and truthfulness, serving thereby, at home, their fathers and elder brothers, and, abroad, their elders and superiors — you will then have a people who can be employed, with sticks which they have prepared, to oppose the strong mail and sharp weapons of the troops of Qin and Chu. *The rulers of those states*, rob their people of their time, so that they cannot plough and weed their fields, in order to support their parents. Their parents suffer from cold and hunger. Brothers, wives, and children, are separated and scattered abroad. Those *rulers, as it were*, drive their people into pit-falls, or drown them. Your Majesty will go to punish them. In such a case, who will oppose Your Majesty? In accordance with this is the saying, 'The benevolent has no enemy.' I beg Your Majesty not to doubt *what I say*."

1.6 　孟子见梁襄王，出，语人曰：“望之不似人君，就之而不见所畏焉。卒然问曰：‘天下恶乎定？’吾对曰：‘定于一。’‘孰能一之？’对曰：‘不嗜杀人者能一之。’‘孰能与之？’对曰：‘天下莫不与也。王知夫苗乎？七八月之间旱，则苗槁矣。天油然作云，沛然下雨，则苗浡然兴之矣。其如是，孰能御之？今夫天下之人牧，未有不嗜杀人者也。如有不嗜杀人者，则天下之民皆引领而望之矣。诚如是也，民归之，由水之就下，沛然谁能御之？’”

1.6　Mencius went to see the king Xiang of Liang. On coming out *from the interview*, he said to some persons: "When I looked at him from a distance, he did not appear like a sovereign; when I drew near to him, I saw nothing venerable about him. Abruptly he asked me: 'How can the empire be settled?' I replied, 'It will be settled by being united under one sway.' 'Who can so unite it?' I replied: 'He who has no pleasure in killing men can so unite it.' 'Who can give it to him?' I replied: 'All the people of the empire will unanimously give it to him. Does Your Majesty understand the way of the growing grain? During the seventh and the eighth months, when drought prevails, the plants become dry. Then the clouds collect densely in the heavens, they send down torrents of rain, and the grain erects itself, as if by a shoot. When it does so, who can keep it back? Now among the shepherds of men throughout the empire, there is not one who does not find pleasure in killing men. If there were one who did not find pleasure in killing men, all the people in the empire would look towards him with outstretched necks. Such being indeed the case, the people would flock to him, as water flows downwards with a rush, which no one can repress.'"

1.7　齐宣王问曰:"齐桓、晋文之事可得闻乎?"孟子对曰:"仲尼之徒无道桓、文之事者,是以后世无传焉,臣未之闻也。无以,则王乎?"曰:"德何如则可以王矣?"曰:"保民而王,莫之能御也。"曰:"若寡人者,可以保民乎哉?"曰:"可。"曰:"何由知吾可也?"曰:"臣闻之胡龁曰,王坐于堂上,有牵牛而过堂下者,王见之,曰:'牛何之?'对曰:'将以衅钟。'王曰:'舍之!吾不忍其觳觫,若无罪而就死地。'对曰:'然则废衅钟与?'曰:'何可废也?以羊易之!'不识有诸?"曰:"有之。"曰:"是心足以王矣。百姓皆以王为爱也,臣固知王之不忍也。"王曰:"然。诚有百姓者。齐国虽褊小,吾何爱一牛?即不忍其觳觫,若无罪而就死地,故以羊易之也。"曰:"王无异于百姓之以王为爱也。以小易大,彼恶知之?王若隐其无罪而就死地,则牛羊何择焉?"王笑曰:"是诚何心哉?我非爱其财而易之以羊也。宜乎百姓之谓我爱也。"曰:"无伤也,是乃仁术也,见牛未见羊也。君子之于禽兽也,见其生,不忍见其死;闻其声,不忍食其肉。是以君子远庖厨也。"王说曰:"《诗》云:'他人有心,予忖度之。'夫子之谓也。夫我乃行之,反而求之,不得吾心。夫子言之,于我心有戚戚焉。此心之所以合于王者,何也?"曰:"有复于王者曰:'吾力足以举百钧,而不足以举一羽;明足以察秋毫之末，而不见舆薪，则王许之乎？"曰："否。""今恩足以及禽兽，而功不至于百姓者，独何与？然则一羽之不举，为不用力焉；舆薪之不见，为不用明焉；百姓之不见保，为不用恩焉。故王之不王，不为也，非不能也。"曰："不为者与不能者之形何以异？"曰："挟太山以超北海，语人曰：'我不能。'是诚不能也。为长者折枝，语人曰：'我不能。'是不为也，非不能也。故王之不王，非挟太山以超北海之类也；王之不王，是折枝之类也。老吾老，以及人之老；幼吾幼，以及人之幼。天下可运于掌。《诗》云：'刑于寡妻，至于兄弟，以御于家邦。'言举斯心加诸彼而已。故推恩足以保四海，不推恩无以保妻子。古之人所以大过人者，无他焉，善推其所为而已矣。今恩足以及禽兽，而功不至于百姓者，独何与？权，然后知轻重；度，然后知长短。物皆然，心为甚。王请度之！抑王兴甲兵，危士臣，构怨于诸侯，然后快于心与？"王曰："否，吾何快于是？将以求吾所大欲也。"曰："王之所大欲可得闻与？"王笑而不言。

曰："为肥甘不足于口与？轻暖不足于体与？抑为采色不足视于目与？声音不足听于耳与？便嬖不足使令于前与？王之诸臣皆足以供之，而王岂为是哉？"曰："否。吾不为是也。"曰："然则王之所大欲可知已，欲辟土地，朝秦楚，莅中国而抚四夷也。以若所为求若所欲，犹缘木而求鱼也。"王曰："若是其甚与？"曰："殆有甚焉。缘木求鱼，虽不得鱼，无后灾。以若所为求若所欲，尽心力而为之，后必有灾。"曰："可得闻与？"

曰：“邹人与楚人战，则王以为孰胜？”曰：“楚人胜。”曰：“然则小固不可以敌大，寡固不可以敌众，弱固不可以敌强。海内之地方千里者九，齐集有其一。以一服八，何以异于邹敌楚哉？盖亦反其本矣。今王发政施仁，使天下仕者皆欲立于王之朝，耕者皆欲耕于王之野，商贾皆欲藏于王之市，行旅皆欲出于王之涂，天下之欲疾其君者皆欲赴愬于王。其若是，孰能御之？”

王曰：“吾惛，不能进于是矣。愿夫子辅吾志，明以教我。我虽不敏，请尝试之。”曰：“无恒产而有恒心者，惟士为能。若民，则无恒产，因无恒心。苟无恒心，放辟邪侈，无不为已。及陷于罪，然后从而刑之，是罔民也。焉有仁人在位罔民而可为也？是故明君制民之产，必使仰足以事父母，俯足以畜妻子，乐岁终身饱，凶年免于死亡；然后驱而之善，故民之从之也轻。今也制民之产，仰不足以事父母，俯不足以畜妻子；乐岁终身苦，凶年不免于死亡。此惟救死而恐不赡，奚暇治礼义哉？王欲行之，则盍反其本矣：五亩之宅，树之以桑，五十者可以衣帛矣。鸡豚狗彘之畜，无失其时，七十者可以食肉矣。百亩之田，勿夺其时，八口之家可以无饥矣。谨庠序之教，申之以孝悌之义，颁白者不负戴于道路矣。老者衣帛食肉，黎民不饥不寒，然而不王者，未之有也。”

1.7 The king Xuan of Qi asked: "May I be informed by you of the transactions of Huan of Qi and Wen of Jin?" Mencius replied: "There were none of the disciples of Zhongni who spoke about the affairs of Huan and Wen, and therefore they have not been transmitted to these after ages; — your servant has not heard them. If you will have me speak, let it be about Imperial government." The king said, "What virtue must there be in order to the attainment of Imperial sway?" Mencius answered: "The love and protection of the people; with this there is no power which can prevent a ruler from attaining it." *The king* asked again: "Is such an one as I competent to love and protect the people?" *Mencius* said, "Yes." The king said: "From what do you know that I am competent for that?" Mencius replied: "I heard the following incident from Hu He, he said: 'The king was sitting aloft in the hall, when a man appeared, leading an ox past the lower part of it. The king saw him, and asked, "Where is the ox going?" The man replied, "We are going to consecrate a bell with its blood." The king said, "Let it go. I cannot bear its frightened appearance, as if it were an innocent person, going to the place of death." The man answered, "Shall we then omit the consecration of the bell?" *The king* said: "How can that be omitted? Change it for a sheep." ' I do not know whether this incident really occurred." *The king* replied, "It did." *Then Mencius* said, "The heart seen in this is sufficient to carry you to the Imperial sway. The people all supposed that Your Majesty grudged *the animal*, but your servant knows surely, that it was Your Majesty's not being able to bear *the sight, which made you do as you did." The king* said, "You are right. And yet there really was an appearance of what the people condemned. But though Qi be a small and narrow state, how should I grudge one ox. Indeed it was because I could not bear its frightened appearance, as if it were an innocent person going to the place of death, that therefore I changed it for a sheep." *Mencius* pursued, "Let not Your Majesty deem it strange that the people should think you were grudging *the animal*. When you changed a large one for a small, how should they know the *true reason*? If you felt pained by its being led without guilt to the place of death, what was there to choose between an ox and a sheep?" The king laughed and said, "What really was my mind in the matter? I did not grudge the expense of it, and changed it for a sheep! — There was reason in the people's saying that I grudged it." "There is no harm *in their saying so*," said *Mencius*, "Your conduct was an artifice of benevolence. You saw the ox, and had not seen the sheep. So is the superior man affected towards animals, that, having seen them alive, he cannot bear to see them die; having heard their dying cries, he cannot bear to eat their flesh. Therefore he keeps away from his cook-room." The king was pleased, and said, "It is said in the *Book of Poetry*, 'The minds of others, I am able by reflection to measure;' — this is verified, my Master, in your discovery of my motive. I indeed did the thing, but when I turned my thoughts inward, and examined into it, I could not discover my own mind. When you, Master, spoke those words, the movements of compassion began to work in my mind. How is it that this heart has in it what is equal to the Imperial sway?" *Mencius* replied, "Suppose a man were to make this statement to Your Majesty: — 'My strength is sufficient to lift three thousand cattles, but it is not sufficient to lift one feather; — my eye-sight is sharp enough to examine the point of an autumn hair, but I do not see a waggon-load of faggots.' — Would Your

Majesty allow what he said?" *The answer was* "No". "Now here is kindness sufficient to reach to animals, and no benefits are extended from it to the people. — How is this? Is an exception to be made here? The truth is, the feather's not being lifted, is because strength is not used; the waggon-load of firewood's not being seen, is because the vision is not used; and the people's not being loved and protected, is because the kindness is not employed. Therefore Your Majesty's not exercising the Imperial sway, is because you do not do it, not because you are not able to do it." *The king* asked: "How may the difference between the not doing a thing and the not being able to do it, be represented?" Mencius replied, "In such a thing as taking the Tai mountain under your arm, and leaping over the north sea with it, if you say to people — 'I am not able to do it,' that is a real case of not being able. In such a matter as breaking off a branch from a tree at the order of a superior, if you say to people — 'I am not able to do it,' that is a case of not doing it, it is not a case of not being able to do it. Therefore Your Majesty's not exercising the Imperial sway is not such a case as that of taking the Tai mountain under your arm, and leaping over the north sea with it. Your Majesty's not exercising the Imperial sway is a case like that of breaking off a branch from a tree. Treat with the reverence due to age the elders in your own family, so that the elders in the families of others shall be similarly treated; treat with the kindness due to youth the young in your own family, so that the young in the families of others shall be similarly treated: — do this, and the empire may be made to go round in your palm. It is said in the *Book of Poetry*,

'His example affected his wife. It reached to his brothers, and his family of the state was governed by it.' The language shows how *King Wen* simply took his *kindly* heart, and exercised it towards those parties. Therefore the carrying out his kindly heart *by a prince* will suffice for the love and protection of all within the four seas, and if he do not carry it out, he will not be able to protect his wife and children. The way in which the ancients came greatly to surpass other men, was no other than this: — simply that they knew well how to carry out, so as to affect others, what they themselves did. Now your kindness is sufficient to reach to animals, and no benefits are extended from it to reach the people. — How is this? Is an exception to be made here? By weighing, we know what things are light, and what heavy. By measuring, we know what things are long, and what short. The relations of all things may be thus determined, and it is of the greatest importance to estimate *the motion of* the mind. I beg Your Majesty to measure it. You collect your equipments of war, endanger your soldiers and officers, and excite the resentment of the other princes, — do these things cause you pleasure in your mind?" The king replied, "No. How should I derive pleasure from these things? My object in them is to seek for what I greatly desire." *Mencius* said, "May I hear from you what it is that you greatly desire?" The king laughed and did not speak. *Mencius* resumed, "*Are you led to desire it*, because you have not enough of rich and sweet food for your mouth? Or because you have not enough of light and warm *clothing* for your body? Or because you have not enough of beautifully colored objects to delight your eyes? Or because you have not voices and tones enough to please your ears? Or because you have not enough of attendants and favorites to stand before you and receive your orders? Your Majesty's various officers are sufficient to supply you with those things. How can Your Majesty be led to entertain such a desire on account of them?" "No," said *the king*. "My desire is not on account of them." *Mencius* added, "Then, what Your Majesty greatly desires may be known. You wish to enlarge your territories, to have Qin and Chu wait at your court, to rule the Middle Kingdom, and to attract to you the barbarous tribes that surround it. But to do what you do to seek for what you desire, is like climbing a tree to seek for fish." *The king* said, "Is it so bad as that?" The reply was: "It is even worse. If you climb a tree to seek for fish, although you do not get the fish, you will not suffer any subsequent calamity. But if you do what you do to seek for what you desire, doing it moreover with all your heart, you will assuredly afterwards meet with calamity." *The king* said, "May I hear *from you the proof of* that?" *Mencius* said, "If the people of Zou should fight with the people of Chu, which of them does Your Majesty think would conquer?" "The people of Chu would conquer." *Mencius* said, "Yes, and so it is certain that a small country cannot contend with a great, that few cannot contend with many, that the weak cannot contend with the strong. The territory within the *four* seas embraces nine divisions, each of a thousand *li* square. All Qi together is but one of them. If with one part you try to subdue the other eight, what is the difference between that and Zou's contending with Chu? For, *with the desire which you have*, you must likewise turn back to the radical course *for its attainment*. Now, if Your Majesty will institute a government whose action shall all be benevolent, this will cause all the officers in the empire to wish to stand in Your Majesty's court, and the farmers all to wish to plough in Your Majesty's fields, and the merchants, both traveling and stationary, all to wish to store their goods in Your Majesty's market places, and traveling strangers all to wish to make their tours on Your Majesty's roads, and all throughout the empire who feel aggrieved by their rulers to wish to come and complain to Your Majesty. And when they are so bent, who will be able to keep them back?" The king said, "I am stupid, and not able to advance to this. I wish you, my Master, to assist my intentions. Teach me clearly; although I am deficient in intelligence and vigor, I will essay and try to carry your instructions into effect." *Mencius* replied, "They are only men of education, who, without a certain livelihood are able to maintain a fixed heart. As to the people, if they have not a certain livelihood, it follows that they will not have a fixed heart. And if they have not a fixed heart, there is nothing which they will not do, in the way of self-abandonment, of moral deflection, of depravity, and of wild license. When they thus have been involved in crime, to follow them up and punish them, — this is to entrap the people. How can such a thing as entrapping the people be done under the rule of a benevolent man? Therefore an intelligent ruler will regulate the livelihood of the people, so as to make sure that, above, they shall have sufficient wherewith to serve their parents, and, below, sufficient wherewith to support their wives and children; that in good years they shall always be abundantly satisfied, and that in bad years they shall escape the danger of perishing. After this he may urge them, and they will proceed to what is good, for in this case the people will follow after that with ease. Now, the livelihood of the people is so regulated, that, above, they have not sufficient wherewith to serve their parents, and below, they have not sufficient wherewith to support their wives and children. *Notwithstanding* good years, their lives are continually embittered, and, in bad years, they do not escape perishing. In such circumstances they only try to save themselves from death, and are afraid they will not succeed. What leisure have they to cultivate propriety and righteousness? If Your Majesty wishes to effect this *regulation of the livelihood of the people*, why not turn to that which is the essential step to it? Let mulberry trees be planted about the homesteads with their five *mu*, and persons of fifty years may be clothed with silk. In keeping fowls, pigs, dogs, and swine, let not their times of breeding be neglected, and persons of seventy years may eat flesh. Let there not be taken away the time that is proper for the cultivation of the farm with its hundred *mu*, and the family of eight mouths that is supported by it shall not suffer from hunger. Let careful attention be paid to education in schools, — the inculcation in it especially of the filial and fraternal duties, and grey-haired men will not be seen upon the roads carrying burdens on their backs or on their heads. It never has been that the rulers of a state where such results were seen, — the old wearing silk and eating flesh, and the black-haired people suffering neither from hunger nor cold, — did not attain to the Imperial dignity."

卷二　梁惠王章句下
BOOK II　KING HUI OF LIANG　PART II

2.1　庄暴见孟子，曰："暴见于王，王语暴以好乐，暴未有以对也。"曰："好乐何如?"孟子曰："王之好乐甚，则齐国其庶几乎!"他日，见于王曰："王尝语庄子以好乐，有诸?"王变乎色，曰："寡人非能好先王之乐也，直好世俗之乐耳。"曰："王之好乐甚，则齐其庶几乎! 今之乐由古之乐也。"曰："可得闻与?"曰："独乐乐，与人乐乐，孰乐?"曰："不若与人。"曰："与少乐乐，与众乐乐，孰乐?"曰："不若与众。""臣请为王言乐。今王鼓乐于此，百姓闻王钟鼓之声，管龠之音，举疾首蹙頞而相告曰：'吾王之好鼓乐，夫何使我至于此极也? 父子不相见，兄弟妻子离散。'今王田猎于此，百姓闻王车马之音，见羽旄之美，举疾首蹙頞而相告曰：'吾王之好田猎，夫何使我至于此极也? 父子不相见，兄弟妻子离散。'此无他，不与民同乐也。今王鼓乐于此，百姓闻王钟鼓之声，管龠之音，举欣欣然有喜色而相告曰：'吾王庶几无疾病与，何以能鼓乐也?'今王田猎于此，百姓闻王车马之音，见羽旄之美，举欣欣然有喜色而相告曰：'吾王庶几无疾病与，何以能田猎也?'此无他，与民同乐也。今王与百姓同乐，则王矣。"

2.1 Zhuang Bao, seeing Mencius, said to him, "I had an audience of the king. His Majesty told me that he loved music, and I was not prepared with anything to reply to him. What do you pronounce about that love of music?" Mencius replied, "If the king's love of music were very great, the kingdom of Qi would be near to a *state of good government*." Another day, *Mencius*, having an audience of the king, said, "Your Majesty, *I have heard*, told the officer Zhuang, that you love music, — was it so?" The king changed color, and said, "I am unable to love the music of the ancient sovereigns; I only love the music that suits the manners of the *present* age." *Mencius* said, "If Your Majesty's love of music were very great, Qi would be near *to a state of good government*! The music of the present day is just like the music of antiquity, *in regard to effecting that*." *The king* said, "May I hear from you the proof of that?" *Mencius* asked, "Which is the more pleasant to enjoy music by yourself alone, or to enjoy it with others?" The reply was: "To enjoy it along with others." "And which is the more pleasant — to enjoy music along with a few, or to enjoy it along with many?" "To enjoy it along with many." *The king* answered. *Mencius proceeded*, "Your servant begs to explain what I have said about music to Your Majesty. Now Your Majesty is having music here, the people hear the noise of your bells and drums, and the notes of your fifes and pipes, and they all, with aching heads, knit their brows, and say to one another, 'That's how our king likes his music! But why does he reduce us to this extremity of *distress*? — Fathers and sons cannot see one another. Elder brothers and younger brothers, wives and children, are separated and scattered abroad.' Now, Your Majesty is hunting here. — The people hear the noise of your carriages and horses, and see the beauty of your plumes and streamers and they all, with aching heads, knit their brows, and say to one another, 'That's how our king likes his hunting! But why does he reduce us to this extremity of *distress*? — Fathers and sons cannot see one another. Elder brothers and younger brothers, wives and children, are separated and scattered abroad. Their feeling thus is from no other reason but that you do not give the people to have pleasure as well as yourself. Now, Your Majesty is having music here. The people hear the noise of your bells and drums, and the notes of your fifes and pipes, they all, delighted, and with joyful looks, say to one another, 'That sounds as if our king were free from all sickness! If he were not, how could he enjoy this music?' Now, Your Majesty is hunting here. The people hear the noise of your carriages and horses, and see the beauty of your plumes and streamers, and they all, delighted and with joyful looks, say to one another, 'That looks as if our king were free from all sickness! If he were not, how could he enjoy this hunting?' Their feeling thus is from no other reason but that you cause them to have their pleasure as you have yours. If Your Majesty now will make pleasure a thing common to the people and yourself, the Imperial sway awaits you."

2.2　齐宣王问曰："文王之囿方七十里，有诸？"孟子对曰："于传有之。"曰："若是其大乎？"曰："民犹以为小也。"曰："寡人之囿方四十里，民犹以为大，何也？"曰："文王之囿方七十里，刍荛者往焉，雉兔者往焉，与民同之。民以为小，不亦宜乎？臣始至于境，问国之大禁，然后敢入。臣闻郊关之内有囿方四十里，杀其麋鹿者如杀人之罪。则是方四十里为阱于国中。民以为大，不亦宜乎？"

2.2   The king Xuan of Qi, asked, "Was it so, that the park of King Wen contained seventy square *li*?" Mencius replied, "It is so in the records." Exclaimed *the king*, "Was it so large as that?" *Mencius* said, "The people still looked on it as small." *The king* added, "My park contains *only* forty square *li*, and the people still look on it as large. How is this?" The reply was, "The park of King Wen contained seventy square *li*, but the grass-cutters and fuel-gatherers had the privilege of entrance into it; so also had the catchers of pheasants and hares. He shared it with the people, and was it not with reason that they looked on it as small? When I first arrived at the borders of *your state*, I enquired about the great prohibitory regulations, before I would venture to enter it; and I heard, that inside the border gates there was a park of forty square *li*, and that he who killed a deer in it, was held guilty of the same crime as if he had killed a man. Thus those forty square *li* are a pitfall in the middle of the kingdom. Is it not with reason that the people look upon them as large?"

2.3   齐宣王问曰："交邻国有道乎？"孟子对曰："有。惟仁者为能以大事小，是故汤事葛，文王事昆夷。惟智者为能以小事大，故太王事獯鬻，勾践事吴。以大事小者，乐天者也；以小事大者，畏天者也。乐天者保天下，畏天者保其国。《诗》云：'畏天之威，于时保之。'王曰："大哉言矣！寡人有疾，寡人好勇。"对曰:"王请无好小勇。夫抚剑疾视曰,'彼恶敢当我哉!'此匹夫之勇,敌一人者也。王请大之!《诗》云:'王赫斯怒,爰整其旅,以遏徂莒,以笃周祜,以对于天下。'此文王之勇也。文王一怒而安天下之民。《书》曰:'天降下民,作之君,作之师,惟曰其助上帝宠之。四方有罪无罪惟我在,天下曷敢有越厥志?'一人衡行于天下,武王耻之。此武王之勇也。而武王亦一怒而安天下之民。今王亦一怒而安天下之民,民惟恐王之不好勇也。"

2.3   The king Xuan of Qi, asked, saying, "Is there any way *to regulate one's maintenance of* intercourse with neighboring kingdoms?" Mencius replied, "There is. But it requires a perfectly virtuous *prince* to be able, with a great *country*, to serve a small one, — as, for instance, Tang served Ge, and King Wen served the Kun barbarians. And it requires a wise *prince* to be able, with a small *country*, to serve a large one, — as the King Tai served the Xunyu, and Goujian served Wu. He who with a great *state* serves a small one, delights in Heaven. He who with a small *state* serves a large one stands in awe of Heaven. He who delights in Heaven, will affect with his love and protection the whole empire. He who stands in awe of Heaven will effect with his love and protection his own kingdom. It is said in the *Book of Poetry*, 'I fear the Majesty of Heaven, and will thus preserve its favoring decree.'" The king said, "A great saying! But I have an infirmity; — I love valour." "I beg Your Majesty," Mencius replied, "not to love small valour. If a man brandishes his sword, looks fiercely, and says, 'How dare he withstand me?'— this is the valour of a common man, who can be the opponent only of a single individual. I beg Your Majesty to greaten it! It is said in the *Book of Poetry*, 'The king blazed with anger, and he marshalled his hosts, to stop the march to Ju, to consolidate the prosperity of Zhou. To meet the expectations of the empire.' This was the valour of King Wen. King Wen in one burst of his anger, gave repose to all the people of the empire. In the *Book of History* it is said: 'Heaven having produced the inferior people, appointed for them rulers and teachers, with the purpose that they should be assisting to God, and therefore distinguished them throughout the four quarters of the empire. Whoever are offenders, and whoever are innocent, here am I *to deal with them*. How dare any under Heaven give indulgence to their refractory wills?' There was one man pursuing a violent and disorderly course in the empire, and King Wu was ashamed of it. This was the valour of King Wu. He also, by one display of his anger, gave repose to all the people of the empire. Let now Your Majesty also, in one burst of anger, give repose to all the people of the empire. The people are only afraid that Your Majesty does not love valour."

2.4　齐宣王见孟子于雪宫。王曰:"贤者亦有此乐乎?"孟子对曰:"有。人不得,则非其上矣。不得而非其上者,非也;为民上而不与民同乐者,亦非也。乐民之乐者,民亦乐其乐;忧民之忧者,民亦忧其忧。乐以天下,忧以天下,然而不王者,未之有也。昔者齐景公问于晏子曰:'吾欲观于转附、朝僻，遵海而南，放于琅邪。吾何修而可以比于先王观也?' 晏子对曰：'善哉问也! 天子适诸侯曰巡狩。巡狩者，巡所守也。诸侯朝于天子曰述职。述职者，述所职也。无非事者。春省耕而补不足，秋省敛而助不给。夏谚曰："吾王不游，吾何以休? 吾王不豫，吾何以助? 一游一豫，为诸侯度。"今也不然：师行而粮食，饥者弗食，劳者弗息。睊睊胥谗，民乃作慝。方命虐民，饮食若流。流连荒亡，为诸侯忧。从流下而忘反谓之流，从流上而忘反谓之连，从兽无厌谓之荒，乐酒无厌谓之亡。先王无流连之乐，荒亡之行。惟君所行也。'景公悦，大戒于国，出舍于郊。于是始兴发补不足。召大师曰：'为我作君臣相说之乐!'盖《徵招》、《角招》是也。其诗曰：'畜君何尤?'畜君者，好君也。"

2.4　The king Xuan of Qi had an interview with Mencius in the Snow Palace, and said to him, "Do men of talents and worth likewise find pleasure in these things?" Mencius replied, "They do, and if people *generally* are not able to *enjoy themselves*, they condemn their superiors. For them, when they cannot enjoy themselves, to condemn their superiors is wrong, but when superiors of the people do not make enjoyment a thing common to the people and themselves, they also do wrong. When a ruler rejoices in the joy of his people, they also rejoice in his joy; when he grieves at the sorrow of his people, they also grieve at his sorrow. A sympathy of joy will pervade the empire, a sympathy of sorrow will do the same; — in such a state of things, it cannot be but that the ruler attain to the Imperial dignity. Formerly, the

prince Jing of Qi, asked the minister Yan Ying, saying, 'I wish
to pay a visit of inspection to both mountains Zhuangfu and
Zhaowu, and then to bend my course southward along the shore,
till I come to Langya. What shall I do that my tour may be fit to
be compared with the visits of inspection made by the ancient
emperors?' The minister Yan replied, 'An excellent inquiry!
When the emperor visited the princes, it was called a tour of
inspection, that is, he surveyed the *states* under their care. When
the princes attended at the court of the emperor, it was called a
report of office, that is, they reported their administration of their
offices. Thus neither of the proceedings was without a purpose.
And moreover, in the spring, they examined the ploughing, and
supplied any deficiency *of seed*; in the autumn, they examined
the reaping, and supplied any deficiency of field. There is the
saying of the Xia Dynasty, — "If our king do not take his ramble,
what will become of our happiness? If our king do not make his
excursion, what will become of our help? That ramble, and that
excursion, were a pattern to the princes." Now, the state of things
is different. — A host marches *in attendance on the ruler*, and
stores of provisions are consumed. The hungry are deprived of
their food, and there is no rest for those who are called to toil.
Maledictions are uttered by one to another with eyes askance, and
the people proceed to the commission of wickedness. Thus the
Imperial ordinances are violated, and the people are oppressed,
and *the supplies* of food and drink flow away like water. *The rulers*
yield themselves to the current, or they urge their way against
it; they are wild; they are utterly lost: — these things proceed to

the grief of their subordinate governors. Descending along with the current, and forgetting to return, is what I call yielding to it. Pressing up against it, and forgetting to return, is what I call urging their way against it. Pursuing the chase without satiety is what I call being wild. Delighting in wine without satiety is what I call being lost. The ancient emperors had no pleasures to which they gave themselves as on the flowing stream; no doings which might be so characterized as wild and lost. It is for you, my prince, to pursue your course.' The Prince Jing was pleased. He issued a proclamation throughout his state, and went out and occupied a shed in the borders. From that time he began to open his granaries to supply the wants of the people, and calling the grand music-master, he said to him, — 'Make for music to suit a prince and his minister pleased with each other.' And it was then the *Zhishao* and *Jueshao* were made, in the poetry to which it was said, 'What fault is it to restrain one's prince?' He who restrains his prince loves his prince."

2.5 齐宣王问曰：“人皆谓我毁明堂。毁诸？已乎？”孟子对曰：“夫明堂者，王者之堂也。王欲行王政，则勿毁之矣。”王曰：“王政可得闻与？”对曰：“昔者文王之治岐也，耕者九一，仕者世禄，关市讥而不征，泽梁无禁，罪人不孥。老而无妻曰鳏，老而无夫曰寡，老而无子曰独，幼而无父曰孤。此四者，天下之穷民而无告者。文王发政施仁，必先斯四者。《诗》云：‘哿矣富人，哀此茕独。’”王曰：“善哉言乎！”曰：“王如善之，则何为不行？”王曰：“寡人有疾，寡人好货。”对曰：“昔者公刘好货,《诗》云:'乃积乃仓,乃裹餱粮,于橐于囊。思戢用光。弓矢斯张,干戈戚扬,爰方启行。'故居者有积仓,行者有裹囊也,然后可以爰方启行。王如好货,与百姓同之,于王何有?"

王曰:"寡人有疾,寡人好色。"对曰:"昔者大王好色,爱厥妃。《诗》云:'古公亶父,来朝走马,率西水浒,至于岐下。爰及姜女,聿来胥宇。'当是时也,内无怨女,外无旷夫。王如好色,与百姓同之,于王何有?"

2.5 The king Xuan of Qi said, "People all tell me to pull down and remove the Brilliant Palace. Shall I pull it down, or stop *the movement for that object*?" Mencius replied, "The Brilliant Palace appropriate to the emperors. If Your Majesty wished to practise the true imperial government, then do not pull it down." The king said, "May I hear from you what the true imperial government is?" The reply was, "Formerly, King Wen's government of Qi, the old capital of Zhou, was as follows: — The husbandmen *cultivated for the government* one-ninth of the land; the descendants of officers were salaried; at the passes and in the markets, *strangers* were inspected, but *goods* were not taxed; there were no prohibitions respecting the ponds and weirs; the wives and children of criminals were not involved in their guilt. There were the old and wifeless, or widowers; the old and husbandless, or widows; the old and childless, or solitaries; the young and fatherless, or orphans, — these four classes are the most destitute of the people, and have none to whom they can tell their wants, and King Wen, in the institution of his government with its benevolent action, made them the first objects of his regard, as it is said in the *Book of Poetry*, 'The rich may get through. But alas! for the miserable and solitary!' " The king said, "O excellent words!" *Mencius* said, "Since Your Majesty deems them excellent, why do you not practise them?" Said the king, "I have an infirmity: I am fond of wealth." The reply was, "Formerly, Gongliu was fond of wealth. It is said in the *Book of Poetry*, 'He reared his ricks, and filled his granaries. He tied up dried provisions and grain, in bottomless bags, and sacks, that he might gather his people together, and glorify *his state*. With bows and arrows all-displayed. With shields, and spears, and battle-axes, large and small, he commenced his march.' In this way those who remained in their old seat had their ricks and granaries, and those who marched had their bags of provisions. It was not till after this that he thought he could commence his march. If Your Majesty loves wealth, let the people be able to gratify the same feeling, and what difficulty will there be in your attaining the Imperial sway?" The king said, "I have an infirmity: I am fond of beauty." The reply was, "Formerly, King Tai was fond of beauty, and loved his wife. It is said in the *Book of Poetry*, 'Gugong Danfu came in the morning, galloping his horse, by the banks of the western waters, as far as the foot of Qi hill, along with the lady of Jiang; they came and together chose the site of settlement.' At that time, in the seclusion of the house, there were no dissatisfied women, and abroad, there were no unmarried men. If Your Majesty loves beauty, let the people be able to gratify the same feeling, and what difficulty will there be in your attaining the Imperial sway?"

2.6 孟子谓齐宣王曰:"王之臣有托其妻子于其友而之楚游者,比其反也,则冻馁其妻子,则如之何?"王曰:"弃之。"曰:"士师不能治士,则如之何?"王曰:"已之。"曰:"四境之内不治,则如之何?"王顾左右而言他。

2.6 Mencius said to the King Xuan of Qi, "Suppose that one of Your Majesty's ministers were to entrust his wife and children to the care of his friend, while he himself went into Chu to travel, and that, on his return, *he should find*, that the friend had caused his wife and children to suffer from cold and hunger; — how ought he to deal with him?" The king said, "He should cast him off." *Mencius* said, "Suppose that the chief criminal judge could not regulate the officers *under him*, how would you deal with him?" The king said, "Dismiss him." *Mencius proceeded*, "If within the four borders *of your kingdom* there is not good government, what is to be done?" The king looked to the right and left, and spoke of other matters.

2.7 孟子见齐宣王,曰:"所谓故国者,非谓有乔木之谓也,有世臣之谓也。王无亲臣矣,昔者所进,今日不知其亡也。"王曰:"吾何以识其不才而舍之?"曰:"国君进贤,如不得已,将使卑逾尊,疏逾戚,可不慎与?左右皆曰贤,未可也;诸大夫皆曰贤,未可也;国人皆曰贤,然后察之;见贤焉,然后用之。左右皆曰不可,勿听;诸大夫皆曰不可,勿听;国人皆曰不可,然后察之;见不可焉,然后去之。左右皆曰可杀,勿听;诸大夫皆曰可杀,勿听;国人皆曰可杀,然后察之;见可杀焉,然后杀之。故曰，国人杀之也。如此，然后可以为民父母。"

2.7 Mencius, having an interview with the king Xuan of Qi, said to him, "When men speak of an ancient kingdom, it is not meant thereby that it has lofty trees in it but that it has ministers *sprung from families which have been noted in it* for generations. Your Majesty has no intimate ministers *even*. Those whom you advanced yesterday are gone today, and you do not know it." The king said, "How shall I know that they have not ability, and so avoid employing them at all?" The reply was, "The ruler of a state advances to office men of talents and virtue, only as a matter of necessity. Since he will thereby cause the low to overstep the honourable, and strangers to overstep his relatives, may he do so but with caution? When all those about you say, — 'This is a man of talents and worth,' you may not for that believe it. When your great officers all say, — 'This is a man of talents and virtue,' neither may you for that believe it. When all the people say, — 'This is a man of talents and virtue,' then examine into the case, and when you find that the man is such, employ him. When all those about you say, — 'This man won't do,' don't listen to them. When all your great officers say, — 'This man won't do,' don't listen to them. When the people all say, — 'This man won't do,' then examine into the case, and when you find that the man won't do, send him away. When all those about you say, — 'This man deserves death,' don't listen to them. When all your great officers say, — 'This man deserves death,' don't listen to them. When the people all say, — 'This man deserves death,' then inquire into the case, and when you see that the man deserves death, put him to death. In accordance with this, we have the saying, 'The people killed him.' You must act in this way in order to be the parent of the people."

2.8　齐宣王问曰："汤放桀，武王伐纣，有诸?"孟子对曰："于传有之。"曰："臣弑其君，可乎?"曰："贼仁者谓之'贼'，贼义者谓之'残'。残贼之人谓之'一夫'。闻诛一夫纣矣，未闻弑君也。"

2.8　The king Xuan of Qi asked, saying, "Was it so, that Tang banished Jie of Xia, and that King Wu smote Zhou of Yin?" Mencius replied, "It is so in the records." *The king* said, "May a minister *then* put his sovereign to death?" *Mencius* said, "He who outrages the benevolence *proper to his nature*, is called a robber; he who outrages righteousness, is called a ruffian. The robber and ruffian we call a mere fellow. I have heard of the cutting off of the fellow Zhou of Yin, but I have not heard of the putting a sovereign to death, *in his case*."

2.9　孟子见齐宣王，曰："为巨室，则必使工师求大木。工师得大木，则王喜，以为能胜其任也。匠人斫而小之，则王怒，以为不胜其任矣。夫人幼而学之，壮而欲行之，王曰，'姑舍女所学而从我，'则何如? 今有璞玉于此，虽万镒，必使玉人雕琢之。至于治国家，则曰，'姑舍女所学而从我，'则何以异于教玉人雕琢玉哉?"

2.9   Mencius, having an interview with the king Xuan of Qi, said to him, "If you are going to build a large mansion, you will surely cause the Master of the workmen to look out for large trees, and when he has found such large trees, you will be glad, thinking that they will answer for the intended object. Should the workmen hew them so as to make them too small, then Your Majesty will be angry, thinking that they will not answer for the purpose. Now, a man spends his youth in learning *the principles of right government*, and, being grown up to vigor, he wishes to put them in practice. — If Your Majesty says to him, 'For the present put aside what you have learned, and follow me,' what shall we say? Here now you have a gem unwrought, in the stone. Although it may be worth 240,000 taels, you will surely employ a lapidary to cut and polish it. But when you come to the government of the state, then you say, — 'For the present put aside what you have learned, and follow me.' How is it that you herein act so differently from your conduct in calling in the lapidary to cut the gem?"

2.10   齐人伐燕，胜之。宣王问曰："或谓寡人勿取，或谓寡人取之。以万乘之国伐万乘之国，五旬而举之，人力不至于此。不取，必有天殃。取之，何如？"孟子对曰："取之而燕民悦，则取之。古之人有行之者，武王是也。取之而燕民不悦，则勿取。古之人有行之者，文王是也。以万乘之国伐万乘之国，箪食壶浆以迎王师，岂有他哉？避水火也。如水益深，如火益热，亦运而已矣。"

2.10   The people of Qi attacked Yan, and conquered it. The king Xuan asked, saying, "Some tell me not to take possession of it for myself, and some tell me to take possession of it. For a kingdom of ten thousand chariots, attacking another of ten thousand chariots, to complete the conquest of it in fifty days, is an achievement beyond *mere* human strength. If I do not take possession of it, calamities from Heaven will surely come upon me. What do you say to my taking possession of it?" Mencius replied, "If the people of Yan will be pleased with your taking possession of it, then do so. Among the ancients there was *one* who acted on this principle, namely King Wu. If the people of Yan will not be pleased with your taking possession of it, then do not do so. Among the ancients there was *one* who acted on this principle, namely King Wen. When, with *all the strength* of your country of ten thousand chariots, you attacked another country of ten thousand chariots, and *the people brought* baskets of rice and vessels of congee, to meet Your Majesty's host, was there any other reason for this but that they hoped to escape out of fire and water? If you make the water more deep and the fire more fierce, they will just in like manner make *another* revolution."

2.11   齐人伐燕，取之。诸侯将谋救燕。宣王曰："诸侯多谋伐寡人者，何以待之?"孟子对曰:"臣闻七十里为政于天下者，汤是也。未闻以千里畏人者也。《书》曰:'汤一征，自葛始。'天下信之，东面而征，西夷怨;南面而征，北狄怨。曰:'奚为后我?'民望之，若大旱之望云霓也。归市者不止，耕者不变，诛其君而吊其民，若时雨降。民大悦。《书》曰：'徯我后，后来其苏。'今燕虐其民，王往而征之，民以为将拯己于水火之中也，箪食壶浆以迎王师。若杀其父兄，系累其子弟，毁其宗庙，迁其重器，如之何其可也？天下固畏齐之强也，今又倍地而不行仁政，是动天下之兵也。王速出令，反其旄倪，止其重器，谋于燕众，置君而后去之，则犹可及止也。"

2.11　The people of Qi having smitten Yan, took possession of it, *and upon this*, the princes of the various states deliberated together, and resolved to deliver Yan *from their power*. The king Xuan said *to Mencius*, "The princes have formed many plans to attack me: — how shall I prepare myself for them?" Mencius replied, "I have heard of one who with seventy *li* exercised all the functions of government throughout the empire. That was Tang. I have never heard of a *prince* with a thousand *li* standing in fear of others. It is said in the *Book of History*, 'As soon as Tang began his work of executing justice, he commenced with Ge.' The whole empire had confidence in him. When he pursued his work in the east, the rude tribes on the west murmured, so did those on the north, when he was engaged in the south. Their cry was, — 'Why does he make us last?' *Thus*, the looking of the people to him, was like the looking in a time of great drought to the clouds and rainbows. The frequenters of the markets stopped not. The husbandmen made no change *in their operations*. While he punished their rulers, he consoled the people. *His progress* was like the falling of opportune rain, and the people were delighted. It is said *again* in the *Book of History*, 'We have waited for our prince *long*; the prince's coming will be our reviving!' *Now the ruler of Yan* was tyrannizing over his people, and Your Majesty went and punished him. The people, supposed that you were going to deliver them out of the water and the fire, and brought baskets of rice and vessels of congee, to meet Your Majesty's host. But you have slain their fathers and elder brothers, and put their sons and younger brothers in chains. You have pulled down the ancestral temple *of the State*, and are removing to Qi its precious vessels. How can such a course be deemed proper? *The rest of* the empire is indeed *jealously* afraid of the strength of Qi, and now, when with a doubled territory you do not put in practice a benevolent government; — it is this which sets the arms of the empire in motion. If Your Majesty will make haste to issue an ordinance, restoring *your captives*, old and young, stopping *the removal of* the precious vessels, *and saying that, after* consulting with the people of Yan, you will appoint them a ruler, and withdraw from the country; — in this way you may still be able to stop *the threatened attack*."

2.12　邹与鲁哄。穆公问曰：“吾有司死者三十三人，而民莫之死也。诛之，则不可胜诛；不诛，则疾视其长上之死而不救，如之何则可也？”孟子对曰：“凶年饥岁，君之民老弱转乎沟壑，壮者散而之四方者，几千人矣；而君之仓廪实，府库充，有司莫以告，是上慢而残下也。曾子曰：‘戒之戒之！出乎尔者，反乎尔者也。’夫民今而后得反之也。君无尤焉！君行仁政，斯民亲其上，死其长矣。”

2.12 There had been a brush between Zou and Lu, when the prince Mu asked Mencius, saying, "Of my officers there were killed thirty-three men, and none of the people would die in their defence. If I put them to death *for their conduct*, it is impossible to put such a multitude to death. If I do not put them to death, then there is *the crime unpunished of* their looking angrily on at the death of their officers, and not saving them. How is the exigency of the case to be met?" Mencius replied, "In calamitous years and years of famine, the old and weak of your people, who have been found lying in the ditches and water-channels, and the able-bodied who have been scattered about to the four quarters, have amounted to several thousands. All the while, your granaries, O prince, have been stored with grain, and your treasuries and arsenals have been full, and not one of your officers has told you *of the distress*. Thus negligent have the superiors *in your state* been, and cruel to their inferiors. The philosopher Zeng said, 'Beware, beware. What proceeds from you, will return to you again.' Now at length the people have returned their conduct to the officers. Do not you, O prince, blame them. If you will put in practice a benevolent government, this people will love you and all above them, and will die for their officers."

2.13　滕文公问曰：“滕，小国也，间于齐、楚。事齐乎？事楚乎？”孟子对曰：“是谋非吾所能及也。无已，则有一焉：凿斯池也，筑斯城也，与民守之，效死而民弗去，则是可为也。”

2.13   The prince Wen of Teng asked *Mencius*, saying, "Teng is a small kingdom, and lies between Qi and Chu. Shall I serve Qi? Or shall I serve Chu?" Mencius replied, "This plan *which you propose* is beyond me. If you will have me counsel you, there is one thing I can suggest. Dig deeper your moats; build higher your walls; guard them along with your people. *In case of attack*, be prepared to die *in your defence*, and have the people so that they will not leave you. — This is a proper course."

2.14   滕文公问曰："齐人将筑薛，吾甚恐，如之何则可？"孟子对曰："昔者大王居邠，狄人侵之，去之岐山之下居焉。非择而取之，不得已也。苟为善，后世子孙必有王者矣。君子创业垂统，为可继也。若夫成功，则天也。君如彼何哉？强为善而已矣。"

2.14   The prince Wen of Teng asked *Mencius*, saying, "The people of Qi are going to fortify Xue. *The movement* occasions me great alarm. What is the proper course for me to take in the case?" Mencius replied, "Formerly, when King Tai dwelt in Bin, the barbarians of the north were *continually* making incursions upon it. He *therefore* left it, went to the foot of mount Qi, and there took up his residence. He did not take that situation, as having selected it. It was a matter of necessity with him. If you do good, among your descendants, in after generations, there shall be one who will attain to the Imperial dignity. A prince lays the foundation of the inheritance, and hands down the beginning *which he has made*, doing what may be continued *by his successors*. As to the accomplishment of the great result, that is with Heaven. What is that *Qi* to you, O prince? Be strong to do good. That is all your business."

2.15 滕文公问曰:"滕,小国也;竭力以事大国,则不得免焉,如之何则可?"孟子对曰:"昔者大王居邠,狄人侵之。事之以皮币,不得免焉;事之以犬马,不得免焉;事之以珠玉,不得免焉。乃属其耆老而告之曰:'狄人之所欲者,吾土地也。吾闻之也:君子不以其所以养人者害人。二三子何患乎无君?我将去之。'去邠,逾梁山,邑于岐山之下居焉。邠人曰:'仁人也,不可失也。'从之者如归市。或曰:'世守也,非身之所能为也。效死勿去。'君请择于斯二者。"

2.15 The prince Wen of Teng asked Mencius, saying, "Teng is a small kingdom. Though I do my utmost to serve those large kingdoms *on either side of it*, we cannot escape *suffering from them*. What course shall I take that we may do so?" Mencius replied, "Formerly, when King Tai dwelt in Bin, the barbarians of the north were *constantly* making incursions upon it. He served them with skins and silks, and still he suffered from them. He served them with dogs and horses, and still he suffered from them. He served them with pearls and gems, and still he suffered from them. Seeing this, he assembled the old men, and announced to them, saying, 'What the barbarians want is my territory. I have heard this, — that a ruler does not injure his people with that wherewith he nourishes them. My children, why

should you be troubled about having no prince. I will leave this.'
Accordingly, he left Bin, crossed the mountain Liang, *built* a town at the foot of mount Qi, and dwelt there. The people of Bin said, 'He is a benevolent man. We must not lose him.' Those who followed him looked like crowds hastening to market. *On the other hand*, some say, '*The kingdom* is a thing to be kept from generation to generation. One individual cannot undertake to dispose of it in his own person. Let him be prepared to die for it. Let him not quit it.' I ask you, prince, to make your selection between these two courses."

2.16　魯平公將出。嬖人臧倉者請曰："他日君出，則必命有司所之。今乘輿已駕矣，有司未知所之，敢請。"公曰："將見孟子。"曰："何哉，君所為輕身以先于匹夫者？以為賢乎？禮義由賢者出，而孟子之後喪逾前喪。君無見焉！"公曰："諾。"樂正子入見，曰："君奚為不見孟軻也？"曰："或告寡人曰：'孟子之後喪逾前喪，'是以不往見也。"曰："何哉，君所謂逾者？前以士，後以大夫；前以三鼎，而後以五鼎與？"曰："否；謂棺椁衣衾之美也。"曰："非所謂逾也，貧富不同也。"樂正子見孟子，曰："克告于君，君為來見也。嬖人有臧倉者沮君，君是以不果來也。"曰："行，或使之；止，或尼之。行止，非人所能也。吾之不遇魯侯，天也。臧氏之子焉能使予不遇哉？"

2.16　The prince Ping of Lu was about to leave *his palace*, when his favorite one Zang Cang made a request to him, saying, "On other day, when you have gone out, you have given instructions to the officers as to where you were going. But now, the horses have been put to the carriage, and the officers do not yet know where you are going. I venture to ask." The prince said, "I am going to see the scholar Meng." Said the other, "How is this! That you demean yourself, prince in paying the honor of the first visit to a common man, is, I apprehend because you think that he is a man of talents and virtue. By such men the rules of ceremonial proprieties and right are observed. But on the occasion of this Meng's second mourning, his observances exceeded those of the former. Do not go to see him, my prince." The prince said, "I will not." The officer Yue Zheng entered *the court*, and had an audience. He said, "Prince, why have you not gone to see Meng Ke?" The prince said, "One told me that on the occasion of the scholar Meng's second mourning, his observances exceeded those of the former. It is on that account that I have not gone to see him." Yue Zheng answered, "How is this! By what you call 'exceeding', you mean, I suppose, that, on the first occasion, he used the rites appropriate to a scholar, and, on the second, those appropriate to a great officer; that he first used three tripods, and afterwards five tripods." *The prince* said, "No. I refer to the greater excellence of the coffin, the shell, the grave-clothes, and the shroud." Yue Zheng said, "That cannot be called 'exceeding'. That was the difference between being poor and being rich." *After this*, Yue Zheng saw Mencius, and said to him, "I told the prince about you, and he was consequently coming to see you, when one of his favorites, named Zang Cang, stopped him, and therefore he did not come according to his purpose." *Mencius* said, "A man's advancement is effected, it may be, by others, and the stopping him is, it may be, from the efforts of others. But to advance a man or to stop his advance is really *beyond* the power of other men. My not finding in the prince of Lu a *ruler who would confide in me, and put my counsels into practice*, is from Heaven. How could that scion of the Zang family cause me not to find *the ruler that would suit me*?"

卷三 公孙丑章句上
BOOK III GONGSUN CHOU PART I

3.1　公孙丑问曰：“夫子当路于齐，管仲、晏子之功，可复许乎？”孟子曰：“子诚齐人也，知管仲、晏子而已矣。或问乎曾西曰：‘吾子与子路孰贤？’曾西蹴然曰：‘吾先子之所畏也。’曰：‘然则吾子与管仲孰贤？’曾西艴然不悦，曰：‘尔何曾比予于管仲？管仲得君如彼其专也，行乎国政如彼其久也，功烈如彼其卑也，尔何曾比予于是？’”曰：“管仲，曾西之所不为也，而子为我愿之乎？”曰：“管仲以其君霸，晏子以其君显。管仲、晏子犹不足为与？”曰：“以齐王，由反手也。”曰：“若是，则弟子之惑滋甚。且以文王之德，百年而后崩，犹未洽于天下；武王、周公继之，然后大行。今言王若易然，则文王不足法与？”曰：“文王何可当也？由汤至于武丁，贤圣之君六七作，天下归殷久矣，久则难变也。武丁朝诸侯，有天下，犹运之掌也。纣之去武丁未久也，其故家遗俗，流风善政，犹有存者；又有微子、微仲、王子比干、箕子、胶鬲——皆贤人也——相与辅相之，故久而后失之也。尺地，莫非其有也；一民，莫非其臣也；然而文王犹方百里起，是以难也。齐人有言曰：‘虽有智慧，不如乘势；虽有镃基，不如待时。’今时则易然也：夏后、殷、周之盛，地未有过千里者也，而齐有其地矣；鸡鸣狗吠相闻，而达乎四境，而齐有其民矣。地不改辟矣，民不改聚矣，行仁政而王，莫之能御也。且王者之不作，未有疏于此时者也；民之憔悴于虐政，未有甚于此时者也。饥者易为食，渴者易为饮。孔子曰：'德之流行，速于置邮而传命。'当今之时，万乘之国行仁政，民之悦之，犹解倒悬也。故事半古之人，功必倍之，惟此时为然。"

3.1　Gongsun Chou asked *Mencius*, saying, "Master, if you were to obtain the ordering of the government in Qi, could you promise yourself to accomplish anew such results as those realized by Guan Zhong and Yan?" Mencius said, "You are indeed a *true* man of Qi. You know about Guan Zhong and Yan, and nothing more. Some one asked Zeng Xi, saying, 'Sir, to which do you give the superiority, — to yourself or to Zilu?' Zeng Xi looked uneasy, and said, 'He was an object of veneration to my grandfather.' 'Then,' pursued the other, 'Do you give the superiority to yourself or to Guan Zhong?' Zeng Xi flushed with anger and displeased, said, 'How dare you compare me with Guan Zhong? Considering how entirely Guan Zhong possessed *the confidence of* his prince, how long he enjoyed the direction of the government of the kingdom, and how low, *after all*, was what he accomplished, — how is it that you liken me to him?' " Mencius concluded: "Thus Zeng Xi would not play Guan Zhong, and is it what you desire for me, that I should do so?" *Gongsun* Chou said, "Guan Zhong raised his prince to be the leader of all the other princes, and Yan made his prince illustrious, and do you still think it would not be enough for you to do what they did?" *Mencius* answered, "To raise Qi to the Imperial dignity would be as easy as it is to turn round the hand." "So!" returned the other, "The perplexity of your disciple is hereby very much increased. There was King Wen, with all the virtue which belonged to him; and who did not die till he had reached a hundred years; — and still *his influence* had not penetrated throughout the empire. It required King Wu and the duke of Zhou to continue his course, before that influence greatly prevailed. Now you say that the Imperial dignity might be so easily obtained; — is King Wen then not a sufficient object for imitation?" Mencius said, "How can King Wen be matched? From Tang to Wuding, there had appeared six or seven worthy and sage sovereigns. The empire had been attached to Yin for a long time, and this length of time made a change difficult. Wuding had all the princes coming to his court, and possessed the empire as if it had been a thing which he moved round in his palm. *Then* Zhou was removed from Wuding by no great interval of time. There were still remaining some of the ancient families and of the old manners, of the influence also which had emanated *from the earlier sovereign*, and of their good government. Moreover, there were the viscount of Wei and his second son, their Royal Highnesses Bigan and the viscount of Ji, and Jiaoge, all, men of ability and virtue, who gave their joint assistance to Zhou *in his government*. In consequence of these things, it took a long time for him to *lose the empire*. There was not a foot of ground which he did not possess. There was not one of all the people who was not his subject. So it was on *his side*, and King Wen made his beginning from a territory of *only* one hundred square *li*. On all these accounts, it was difficult for him *immediately to attain to the Imperial dignity*. The people of Qi have a saying — 'A man may have wisdom and discernment, but that is not like embracing the favorable opportunity. A man may have instruments of husbandry, but that is not like waiting for the *farming* seasons.' The present time is one in which *the Imperial dignity* may be easily attained. In the flourishing periods of the Xia, Yin, and Zhou dynasties, the *Imperial* domain did not exceed a thousand *li*, and Qi embraces so much territory. Cocks crow and dogs bark to each other, all the way to the four borders of the state: — so Qi possesses the people. No change is needed for the enlarging of its territory; no change is needed for the collecting of a population. If its ruler will put in practice a benevolent government, no power will be able to prevent his becoming Emperor. Moreover, never was there a time further removed than the present from the appearance of a true sovereign; never was there a time when the sufferings of the people from tyrannical government were more intense than the present. The hungry are easily supplied with food, and the thirsty are easily supplied with drink. Confucius said, 'The flowing progress of virtue is more rapid than the transmission of *imperial* orders by stages and couriers.' At the present time, in a country of ten thousand chariots, let benevolent government be put in practice, and the people will be delighted with it, as if they were relieved from hanging by the heels. With half the merit of the ancients, double their achievements is sure to be realized. It is only at this time that such could be the case."

3.2 公孙丑问曰："夫子加齐之卿相，得行道焉，虽由此霸王，不异矣。如此，则动心否乎？"孟子曰："否；我四十不动心。"曰："若是，则夫子过孟贲远矣。"曰："是不难，告子先我不动心。"曰："不动心有道乎？"曰："有。北宫黝之养勇也：不肤挠，不目逃，思以一豪挫于人，若挞之于市朝；不受于褐宽博，亦不受于万乘之君；视刺万乘之君，若刺褐夫；无严诸侯，恶声至，必反之。孟施舍之所养勇也，曰：'视不胜犹胜也；量敌而后进，虑胜而后会，是畏三军者也。舍岂能为必胜哉？能无惧而已矣。'孟施舍似曾子，北宫黝似子夏。夫二子之勇，未知其孰贤，然而孟施舍守约也。昔者曾子谓子襄曰：'子好勇乎？吾尝闻大勇于夫子矣：自反而不缩，虽褐宽博，吾不惴焉；自反而缩，虽千万人，吾往矣。'孟施舍之守气，又不如曾子之守约也。"曰："敢问夫子之不动心与告子之不动心，可得闻与？""告子曰：'不得于言，勿求于心，不得于心，勿求于气。'不得于心，勿求于气，可；不得于言，勿求于心，不可。夫志，气之帅也；气，体之充也。夫志至焉，气次焉。故曰：'持其志，无暴其气。'""既曰，'志至焉，气次焉。'又曰，'持其志，无暴其气。'者，何也？"曰："志壹则动气，气壹则动志也，今夫蹶者趋者，是气也，而反动其心。""敢问夫子恶乎长？"曰："我知言，我善养吾浩然之气。""敢问何谓浩然之气？"曰："难言也。其为气也，至大至刚，以直养而无害，则塞于天地之间。其为气也，配义与道；无是，馁也。是集义所生者，非义袭而取之也。行有不慊于心，则馁矣。我故曰，告子未尝知义，以其外之也。必有事焉，而勿正，心勿忘，勿助长也。无若宋人然。宋人有闵其苗之不长而揠之者，芒芒然归，谓其人曰：'今日病矣！予助苗长矣！'其子趋而往视之，苗则槁矣。天下之不助苗长者寡矣。以为无益而舍之者，不耘苗者也；助之长者，揠苗者也——非徒无益，而又害之。""何谓知言？"曰："诐辞知其所蔽，淫辞知其所陷，邪辞知其所离，遁辞知其所穷。——生于其心，害于其政；发于其政，害于其事。圣人复起，必从吾言矣。""宰我、子贡善为说辞；冉牛、闵子、颜渊善言德行。孔子兼之，曰：'我于辞命，则不能也。'然则夫子既圣矣乎？"曰："恶！是何言也？昔者子贡问于孔子曰：'夫子圣矣乎？'孔子曰：'圣则吾不能，我学不厌而教不倦也。'子贡曰：'学不厌，智也；教不倦，仁也。仁且智，夫子既圣矣。'夫圣，孔子不居——是何言也？""昔者窃闻之：子夏、子游、子张皆有圣人之一体，冉牛、闵子、颜渊则具体而微，敢问所安？"曰："姑舍是。"曰："伯夷、伊尹何如？"曰："不同道。非其君不事，非其民不使；治则进，乱则退，伯夷也。何事非君，何使非民；治亦进，乱亦进，伊尹也。可以仕则仕，可以止则止，可以久则久，可以速则速，孔子也。皆古圣人也，吾未能有行焉；乃所愿，则学孔子也。""伯夷、伊尹于孔子，若是班乎？"曰："否，自有生民以来，未有孔子也。"曰："然则有同与？"曰："有。得百里之地而君之，皆能以朝诸侯，有天下；行一不义，杀一不辜，而得天下，皆不为也。是则同。"曰："敢问其所以异？"曰：

"宰我、子贡、有若，智足以知圣人，污不至阿其所好。宰我曰：

'以予观于夫子，贤于尧舜远矣。'子贡曰：'见其礼而知其政，

闻其乐而知其德。由百世之后，等百世之王，莫之能违也。自

生民以来，未有夫子也。'有若曰：'岂惟民哉？麒麟之于走兽，

凤凰之于飞鸟，泰山之于丘垤，河海之于行潦，类也。圣人之

于民，亦类也。出于其类，拔乎其萃，自生民以来，未有盛于

孔子也。'"

3.2 Gongsun Chou asked *Mencius*, saying, "Master, if you were to be appointed a high noble and the prime minister of Qi, so as to be able to carry *your* principles into practice, though you should thereupon raise the prince to the headship of all the other princes, or *even* to the Imperial dignity, it would not be to be wondered at. — In such a position would your mind be perturbed or not?" Mencius replied, "No. At forty, I attained to an unperturbed mind." *Chou* said, "Since it is so with you, my Master, you are far beyond Meng Ben." "The *mere* attainment," said *Mencius*, "is not difficult. The scholar Gao had attained to an unperturbed mind, at an earlier period of life than I did." *Chou* asked, "Is there any way to an unperturbed mind?" The answer was, "Yes, Beigong You had this way of nourishing his valour: — He did not flinch from any strokes at his body; he did not turn his eyes aside from any thrusts at them; he considered that the slightest push from any one was the same as if he were beaten *before the crowds* in the market place and that what he would not receive *from a common man* in his loose large garments of hair; he viewed stabbing a prince of ten thousand chariots just as stabbing a fellow dressed in cloth of hair; he feared not any of all the princes; a bad word addressed to him be always returned. Meng Shishe had this way of nourishing his valour: — he said, 'I look upon not conquering and conquering in the same way. To measure the enemy and then advance; to calculate the chances of victory and then engage: — this is to stand in awe of the opposing force. How can I make certain of conquering? I can only rise superior to all fear.' Meng Shishe resembled *the philosopher Zeng*, Beigong You resembled Zixia. I do not know to the valour of which of the two the superiority should be ascribed, but yet Meng Shishe attended to what was of the greater importance. Formerly, *the philosopher Zeng* said to Zixiang, 'Do you love valour? I heard an account of great valour from the Master. *It speaks thus*: — If, on self-examination, I find that I am not upright, shall I not be in fear even of a poor man in his loose garments of haircloth? If, on self-examination, I find that I am upright, I will go forward against thousands and tens of thousands. *Yet* what Meng Shishe maintained, being his *merely* physical energy, was after all inferior to what the philosopher Zeng maintained, which was *indeed* of the most importance." *Gongsun Chou* said, "May I venture to ask an explanation from you, Master, of how you maintain an unperturbed mind and how the philosopher Gao does the same?" *Mencius answered*, "Gao says, 'What is not attained in words is not to be sought for in the mind; what produce dissatisfaction in the mind, is not to be helped by passion-effort.' *This last*, — when there is unrest in the mind, not to seek for relief from passion-effort, may be conceded. But not to seek in the mind for what is not attained in words cannot be conceded. The will is the leader of the passion-nature. The passion-nature pervades and animates the body. The will is *first and chief*, and the passion-nature is subordinate to it. Therefore *I* say, '—Maintain firm the will, and do no violence to the passion-nature.' " *Chou observed*, "Since you say — 'The will is chief, and the passion-nature is subordinate,' how do you also say, 'Maintain firm the will, and do no violence to the passion-nature?' " *Mencius* replied, "When it is the will alone which is active, it moves the passion-nature. When it is the passion-nature alone which is active, it moves the will. For instance now, in the case of a man falling or running; — that is from the passion-nature, and yet it moves the mind." "I venture to ask," *said Chou again*, "wherein you, Master, surpass *Gao*." *Mencius* told him, "I understand words, I am skilful in nourishing my vast, flowing passion-nature." *Chou* pursued, "I venture to ask what you mean by your vast, flowing passion-nature!" The reply was, "It is difficult to describe it. This is the passion-nature: — It is exceedingly great, and exceedingly strong; being nourished by rectitude, and sustaining no injury, it fills up all between heaven and earth. This is the passion-nature: — It is the mate and assistant of righteousness and reason. Without it, *man* is in a state of starvation. It is produced by the accumulation of righteous deeds; it is not to be obtained by incidental acts of righteousness. If the mind does not feel complacency in the conduct, *the nature* becomes starved. I therefore said, 'Gao has never understood righteousness, because he makes it something external.' There must be the *constant* practice *of this righteousness, but without the object of thereby nourishing the passion-nature*. Let not the mind forget *its work*, but let there be no assisting the growth *of that nature*. Let us not be like the man of Song. There was a man of Song, who was grieved that his growing corn was not longer, and so he pulled it up. *Having done this,* he returned home, looking very stupid, and said to his people, 'I am tired today. I have been helping the corn to grow long.' His son ran to look at it, and found the corn all withered. There are few in the world, *who do not deal with their passion-nature, as if* they were assisting the corn to grow long. Some indeed consider it of no benefit to them, and let it alone: — they do not weed their corn. They who assist it to grow long pull out their corn. *What they do is* not only of no benefit *to the nature, but it also injures it.*" *Gongsun Chou further asked,* "What do you mean by saying that you understand *whatever words you hear?*" *Mencius* replied, "When words are one-sided, I know how *the mind of the speaker* is clouded over. When words are extravagant, I know how *the mind* is fallen and sunk. When words are all depraved, I know how *the mind* has departed *from principle*. When words are evasive, I know how *the mind* is at its wits' end. *These evils* growing in the mind, do injury to government, and, displayed in the government, are hurtful to the conduct of affairs. When a sage shall again arise, he will certainly follow my words." *On this Chou observed,* "Zai Wo and Zigong were skilful in speaking. Ran Niu, the disciple Min, and Yan Yuan, while their words were good, were distinguished for their virtuous conduct. Confucius united the qualities of the disciples in himself, *but still* he said: 'In the matter of speeches, I am not competent.' — Then, Master, have you attained to be a sage?" *Mencius* said, "Oh! what words are these? Formerly Zigong asked Confucius, saying, 'Master, are you a sage?' Confucius answered him, 'A sage is what I cannot rise to. I learn without satiety, and teach without being tired.' Zigong said, 'You learn without satiety: — that shows your wisdom. You teach without being tired: — that shows your benevolence. Benevolent and wise, — Master, you are a sage.' Now, since Confucius would not have himself regarded as a sage, what words were those?" *Chou said*, "Formerly, I once heard this: — Zixia, Ziyou, and Zizhang had each one member of the sage. Ran Niu, the disciple Min, and Yan Yuan, had all the members, but in small proportions. I venture to ask, — With which of these are you pleased to rank yourself?" *Mencius* replied, "Let us drop speaking about these, if you please." *Chou then* asked, "What do you say of Boyi and Yiyin? Their ways were different from mine," said *Mencius*. "Not to serve a prince whom he did not esteem, nor command a people whom he did not approve; in a time of good government to take office, and on the occurrence of confusion to retire: — this was *the way of* Boyi. *To say*, — 'Whom may I not serve? My serving him makes him my prince. What people may I not command? My commanding them makes them my people.' In a time of good government to take office, and when disorder prevailed, also to take office: — that was *the way of* Yiyin. When it was proper to go into office, then to go into it; when it was proper to keep retired from office, then to keep retired from it; when it was proper to continue in it long, then to continue in it long; when it was proper to withdraw from it quickly, then to withdraw quickly — that was *the way of* Confucius. These were all sages of antiquity, and I have not attained to do what they did. But what I wish to do is to learn to be like Confucius." *Chou* said, "Comparing Boyi and Yiyin with Confucius, are they to be placed in the same rank?" *Mencius* replied, "No. Since there were living men until now, there never was another *Confucius.*" *Chou* said, "Then, did they have *any points* of agreement *with him*?" The reply was, — "Yes. If they had been sovereigns over a hundred *li* of territory, they would, all of them, have brought all the princes to attend in their court, and have obtained the empire. And none of them, in order to obtain the empire, would have committed one act of unrighteousness, or put to death one innocent person. In those things they agreed with him." *Chou* said, "I venture to ask wherein he differed from them." *Mencius* replied, "Zai Wo, Zigong, and You Ruo had wisdom sufficient to know the sage. *Even had they been ranking themselves* low, they would not have demeaned themselves to flatter their favorite. *Now*, Zai Wo said, 'According to my view of our Master, he is far superior to Yao and Shun.' Zigong said, 'By viewing the ceremonial ordinances *of a prince*, we know *the character of* his government. By hearing his music, we know *the character of* his virtue. From the distance of a hundred ages after, I can arrange, according to their merits, the kings of a hundred ages — not one of them can escape me. From the birth of mankind till now, there has never been *another* like our Master.' You Ruo said, 'Is it only among men that it is so? There is the Qilin among quadrupeds, the Fenghuang among birds, the Tai mountain among mounds and anthills, and rivers and seas among rain-pools. *Though different in degree*, they are the same in kind. So the sages among mankind are also the same in kind. But they stand out from their fellows, and rise above the level, and from the birth of mankind till now, there never has been one so complete as Confucius.'"

3.3 　孟子曰：“以力假仁者霸，霸必有大国；以德行仁者王，王不待大——汤以七十里，文王以百里。以力服人者，非心服也，力不赡也；以德服人者，中心悦而诚服也，如七十子之服孔子也。《诗》云：‘自西自东，自南自北，无思不服。’此之谓也。”

3.3　Mencius said, "He who, using force, makes a pretence to benevolence, is the leader *of the princes*. A leader *of the princes* requires a large kingdom. He who, using virtue, practises benevolence, — is the sovereign of the empire. To become the sovereign of the empire, *a prince* need not wait for a large *kingdom*. Tang did it with only seventy *li*, and King Wen with only a hundred. When one by force subdues men, they do not submit to him in heart. *They submit because* their strength is not adequate to resist. When one subdues men by virtue, in their hearts' core they are pleased, and sincerely submit, as was the case with the seventy disciples in their submission to Confucius. What is said in the *Book of Poetry*: 'From the west, from the east, from the south, from the north, there was not one who thought of refusing submission,' is an illustration of this."

3.4 孟子曰："仁则荣，不仁则辱；今恶辱而居不仁，是犹恶湿而居下也。如恶之，莫如贵德而尊士，贤者在位，能者在职；国家闲暇，及是时，明其政刑。虽大国，必畏之矣。《诗》云：'迨天之未阴雨，彻彼桑土，绸缪牖户。今此下民，或敢侮予？'孔子曰：'为此诗者，其知道乎！能治其国家，谁敢侮之？'今国家闲暇，及是时，般乐怠敖，是自求祸也。祸福无不自己求之者。《诗》云：'永言配命，自求多福。'《太甲》曰：'天作孽，犹可违；自作孽，不可活。'此之谓也。"

3.4 Mencius said, "Benevolence brings glory *to a prince*, and the opposite of it brings disgrace. For *the princes of* the present day to hate disgrace and yet to live complacently doing what is not benevolent, is like hating moisture and yet living in a low situation. If *a prince* hates disgrace, the best course for him to pursue, is to esteem virtue and honour *virtuous* scholars, giving the worthiest among them places of *dignity*, and the able offices of *trust*. When throughout his kingdom there is leisure and rest *from external troubles*, taking advantage of such a season, let him clearly *digest* the principles of his government with its legal sanctions, and then even great kingdoms will be constrained to stand in awe of him. It is said in the *Book of Poetry*: — 'Before the heavens were dark with rain, I gathered the bark from the roots of the mulberry trees. And wove it closely to form the window and door *of my nest*; now, *I thought*, ye people below, perhaps ye will not dare to insult me.' Confucius said, 'Did not he who made this ode understand the way of governing? If a prince able rightly to govern his kingdom, who will dare to insult him?' *But* now *the princes* take advantage of the time when throughout their kingdoms there is leisure and rest *from external troubles*, to abandon themselves to pleasure and indolent indifference; — they in fact seek for calamities for themselves. Calamity and happiness in all cases are men's own seeking. This is illustrated by what is said in the *Book of Poetry*, — 'Be always studious to be in harmony with the ordinances of God, so you will certainly get for yourself much happiness'; and by the passage of the *Tai Jia*, — 'When Heaven sends down calamities, it is still possible to escape from them; when we occasion the calamities ourselves, it is not possible any longer to live.' "

3.5　孟子曰：“尊贤使能，俊杰在位，则天下之士皆悦，而愿立于其朝矣；市，廛而不征，法而不廛，则天下之商皆悦，而愿藏于其市矣；关，讥而不征，则天下之旅皆悦，而愿出于其路矣；耕者，助而不税，则天下之农皆悦，而愿耕于其野矣；廛，无夫里之布，则天下之民皆悦，而愿为之氓矣。信能行此五者，则邻国之民仰之若父母矣。率其子弟，攻其父母，自有生民以来未有能济者也。如此，则无敌于天下。无敌于天下者，天吏也。然而不王者，未之有也。”

3.5　Mencius said, "If *a ruler* give honor to men of talents and virtue and employ the able, so that offices shall all be filled by individuals of distinction and mark; — then all the scholars of the empire will be pleased, and wish to stand in his court. If, in the marketplace *of his capital*, he levy a ground rent on the shops but do not tax the goods, or enforce the proper regulations without levying a ground rent, — then all the traders of the empire will be pleased, and wish to store their goods in his marketplace. If, at his frontier-passes, there be an inspection of persons, but no taxes charged *on goods or other articles*, then all the travelers of the empire will be pleased, and wish to make their tours on his roads. If he require that the husbandmen give their mutual aid to *cultivate the public field*, and erect no *other* taxes from them — then all the husbandmen of the empire will be pleased, and wish to plough in his fields. If from the occupiers of the shops in his marketplace he do not exact the fine of the individual idler, or of the hamlet's quota of cloth, then all the people of the empire will be pleased, and wish to come and be his people. If *a ruler* can truly practise these five things, then the people in the neighboring kingdoms will look up to him as a parent. From the first birth of mankind till now, never has any one led children to attack their parent, and succeeded in his design. Thus such a ruler will not have an enemy in all the empire, and he who has no enemy in the empire is the minister of Heaven. Never has there been a ruler in such a case who did not attain to the Imperial dignity."

3.6　孟子曰："人皆有不忍人之心。先王有不忍人之心，斯有不忍人之政矣。以不忍人之心，行不忍人之政，治天下可运之掌上。所以谓人皆有不忍人之心者，今人乍见孺子将入于井，皆有怵惕恻隐之心——非所以内交于孺子之父母也，非所以要誉于乡党朋友也，非恶其声而然也。由是观之，无恻隐之心，非人也；无羞恶之心，非人也；无辞让之心，非人也；无是非之心，非人也。恻隐之心，仁之端也；羞恶之心，义之端也；辞让之心，礼之端也；是非之心，智之端也。人之有是四端也，犹其有四体也。有是四端而自谓不能者，自贼者也；谓其君不能者，贼其君者也。凡有四端于我者，知皆扩而充之矣，若火之始然，泉之始达。苟能充之，足以保四海；苟不充之，不足以事父母。"

3.6 Mencius said, "All men have a mind which cannot bear *to see the sufferings of* others. The ancient kings had this commiserating mind, and they, as a matter of course, had likewise a commiserating government. When with a commiserating mind was practised a commiserating government, the government of the empire was as *easy a matter* as the making any thing go round in the palm. When I say that all men have a mind which cannot bear *to see the sufferings of others*, my meaning may be illustrated thus — even nowadays, if men suddenly see a child about to fall into a well, they will without exception experience a feeling of alarm and distress. *They will feel so*, not as a ground on which they may gain the favor of the child's parents, nor as a ground on which they may seek the praise of their neighbors and friends, nor from a dislike to the reputation of *having been unmoved by* such a thing. From this case we may perceive that the feeling of commiseration is essential to man, that the feeling of shame and dislike is essential to man, that the feeling of modesty and complaisance is essential to man, and that the feeling of approving and disapproving is essential to man. The feeling of commiseration is the principle of benevolence. The feeling of shame and dislike is the principle of righteousness. The feeling of modesty and complaisance is the principle of propriety. The feeling of approving and disapproving is the principle of knowledge. Men have these four principles just as they have their four limbs. When men, having these four principles, yet say of themselves that they cannot *develop them*, they play the thief with themselves, and he who says of his prince that he cannot develop them, plays the thief with his prince. Since all men have these four principles in themselves, let them know to give them all their development and completion and the issue will be like that of fire which has begun to burn, or that of a spring which has begun to find vent. Let them have their complete development, and they will suffice to love and protect all within the four seas. Let them be denied that development, and they will not suffice for a man to serve his parents with."

3.7　孟子曰："矢人岂不仁于函人哉？矢人唯恐不伤人，函人唯恐伤人。巫匠亦然。故术不可不慎也。孔子曰：'里仁为美。择不处仁，焉得智？'夫仁，天之尊爵也，人之安宅也。莫之御而不仁，是不智也。不仁、不智、无礼、无义，人役也。人役而耻为役，由弓人而耻为弓，矢人而耻为矢也。如耻之，莫如为仁。仁者如射：射者正己而后发；发而不中，不怨胜己者，反求诸己而已矣。"

3.7　Mencius said, "Is the arrow-maker less benevolent than the maker of armor of defence? *And yet*, the arrow-maker's only fear is lest men should not be hurt, and the armor-maker's only fear is lest men should be hurt. So it is with the priest and the coffin-maker. *The choice of* a profession, therefore, is a thing in which great caution is required. Confucius said, 'It is virtuous manners which constitute the excellence of a neighborhood. If a man, in selecting a residence, do not fix on one where such prevail, how can he be wise?' Now, benevolence is the most honorable dignity conferred by Heaven, and the quiet home in which man should dwell. Since no one can hinder us from being so, if yet we are not benevolent, — this is being not wise. From the want of benevolence and the want of wisdom will ensue the entire absence of propriety and righteousness, — he who is in such a case must be the servant of other men. To be the servant of men and yet ashamed of such servitude, is like a bow-maker's being ashamed to make bows, or an arrow-maker's being ashamed to make arrows. If he be ashamed of his case, his best course is to practise benevolence. The man who would be benevolent is like the archer. The archer adjusts himself and then shoots. If he misses, he does not murmur against those who surpass himself. He simply turns round and seeks *the cause of his failure* in himself."

3.8　孟子曰: "子路, 人告之以有过, 则喜。禹闻善言, 则拜。大舜有大焉, 善与人同, 舍己从人, 乐取于人以为善。自耕稼、陶、渔以至为帝, 无非取于人者。取诸人以为善, 是与人为善者也。故君子莫大乎与人为善。"

3.8   Mencius said, "When any one told Zilu that he had a fault, he rejoiced. When Yu heard good words, he bowed to the speaker. The great Shun had a still greater *delight in what was good. He regarded* virtue as the common property of himself and others, giving up his own way to follow that of others, and delighting to learn from others to practise what was good. From the time when he ploughed and sowed, exercised the potter's art and was a fisherman, to the time when he became emperor, he was continually learning from others. To take example from others to practise virtue is to help them in the same practice. Therefore, there is no attribute of the superior man greater than his helping men to practise virtue."

3.9   孟子曰："伯夷，非其君，不事；非其友，不友。不立于恶人之朝，不与恶人言；立于恶人之朝，与恶人言，如以朝衣朝冠坐于涂炭。推恶恶之心，思与乡人立，其冠不正，望望然去之，若将浼焉。是故诸侯虽有善其辞命而至者，不受也。不受也者，是亦不屑就已。柳下惠不羞污君，不卑小官；进不隐贤，必以其道；遗佚而不怨，阨穷而不悯。故曰：'尔为尔，我为我，虽袒裼裸裎于我侧，尔焉能浼我哉？'故由由然与之偕而不自失焉，援而止之而止。援而止之而止者，是亦不屑去已。"孟子曰："伯夷隘，柳下惠不恭。隘与不恭，君子不由也。"

3.9   Mencius said, "Boyi would not serve a prince whom he did not approve, nor associate with a friend whom he did not esteem. He would not stand in a bad prince's court, nor speak with a bad man. To stand in a bad prince's court, or to speak with a bad man, would have been to him the same as to sit with his court robes and court cap amid mire and ashes. Pursuing the examination of his dislike to what was evil, *we find* that he *thought it necessary*, if he happened to be standing with a villager whose cap was not rightly adjusted, to leave him with a high air, as if he were going to be defiled. Therefore, although some of the princes made application to him with very proper messages, he would not receive their gifts. — He would not receive their gifts, counting it inconsistent with his purity to go to them. Hui of Liuxia was not ashamed to serve an impure prince, nor did he think it low to be an inferior officer. When neglected and left without office, he did not murmur. When straitened by poverty, he did not grieve. Accordingly, he had a saying, 'You are you, and I am I. Although you stand by my side with breast and arms bare, or with your body naked, how can you defile me?' Therefore, self-possessed, he companied with men indifferently, at the same time not losing himself. *When he wished to leave*, if pressed to remain in office, he would remain. — He would remain in office, when pressed to do so, not counting it required by his purity to go away." Mencius said, "Boyi was narrow-minded, and Hui of Liuxia was wanting in self-respect. The superior man will not follow either narrow-minded, or the want of self-respect."

卷四　公孙丑章句下

BOOK IV　GONGSUN CHOU　PART II

4.1　孟子曰："天时不如地利，地利不如人和。三里之城，七里之郭，环而攻之而不胜。夫环而攻之，必有得天时者矣；然而不胜者，是天时不如地利也；城非不高也，池非不深也，兵革非不坚利也，米粟非不多也；委而去之，是地利不如人和也。故曰：域民不以封疆之界，固国不以山溪之险，威天下不以兵革之利。得道者多助，失道者寡助。寡助之至，亲戚畔之；多助之至，天下顺之。以天下之所顺，攻亲戚之所畔；故君子有不战，战必胜矣。"

4.1　Mencius said, "Opportunities of time *vouchsafed by* Heaven are not equal to advantages of situation *afforded by* the Earth, and advantages of situation afforded by the Earth are not equal to *the union arising from* the accord of Men. *There is a city*, with an inner wall of three *li* in circumference, and an outer wall of seven. — *The enemy* surround and attack it, but they are not able to take it. Now, to surround and attack it, there must have been vouchsafed to them by Heaven the opportunity of time, and in such case their not taking it is because opportunities of time vouchsafed by Heaven are not equal to advantages of situation afforded by the Earth. *There is a city, whose* walls are distinguished for their height, and whose moats are distinguished for their depth, where the arms *of its defenders*, offensive and defensive, are distinguished for their strength and sharpness, and the stores of rice and other grain are very large. *Yet it is obliged* to be given up and abandoned. This is because advantages of situation afforded by the Earth are not equal to the union arising from the accord of Men. In accordance with these principles it is said, 'A people is bounded in, not by the limits of dikes and borders; a kingdom is secured, not by the strengths of mountains and rivers; the empire is overawed, not by the sharpness *and strength of* arms. He who finds the proper course has many to assist him. He who loses the proper course has few to assist him. When this, — the being assisted by few, — reaches its extreme point, his own relations revolt *from the prince*. When the being assisted by many reaches its highest point, the whole empire becomes obedient *to the prince*. When one to whom the whole empire is prepared to be obedient, attacks those from whom their own relations revolt, *what must be the result*? Therefore, the true ruler will prefer not to fight; but if he do fight, he must overcome."

4.2　孟子将朝王，王使人来曰："寡人如就见者也，有寒疾，不可以风。朝，将视朝。不识可使寡人得见乎？"对曰："不幸而有疾，不能造朝。"明日，出吊于东郭氏。公孙丑曰："昔者辞以病，今日吊，或者不可乎？"曰："昔者疾，今日愈，如之何不吊？"王使人问疾，医来。孟仲子对曰："昔者有王命，有采薪之忧，不能造朝。今病小愈，趋造于朝，我不识能至否乎？"使数人要于路，曰："请必无归，而造于朝！"不得已而之景丑

氏宿焉。景子曰："内则父子，外则君臣，人之大伦也。父子
主恩，君臣主敬。丑见王之敬子也，未见所以敬王也。"曰：
"恶！是何言也！齐人无以仁义与王言者，岂以仁义为不美也？
其心曰，'是何足与言仁义也'云尔，则不敬莫大乎是。我非
尧舜之道，不敢以陈于王前，故齐人莫如我敬王也。"景子曰：
"否；非此之谓也。《礼》曰，'父召，无诺；君命召，不俟驾。'
固将朝也，闻王命而遂不果，宜与夫礼若不相似然。"曰："岂
谓是与？曾子曰：'晋楚之富，不可及也；彼以其富，我以吾
仁；彼以其爵，我以吾义，吾何慊乎哉？'夫岂不义而曾子言
之？是或一道也，天下有达尊三：爵一，齿一，德一。朝廷
莫如爵，乡党莫如齿，辅世长民莫如德。恶得有其一以慢其二
哉？故将大有为之君，必有所不召之臣；欲有谋焉，则就之。
其尊德乐道，不如是，不足与有为也。故汤之于伊尹，学焉而
后臣之，故不劳而王；桓公之于管仲，学焉而后臣之，故不劳
而霸。今天下地丑德齐，莫能相尚，无他，好臣其所教，而不
好臣其所受教。汤之于伊尹，桓公之于管仲，则不敢召。管仲
且犹不可召，而况不为管仲者乎？"

4.2 As Mencius was about to go to court to see the king, the king
sent a person to him *with this message,* — "I was wishing to come
and see you. But I have got a cold, and may not expose myself
to the wind. In the morning I will hold my court. I do not know
whether you will give me the opportunity of seeing you then."
Mencius replied, "Unfortunately, I am unwell, and not able to go

to the court." Next day, he went out to pay a visit of condolence to some one of the Dongguo family, when Gongsun Chou said to him, "Yesterday, you declined *going to the court* on the ground of being unwell, and today you are going to pay a visit of condolence. May this not be regarded as improper?" "Yesterday," said Mencius, "I was unwell; today, I am better; — why should I not pay this visit?" *In the mean time*, the king sent a messenger to inquire about his sickness, and also a physician. Meng Zhong replied to them, "Yesterday, when the king's order came, he was feeling a little unwell, and could not go to the court. Today he was a little better, and hastened to go to court. I do not know whether he can have reached it *by this time* or not." *Having said this*, he sent several men to look for Mencius on the way, and say to him, "I beg that, before you return home, you will go to the court." *On this*, Mencius felt himself compelled to go to Jing Chou's, and there stop the night. Jing said to him, "In the family, there is *the relation of* father and son; abroad, there is *the relation of* prince and minister. These are the two great relations among men. Between father and son, the ruling principle is kindness. Between prince and minister, the ruling principle is respect. I have seen the respect of the king to you, Sir, but I have not seen in what way you show respect to him." *Mencius* replied, "Oh! what words are these? Among the people of Qi, there is no one who speaks to the king about benevolence and righteousness. Are they thus silent because they do not think that benevolence and righteousness are admirable? *No, but* in their hearts they say, 'This man is not fit to be spoken with about benevolence and righteousness.' Thus they manifest a disrespect than which there can be none greater. I do not dare to set forth before the king any but the ways of Yao and Shun. There is therefore no man of Qi who respects the king so much as I do." Jing said, "Not so. That was not what I meant. In the *Book of Rites* it is said, 'When a father calls, the answer must be without a moment's hesitation. When the prince's order calls, the carriage must not be waited for.' You were certainly going to the court, but when you heard the king's order, then you did not carry your purpose out. This does seem as if it were not in accordance with that rule of propriety." *Mencius* answered him, "How can you give that meaning to my conduct? The philosopher Zeng said, 'The wealth of Jin and Chu cannot be equalled. Let *their rulers* have their wealth; — I have my benevolence. Let them have their nobility; — I have my righteousness. Wherein should I be dissatisfied *as inferior to them*?' Now shall we say that these sentiments are not right? Seeing that the philosopher Zeng spoke them, there is in them, I apprehend a real principle — In the empire there are three things universally acknowledged to be honorable. Nobility is one of them; age is one of them; virtue is one of them. In courts, nobility holds the first place of the three; in villages, age holds the first place; and for helping one's generation and presiding over the people, the other two are not equal to virtue. How can the possession of *only* one of these be *presumed on* to despise one who possesses the other two? Therefore a prince who is to accomplish great deeds will certainly have ministers whom he does not call to go to him. When he wishes to consult with them, he goes to them. The prince who does not honor the virtuous, and delight in their ways of doing, to this extent, is not worth having to do with. Accordingly, there was the behavior of Tang to Yiyin: — he first learned of him, and then employed him as his minister; and so without difficulty he became emperor. There was the behavior of the prince Huan to Guan Zhong: — he first learned of him, and then employed him as his minister; and so without difficulty he became chief of all the princes. Now throughout the empire, the territories *of the princes* are of equal extent, and in their achievements they are on a level. Not one of them is able to exceed the others. This is from no other reason, but that they love to make ministers of those whom they teach, and do not love to make ministers of those by whom they might be taught. So did Tang behave to Yiyin, and the prince Huan to Guan Zhong, that they would not venture to call them to go to them. If Guan Zhong might not be called to him by his prince, how much less may he be called, who would not play the part of Guan Zhong."

4.3　陈臻问曰：“前日于齐，王馈兼金一百，而不受；于宋，馈七十镒而受；于薛，馈五十镒而受。前日之不受是，则今日之受非也；今日之受是，则前日之不受非也。夫子必居一于此矣。”孟子曰：“皆是也。当在宋也，予将有远行，行者必以赆；辞曰：‘馈赆。’予何为不受？当在薛也，予有戒心；辞曰：‘闻戒，故为兵馈之。’予何为不受？若于齐，则未有处也。无处而馈之，是货之也。焉有君子而可以货取乎？”

4.3   Chen Zhen asked *Mencius*, saying, "Formerly, when you were in Qi, the king sent you a present of 2,400 taels of fine silver, and you refused to accept it. When you were in Song, 1,680 taels were sent to you, which you accepted; and when you were in Xue, 1,200 taels were sent, which you *likewise* accepted. If your declining to accept the gift in the first case was right, your accepting it in the latter cases was wrong. If your accepting it in the latter cases was right, your declining to do so in the first case was wrong. You must accept, Master, one of these alternatives." Mencius said, "I did right in all the cases. When I was in Song, I was about to take a long journey. Travelers must be provided with what is necessary for their expenses. The prince's message was — 'A present against traveling-expenses.' Why should I have declined the gift? When I was in Xue, I was apprehensive for my safety, and taking measures for my protection. The message was, 'I have heard that you are taking measures to protect yourself, and send this to help you in procuring arms.' Why should I have declined the gift? But when I was in Qi, I had no occasion for money. To send a man a gift when he has no occasion for it, is to bribe him. How is it possible that a superior man should be taken with a bribe?"

4.4   孟子之平陆，谓其大夫曰："子之持戟之士，一日而三失伍，则去之否乎？"曰："不待三。""然则子之失伍也亦多矣。凶年饥岁，子之民，老羸转于沟壑，壮者散而之四方者，几千人矣。"曰："此非距心之所得为也。"曰："今有受人之牛羊而为之牧之者，则必为之求牧与刍矣。求牧与刍而不得，则反诸其人乎？抑亦立而视其死与？"曰："此则距心之罪也。"他日，见于王曰："王之为都者，臣知五人焉。知其罪者，惟孔距心。"为王诵之。王曰："此则寡人之罪也。"

4.4 Mencius having gone to Pinglu, addressed the governor of it, saying, "*If one of* your spearmen should lose his place in the ranks three times in one day, would you, sir, put him to death or not?" The reply was, "I would not wait for three times *to do so*." *Mencius* said, "Well then, you, sir, have likewise lost your place in the ranks many times. In bad calamitous years, and years of famine, the old and feeble of your people, who have been found lying in the ditches and water-channels, and the able-bodied who have been scattered about to the four quarters, have amounted to several thousand." The governor replied, "That is a state of things in which it does not belong to me Juxin to act." "Here," said *Mencius*, "is a man who receives charge of the cattle and sheep of another, and undertakes to feed them for him, — of course he searches for pasture-ground and grass for them. If, after searching for those, he cannot find them, will he return *his charge to* the owner? Or will he stand by and see them die?" "Herein," said the officer, "I am guilty." Another day, *Mencius* had an audience of the king, and said to him, "Of the governors of Your Majesty's cities, I am acquainted with five, but the only one of them who knows his faults is Kong Juxin." He then repeated the conversation to the king. The king said, "In this matter, I am the guilty one."

4.5　孟子谓蚳蛙曰："子之辞灵丘而请士师，似也，为其可以言也。今既数月矣，未可以言与？"蚳蛙谏于王而不用，致为臣而去。齐人曰："所以为蚳蛙则善矣；所以自为，则吾不知也。"公都子以告。曰："吾闻之也：有官守者，不得其职则去；有言责者，不得其言则去。我无官守，我无言责也，则吾进退，岂不绰绰然有余裕哉？"

4.5　Mencius said to Chi Wa, "There seemed to be reason in your declining the governorship of Lingqiu, and requesting to be appointed chief criminal judge, because the *latter office* would afford you the opportunity of speaking *your views*. Now several months have elapsed, and have you yet found nothing of which you might speak?" *On this*, Chi Wa remonstrated *on some matter* with the king, and, his counsel not being taken, resigned his office, and went away. The people of Qi said: "In the course which he marked out for Chi Wa, he did well, but we do not know as to the course which he pursues for himself." His disciple Gongdu told him *these remarks*. *Mencius* said, "I have heard that he who is in charge of an office, when he is prevented from fulfilling its duties, ought to take his departure, and that he on whom is the responsibility of giving his opinion, when he finds his words unattended to, ought to do the same. But I am in charge of no office; on me devolves no duty of speaking out my opinion: — may not I therefore act freely and without any constraint, either in going forward or in retiring?"

4.6 孟子为卿于齐，出吊于滕，王使盖大夫王驩为辅行。王驩朝暮见，反齐滕之路，未尝与之言行事也。公孙丑曰："齐卿之位，不为小矣；齐滕之路，不为近矣，反之而未尝与言行事，何也？"曰："夫既或治之，予何言哉？"

4.6 Mencius, occupying the position of a high dignitary in Qi, went on a mission of condolence to Teng. The king *also* sent Wang Huan, the governor of Gai, assistant-commissioner. Wang Huan, morning and evening, waited upon Mencius, who, during all the way to Teng and back, never spoke to him about the business of their mission. Gongsun Chou said to Mencius, "The position of a high dignitary of Qi is not a small one; the road from Qi to Teng is not short. How was it that during all the way there and back, you never spoke to Huan about the matters of your mission?" Mencius replied, "There were the proper officers who attended to them. What occasion had I to speak to him about them?"

4.7 孟子自齐葬于鲁，反于齐，止于嬴。充虞请曰："前日不知虞之不肖，使虞敦匠事。严，虞不敢请。今愿窃有请也：木若以美然。"曰："古者棺椁无度，中古棺七寸，椁称之。自天子达于庶人，非直为观美也，然后尽于人心。不得，不可以为悦；无财，不可以为悦。得之为有财，古之人皆用之，吾何为独不然？且比化者无使土亲肤，于人心独无恔乎？吾闻之也：君子不以天下俭其亲。"

4.7 Mencius went from Qi to Lu to bury *his mother*. On his return to Qi, he stopped at Ying. Chong Yu begged to put a question to him and said, "Formerly, in ignorance of my incompetency, you employed me to superintend the making of the coffin. *As you were then pressed by* the urgency *of the business*, I did not venture to put any question to you. Now, however, I wish to take the liberty to submit the matter. The wood *of the coffin*, it appeared to me, was too good." *Mencius* replied, "Anciently, there was no rule for the size of either the inner or the outer coffin. In middle antiquity, the inner coffin was made seven inches thick, and the outer one the same. This *was done by all*, from the emperor to the common people, and not simply for the beauty of the appearance, but because they thus satisfied *the natural feelings of* their hearts. If prevented by *statutory regulations from making their coffins in this way*, men cannot have the feeling of pleasure. If they have not the money *to make them in this way*, they cannot have the feeling of pleasure. When they were not prevented, and had the money, the ancients all used this style. Why should I alone not do so? And moreover, is there no satisfaction to the natural feelings of a man, in preventing the earth from getting near to the bodies of his dead? I have heard that the superior man will not for all the world be niggardly to his parents."

4.8　沈同以其私问曰："燕可伐与?"孟子曰："可;子哙不得与人燕,子之不得受燕于子哙。有仕于此,而子悦之,不告于王而私与之吾子之禄爵;夫士也,亦无王命而私受之于子,则可乎?——何以异于是?"齐人伐燕。或问曰:"劝齐伐燕,有诸?"曰:"未也;沈同问'燕可伐与',吾应之曰,'可',彼然而伐之也。彼如曰，'孰可以伐之?'则将应之曰，'为天吏，则可以伐之。'今有杀人者，或问之曰，'人可杀与?'则将应之曰，'可。'彼如曰，'孰可以杀之?'则将应之曰：'为士师，则可以杀之。'今以燕伐燕，何为劝之哉?"

4.8 Shen Tong, on his own impulse, asked Mencius, saying, "May Yan be smitten?" *Mencius* replied, "It may. Zikuai had no right to give Yan to another man, and Zizhi had no right to receive Yan from Zikuai. *Suppose* there were an officer here, with whom you, sir, were pleased, and that, without informing the king, you were privately to give to him your salary and rank; and suppose that this officer, also without the king's orders, were privately to receive them from you: — would *such a transaction* be allowable? And where is the difference between *the case of Yan and* this?" The people of Qi smote Yan. Some one asked Mencius, saying, "Is it really the case that you advised Qi to smite Yan?" He replied, "No. Shen Tong asked me whether Yan might be smitten, and I answered him, 'It may.' They accordingly went and smote it. If he had asked me — 'Who may smite it?' I would have answered him, 'He who is the minister of Heaven may smite it.' Suppose the case of a murderer, and that one asks me — 'May this man be put to death?' I will answer him, — 'He may.' If he ask me, — 'Who may put him to death?' I will answer him, — 'The chief criminal judge may put him to death.' But now with one Yan to smite another Yan; — how should I have advised this?"

4.9 燕人畔。王曰："吾甚惭于孟子。"陈贾曰："王无患焉。王自以为与周公孰仁且智?"王曰："恶!是何言也!"曰："周公使管叔监殷,管叔以殷畔;知而使之,是不仁也;不知而使之,是不智也。仁智,周公未之尽也,而况于王乎?贾请见而解之。"见孟子,问曰："周公何人也?"曰："古圣人也。"曰："使管叔监殷,管叔以殷畔也,有诸?"曰："然。"曰:"周公知其将畔而使之与?"曰:"不知也。""然则圣人且有过与?"曰:"周公,弟也;管叔,兄也。周公之过,不亦宜乎?且古之君子,过则改之;今之君子,过则顺之。古之君子,其过也,如日月之食,民皆见之,及其更也,民皆仰之。今之君子,岂徒顺之,又从为之辞。"

4.9 The people of Yan having rebelled, the king of Qi said, "I feel very much ashamed *when I think* of Mencius." Chen Jia said to him, "Let not Your Majesty be grieved. Whether does Your Majesty consider yourself or Zhougong the more benevolent and wise?" The king replied, "Oh! what words are those!" "The duke of Zhou," said *Jia*, "appointed Guanshu to oversee *the heir of* Yin, but Guanshu with the power of the Yin State rebelled. If knowing that this would happen he appointed Guanshu, he was deficient in benevolence. If he appointed him not knowing that it would happen, he was deficient in knowledge. If the duke of Zhou was not completely benevolent and wise, how much less can Your Majesty be expected to be so! I beg to go and see Mencius, and relieve Your Majesty from that feeling." *Chen Jia* accordingly saw Mencius, and asked him saying, "What kind of man was the duke of Zhou?" "An ancient sage," was the reply. "Is it the fact that he appointed Guanshu oversee *the heir of* Yin, and that Guanshu with the state of Yin rebelled?" "It is." "Did the duke of Zhou know that he would rebel, and *purposely appoint him to that office*?" Mencius said, "He did not know." "Then, though a sage, he still fell into error?" "The duke of Zhou," answered *Mencius*, "was the younger brother. Guanshu was his elder brother. Was not the error of Zhougong in accordance with what is right? Moreover, when the superior men of old had errors, they reformed them. The superior men of the present time, when they have errors, persist in them. The errors of the superior men of old were like eclipses of the sun and moon. All the people witnessed them, and when they had reformed them, all the people looked up to them *with their former admiration. But* do the superior men of the present day only persist in their errors? They go on to raise apologizing discussions about them likewise."

4.10　孟子致为臣而归。王就见孟子，曰："前日愿见而不可得，得侍同朝，甚喜；今又弃寡人而归，不识可以继此而得见乎？"对曰："不敢请耳，固所愿也。"他日，王谓时子曰："我欲中国而授孟子室，养弟子以万钟，使诸大夫国人皆有所矜式。子盍为我言之！"时子因陈子而以告孟子，陈子以时子之言告孟子。孟子曰："然；夫时子恶知其不可也？如使予欲富，辞十万而受万，是为欲富乎？季孙曰：'异哉子叔疑！使己为政，不用，则亦已矣，又使其子弟为卿。人亦孰不欲富贵？而独于富贵之中有私龙断焉。'古之为市也，以其所有，易其所无者，有司者治之耳。有贱丈夫焉，必求龙断而登之，以左右望，而罔市利。人皆以为贱，故从而征之。征商自此贱丈夫始矣。"

4.10 Mencius gave up his office, and *made arrangements for* returning *to his native state.* The king came to visit him, and said, "Formerly, I wished to see you, but in vain. Then, I got the opportunity of being by your side, and all my court joyed exceedingly along with me. Now again you abandon me, and are returning home. I do not know if hereafter I may expect to have another opportunity of seeing you." Mencius replied, "I dare not request permission to visit you at any particular time, but indeed, it is what I desire." Another day, the king said to the officer Shi, "I wish to give Mencius a house, somewhere in the middle of the kingdom, and to support his disciples with *an allowance of 10,000 zhong*, that all the officers and the people may have *such an example* to reverence and imitate. Had you not better tell him this for me?" Shi took advantage to convey this message by means of the disciple Chen, who reported his words to Mencius. Mencius said, "Yes; but how should the officer Shi know that the thing may not be? Suppose that I wanted to be rich, having formerly declined 100,000 zhong, would my now accepting 10,000 be the conduct of one desiring riches? Jisun said, 'A strange man was Zishu Yi. He pushed himself into the service of government. *The prince* declined to employ him, he had to retire indeed, but he again schemed that his son or younger brother should be made a high officer. Who indeed is there of men but wishes for riches and honor? But he only, among the seekers of these, tried to monopolize the conspicuous mound.' Of old time, the market-dealers exchanged the articles which they had for others which they had not, and simply had certain officers to keep order among them. It happened that there was a mean fellow, who made it a point to look out for a conspicuous mound, and get up upon it. Thence he looked right and left, to catch in his net the whole of the market. The people all thought his conduct mean, and therefore they proceeded to lay a tax upon his wares. The taxing of traders took its rise from this mean fellow."

4.11 孟子去齐，宿于昼。有欲为王留行者，坐而言。不应，隐几而卧。客不悦曰："弟子齐宿而后敢言，夫子卧而不听，请勿复敢见矣。"曰："坐！我明语子。昔者鲁缪公无人乎子思之侧，则不能安子思；泄柳、申详无人乎缪公之侧，则不能安其身。子为长者虑，而不及子思；子绝长者乎？长者绝子乎？"

4.11 Mencius, having taken his leave of Qi, was passing the night in Zhou county. A person who wished to detain him on behalf of the king, *came and* sat down, and began to speak to him. *Mencius* gave him no answer, but leaned upon his stool and slept. The stranger was displeased, and said, "I passed the night in careful vigil, before I would venture to speak to you, and you, Master, sleep and do not listen to me. Allow me to request that I may not again presume to see you." *Mencius* replied, "Sit down, and I will explain the case clearly to you. Formerly, if the prince Mu had not kept a person by the side of Zisi, he could not have induced Zisi to remain with him. If Xie Liu and Shen Xiang had not had a *remembrancer* by the side of the prince Mu, he would not have been able to make them feel at home and remain with him. You anxiously form plans with reference to me, but you do not treat me as Zisi was treated. Is it you, Sir, who cut me? Or is it I, who cut you?"

4.12　孟子去齐。尹士语人曰："不识王之不可以为汤武，则是不明也；识其不可，然且至，则是干泽也。千里而见王，不遇故去。三宿而后出昼,是何濡滞也？士则兹不悦。"高子以告。曰："夫尹士恶知予哉？千里而见王，是予所欲也；不遇故去，岂予所欲哉？予不得已也。予三宿而出昼，于予心犹以为速。王庶几改之！王如改诸，则必反予。夫出昼，而王不予追也，予然后浩然有归志。予虽然，岂舍王哉！王由足用为善；王如用予,则岂徒齐民安，天下之民举安。王庶几改之！予日望之！予岂若是小丈夫然哉？谏于其君而不受，则怒，悻悻然见于其面，去则穷日之力而后宿哉？"尹士闻之，曰："士诚小人也。"

4.12　When Mencius had left Qi, Yin Shi spoke about him to others, saying, "If he did not know that the king could not be made a Tang or a Wu, that showed his want of intelligence. If he knew that he could not be made such, and came notwithstanding, that showed he was seeking his own benefit. He came a thousand *li* to wait on the king; because he did not find in him a ruler to suit him, he took his leave, but how dilatory and lingering was his departure, stopping three nights before he quitted Zhou! I am dissatisfied on account of this." The disciple Gao informed

Mencius *of these remarks. Mencius* said, "How should Yin Shi know me! When I came a thousand *li* to wait on the king, it was what I desired to do. When I went away because I did not find in him a ruler to suit me, was that what I desired to do? I felt myself constrained to do it. When I stopped three nights before I quitted Zhou, in my own mind I still considered my departure speedy. I was hoping that the king might change. If the king had changed, he would certainly have recalled me. When I quitted Zhou, and the king had not sent after me, then, and only till then, was my mind resolutely bent on returning *to Zou*. But, notwithstanding that, how can *it be said that* I give up the king? The king, after all, is one who may be made to do what is good. If he were to use me, would it be for the happiness of the people of Qi only? It would be for the happiness of the people of the whole empire. I am hoping that the king will change. I am daily hoping for this. Am I like one of your little-minded people? They will remonstrate with their prince, and *on their remonstrance not* being accepted, they get angry, and, with their passion displayed in their countenance, they take their leave, and travel with all their strength for a whole day before they will stop for the night." When Yin Shi heard this explanation, he said, "I am indeed a small man."

4.13 孟子去齐，充虞路问曰："夫子若有不豫色然。前日虞闻诸夫子曰：'君子不怨天，不尤人。'"曰："彼一时，此一时也。五百年必有王者兴，其间必有名世者。由周而来，七百有余岁矣。以其数，则过矣；以其时考之，则可矣。夫天未欲平治天下也；如欲平治天下，当今之世，舍我其谁也？吾何为不豫哉？"

4.13　When Mencius left Qi, Chong Yu questioned him upon the way, saying, "Master, you look like one who carries an air of dissatisfaction in his countenance. But formerly I heard you say — 'The superior man does not murmur against Heaven, nor grudge against men.' " Mencius said, "That was one time, and this is another. It is a rule that a true Imperial sovereign should arise in the course of five hundred years, and that during that time there should be men illustrious in their generation. From the commencement of the Zhou Dynasty till now, more than 700 years have elapsed. Judging numerically, the date is past. Examining *the character of the present* time, we might *expect the rise of such individuals in* it. But Heaven does not yet wish that the empire should enjoy tranquillity and good order. If it wished this, who is there besides me to bring it about? How should I be otherwise than dissatisfied?"

4.14　孟子去齐，居休。公孙丑问曰："仕而不受禄，古之道乎？"
曰："非也，于崇，吾得见王，退而有去志，不欲变，故不受也。
继而有师命，不可以请。久于齐，非我志也。"

4.14　When Mencius left Qi, he dwelt in Xiu. There Gongsun Chou asked him, saying, "Was it the way of the ancients to hold office without receiving salary?" *Mencius* replied, "No; when I first saw the king in Chong, it was my intention, on retiring from the interview, to go away. Because I did not wish to change this intention, I declined to receive any salary. Immediately after, came orders for the collection of troops when it would have been improper for me to beg permission to leave. But to remain so long in Qi was not my purpose."

卷五　滕文公章句上

BOOK V　TENG WEN GONG　PART I

5.1　滕文公为世子，将之楚，过宋而见孟子。孟子道性善，言必称尧舜。世子自楚反，复见孟子。孟子曰："世子疑吾言乎？夫道一而已矣。成覸谓齐景公曰：'彼，丈夫也；我，丈夫也，吾何畏彼哉？'颜渊曰：'舜，何人也？予，何人也？有为者亦若是。'公明仪曰：'文王，我师也；周公岂欺我哉？'今滕，绝长补短，将五十里也，犹可以为善国。《书》曰：'若药不瞑眩，厥疾不瘳。'"

5.1　When the prince Wen of Teng was crown-prince, having to go to Chu, he went by way of Song and visited Mencius. Mencius discoursed to him how the nature *of man* is good, and, when speaking, always made laudatory reference of Yao and Shun. When the crown-prince was returning from Chu, he again visited Mencius. Mencius said to him, "Prince, do you doubt my words? The path is one, and only one. Cheng Gan said to the prince Jing of Qi, 'They were men. I am a man. Why should I stand in awe of them?' Yan Yuan said, 'What kind of man was Shun? What kind of man am I? He who exerts himself will also become such as he was.' Gongming Yi said, 'King Wen is my teacher. How should the duke of Zhou deceive me *by those words*?' Now, Teng, taking its length with its breadth, will amount, I suppose, to fifty *li. It is small, but* still sufficient to make a good kingdom. It is said in the *Book of History*, 'If medicine do not raise a commotion in the patient, his disease will not be cured by it.' "

5.2 滕定公薨。世子谓然友曰：“昔者孟子尝与我言于宋，于心终不忘。今也不幸至于大故，吾欲使子问于孟子，然后行事。”然友之邹问于孟子。孟子曰：“不亦善乎！亲丧，固所自尽也。曾子曰：‘生，事之以礼；死，葬之以礼，祭之以礼，可谓孝矣。’诸侯之礼，吾未之学也。虽然，吾尝闻之矣。三年之丧，齐疏之服，饘粥之食，自天子达于庶人，三代共之。”然友反命，定为三年之丧。父兄百官皆不欲，曰：“吾宗国鲁先君莫之行，吾先君亦莫之行也，至于子之身而反之，不可。且《志》曰：‘丧祭从先祖。’曰，‘吾有所受之也。’”谓然友曰：“吾他日未尝学问，好驰马试剑。今也父兄百官不我足也，恐其不能尽于大事，子为我问孟子！”然友复之邹问孟子。孟子曰：“然。不可以他求者也。孔子曰：‘君薨，听于冢宰。歠粥，面深墨，即位而哭，百官有司莫敢不哀，先之也。’上有好者，下必有甚焉者矣。君子之德，风也；小人之德，草也。草尚之风，必偃。是在世子。”然友反命。世子曰：“然；是诚在我。”五月居庐，未有命戒。百官族人可，谓曰知。及至葬，四方来观之，颜色之戚，哭泣之哀，吊者大悦。

5.2 When the prince Ding of Teng died, the crown-prince said to Ran You, "Formerly, Mencius spoke with me in Song, and in my mind I have never forgotten *his words*. Now, alas! this great duty to my father devolves upon me; I wish to send you to ask the advice of Mencius, and then to proceed to its *various* services." Ran You *accordingly* proceeded to Zou, and consulted Mencius. Mencius said, "Is this not good? In discharging the funeral duties to parents, men indeed feel constrained to do their utmost. The philosopher Zeng said, 'When parents are alive, they should be served according to propriety; when they are dead, they should be buried according to propriety; and they should be sacrificed to according to propriety; — this may be called filial piety.' The ceremonies to be observed by the princes I have not learned, but I have heard *these points*: — that the three years' mourning, the garment of coarse cloth with its lower edge even, and the eating of congee, were equally prescribed by the three dynasties, and binding on all, from the emperor to the mass of the people." Ran You reported the execution of his commission, and the prince determined that the three years' mourning should be observed. His aged relatives, and the body of the officers, did not wish that it should be so, and said, "The former princes of Lu, that kingdom which we honor, have, none of them, observed this practice, neither have any of our own former princes observed it. For you to act contrary to their example is not proper. Moreover, the *History* says, — 'In the observances of mourning and sacrifice, ancestors are to be followed, meaning that they received those things from *a proper source to hand them down*." *The prince said again* to Ran You, "Hitherto, I have not given myself to the pursuit of learning, but have found my pleasure in horsemanship and sword-exercise, and now I don't come up to the wishes of my aged relatives and the officers. I am afraid I may not be able to discharge my duty in the great business *that I have entered on*; do you again consult Mencius for me." *On this*, Ran You went again to Zou, and consulted Mencius. Mencius said, "It is so, but he may not seek a *remedy* in others, *but only in himself*. Confucius said, 'When a prince dies, his successor entrusts the administration to the prime minister. He sips the congee. His face is of a deep black. He approaches the place of mourning, and weeps. Of all the officers and inferior ministers there is not one who will presume not to join in the lamentation, he setting them this example.' What the superior loves, his inferiors will be found to love exceedingly. The relation between superiors and inferiors is like that between the wind and grass. The grass must bend, when the wind blows upon it. The business depends on the prince." Ran You returned with this answer to his commission, and the prince said, "It is so. The matter does indeed depend on me." So for five months he dwelt in the shed, without issuing an order or a caution. All the officers and his relatives said, "He may be said to understand *the ceremonies*." When the time of interment arrived, from all quarters of the state, they came to witness it. Those who had come *from other states to* condole with him, were greatly pleased with the deep dejection of his countenance and the mournfulness of his wailing and weeping.

5.3 滕文公问为国。孟子曰："民事不可缓也。《诗》云：'昼尔于茅，宵尔索绹；亟其乘屋，其始播百谷。'民之为道也，有恒产者有恒心，无恒产者无恒心。苟无恒心，放辟邪侈，无不为已。及陷乎罪，然后从而刑之，是罔民也。焉有仁人在位罔民而可为也？是故贤君必恭俭礼下，取于民有制。阳虎曰：'为富不仁矣，为仁不富矣。'夏后氏五十而贡，殷人七十而助，周人百亩而彻，其实皆什一也。彻者，彻也；助者，籍也。龙子曰：'治地莫善于助，莫不善于贡。'贡者，挍数岁之中以为常。乐岁，粒米狼戾，多取之而不为虐，则寡取之；凶年，粪其田而不足，则必取盈焉。为民父母，使民盻盻然，将终岁勤动，不得以养其父母，又称贷而益之，使老稚转乎沟壑，恶在其为民父母也？夫世禄，滕固行之矣。《诗》云：'雨我公田，遂及我私。'惟助为有公田。由此观之，虽周亦助也。设为庠序学校以教之。庠者，养也；校者，教也；序者，射也。夏曰校，殷曰序，周曰庠；学则三代共之，皆所以明人伦也。人伦明于上，小民亲于下。有王者起，必来取法，是为王者师也。《诗》云：'周虽旧邦，其命惟新。'文王之谓也。子力行之，亦以新子之国！"使毕战问井地。孟子曰："子之君将行仁政，选择而使子，子必勉之！夫仁政，必自经界始。经界不正，井地不钧，谷禄不平，是故暴君污吏必慢其经界。经界既正，分田制禄，可坐而定也。夫滕，壤地褊小，将为君子焉，将为野人焉。无君子，莫治野人；无野人，莫养君子。请野九一而助，国中什一使自赋。卿以下必有圭田，圭田五十亩；馀夫二十五亩。死徙无出乡，乡田同井，出入相友，守望相助，疾病相扶持，则百姓亲睦。

方里而井，井九百亩，其中为公田。八家皆私百亩，同养公田；公事毕，然后敢治私事，所以别野人也。此其大略也；若夫润泽之，则在君与子矣。"

5.3　The prince Wen of Teng asked Mencius about *the proper way of* governing a kingdom. Mencius said, "The business of the people may not be remissly attended to. It is said in the *Book of Poetry*: 'In the day-light go and gather the grass. And at night twist your ropes, then get up quickly on the roofs; — *soon* must we begin sowing *again* the grain.' The way of the people is this. — If they have a certain livelihood, they will have a fixed heart. If they have not a certain livelihood, they have not a fixed heart. And if they have not a fixed heart, there is nothing which they will not do in the way of self-abandonment, of moral deflection, of depravity, and of wild license. When they have thus been involved in crime, to follow them up and punish them: — this is to entrap the people. How can such a thing as entrapping the people be done under the rule of a benevolent man? Therefore, a ruler who is endowed with talents and virtue will be gravely complaisant and economical, showing a respectful politeness to his ministers, and taking from the people only in accordance with regulated limits. Yang Hu said, 'He who seeks to be rich will not be benevolent. He who wishes to be benevolent will not be rich.' The sovereign of the Xia Dynasty enacted the fifty *mu* allotment, and the payment of a tax. The founder of the Yin enacted the seventy *mu* allotment, and the system of mutual aid. The founder of the Zhou enacted the hundred *mu* allotment, and the share system. In reality, *what was paid* in all these was a tithe. The share system means mutual division. The aid system means mutual dependence. Long, the ancient person of virtue, said, 'For regulating the lands, there is no better system than that of mutual aid, and none which is not better than that of taxing.' By the tax system, the regular amount was fixed by taking the average of several years. In good years, when the grain lies about in abundance, much might be taken without its being oppressive, and the actual exaction would be small. But in bad years, the produce being not sufficient to repay the manuring of the fields, this system still requires the taking of the full amount. When the parent of the people causes the people to wear looks of distress, and, after the whole year's toil, yet not to be able to nourish their parents, so that they proceed to borrowing to increase their means, till the old people and children are found lying in the ditches and water channels: — where, *in such a case*, is his parental relation to the people? As to the system of hereditary salaries, that is already observed in Teng. It is said in the *Book of Poetry*, — 'May the rain come down on our public field, and then upon our private field.' It is only in the system of mutual aid that there is a public field, and from this passage we perceive that even in the Zhou Dynasty this system has been recognized. Establish Xiang, Xu, Xue, and Xiao, — all those educational institutions, — for the instruction of the people. The name Xiang indicates nourishing as its object; Xiao, indicates teaching; and Xu indicates archery. By the Xia Dynasty, the name Xiao was used; by the Yin, that of Xu; and by the Zhou, that of Xiang. As to the Xue, they belonged to the three dynasties, *and by that name.* The object of them all is to illustrate the human relations. When those are thus illustrated by superiors, kindly feeling will prevail among the inferior people below. Should a real sovereign arise, he will certainly come and take an example *from you*; and thus you will be the teacher of the true sovereign. It is said in the *Book of Poetry*: 'Although Zhou was an old country, it received a new destiny.' That is said with reference to King Wen. Do you practise those things with vigor, and you also will by them make new your kingdom." *The prince afterwards* sent Bi Zhan to consult *Mencius* about the nine-squares system of dividing the land. Mencius said to him, "Since your prince, wishing to put in practice a benevolent government, has made choice of you and put you into this employment, you must exert yourself to the utmost. Now, the first thing towards a benevolent government must be to lay down the boundaries. If the boundaries be not defined correctly, the division of the land into squares will not be equal, and the produce *available for* salaries will not be evenly distributed. On this account, oppressive rulers and impure ministers are sure to neglect this defining of the boundaries. When the boundaries have been defined correctly, the division of the fields and the regulation of allowances may be determined by you, sitting at your ease. Although the territory of Teng is narrow and small, yet there must be in it men of a superior grade and there must be in it countrymen. If there were not men of a superior grade, there would be none to rule the countrymen. If there were not countrymen, there would be none to support the men of superior grade. I would ask you, in the remoter districts, observing the nine-squares division, to reserve one division to be cultivated on the system of mutual aid, and in the more central parts of the kingdom, to make the people pay for themselves a tenth part of their produce. From the highest officers down to the lowest, each one must have his holy field, consisting of fifty *mu*. Let the supernumerary males have their twenty-five *mu*. On occasions of death, or removal from one dwelling to another, there will be no quitting the district. In the fields of a district, those who belong to the same nine-squares render all friendly offices to one another in their going out and coming in, aid one another in keeping watch and ward, and sustain one another in sickness. Thus the people are brought to live in affection and harmony. A square *li* covers nine squares of land, which nine squares contain nine hundred *mu*. The central square is the public field, and eight families, each having its private hundred *mu*, cultivate in common the public field. And not till the public work is finished, may they presume to attend to their private affairs. This is the way by which the country-men are distinguished *from those of a superior grade*. Those are the great outlines of the system. Happily to modify and adapt it depends on the prince and you."

5.4　有为神农之言者许行，自楚之滕，踵门而告文公曰："远方之人闻君行仁政，愿受一廛而为氓。"文公与之处。其徒数十人，皆衣褐，捆屦、织席以为食。陈良之徒陈相与其弟辛负耒耜而自宋之滕，曰："闻君行圣人之政，是亦圣人也，愿为圣人氓。"陈相见许行而大悦，尽弃其学而学焉。陈相见孟子，道许行之言曰："滕君则诚贤君也；虽然，未闻道也。贤者与民并耕而食，饔飧而治。今也滕有仓廪府库，则是厉民而以自养也，恶得贤？"孟子曰："许子必种粟而后食乎？"曰："然。""许子必织布而后衣乎？"曰："否，许子衣褐。""许子冠乎？"曰："冠。"曰："奚冠？"曰："冠素。"曰："自织之与？"曰："否，以粟易之。"曰："许子奚为不自织？"曰："害于耕。"曰："许子以釜甑爨，以铁耕乎？"曰："然。""自为之与？"曰："否；以粟易之。""以粟易械器者，不为厉陶冶；陶冶亦以其械器易粟者，岂为厉农夫哉？且许子何不为陶冶，舍皆取诸其宫中而用之？何为纷纷然与百工交易？何许子之不惮烦？"曰："百工之事固不可耕且为也。""然则治天下独可耕且为与？有大人之事，有小人之事，且一人之身，而百工之所为备，如必自为而后用之，是率天下而路也。故曰：或劳心，或劳力，劳心者治人，劳力者治于人；治于人者食人，治人者食于人，天下之通义也。当尧之时，天下犹未平，洪水横流，泛滥于天下，草木畅茂，禽兽繁殖，五谷不登，禽兽逼人，兽蹄鸟迹之道交于中国。尧独忧之，举舜而敷治焉。舜使益掌火，益烈山泽而焚之，禽兽逃匿。禹疏九河，瀹济漯而注诸海，决汝汉，排淮泗，而注之江，然后中国可得而食也。当是时也，禹八年于外，三过其门而不入。虽欲耕，得乎？后稷教民稼穑，树艺五谷；五谷熟而民人育。人之有道也，饱食、暖衣、逸居而无教，则近于禽兽。圣人有忧之，使契为司徒，教以人伦，——父子有亲，君臣有义，夫妇有别，长幼有序，朋友有信。放勋曰：'劳之

来之，匡之直之，辅之翼之，使自得之，又从而振德之。'圣
人之忧民如此，而暇耕乎？尧以不得舜为已忧，舜以不得禹、
皋陶为已忧。夫以百亩之不易为已忧者，农夫也。分人以财谓
之惠，教人以善谓之忠，为天下得人者谓之仁。是故以天下与
人易，为天下得人难。孔子曰：'大哉，尧之为君！惟天为大，
惟尧则之，荡荡乎民无能名焉！君哉舜也！巍巍乎有天下而不
与焉！'尧舜之治天下，岂无所用其心哉？亦不用于耕耳。吾
闻用夏变夷者，未闻变于夷者也。陈良，楚产也。悦周公、仲
尼之道，北学于中国，北方之学者，未能或之先也。彼所谓豪
杰之士也。子之兄弟事之数十年，师死而遂倍之！昔者孔子没，
三年之外，门人治任将归，入揖于子贡，相向而哭，皆失声，
然后归。子贡反，筑室于场，独居三年，然后归。他日，子夏、
子张、子游以有若似圣人，欲以所事孔子事之，强曾子。曾子
曰：'不可；江汉以濯之，秋阳以暴之，皜皜乎不可尚已。'今
也南蛮鴃舌之人，非先王之道，子倍子之师而学之，亦异于曾
子矣。吾闻出于幽谷迁于乔木者，未闻下乔木而入于幽谷者。
《鲁颂》曰：'戎狄是膺，荆舒是惩。'周公方且膺之，子是之学，
亦为不善变矣。从许子之道，则市贾不贰，国中无伪；虽使五
尺之童适市，莫之或欺。布帛长短同，则贾相若；麻缕丝絮轻
重同，则贾相若；五谷多寡同，则贾相若；屦大小同，则贾相
若。"曰："夫物之不齐，物之情也；或相倍蓰，或相什百，或
相千万。子比而同之，是乱天下也。巨屦小屦同贾，人岂为之

哉？从许子之道，相率而为伪者也，恶能治国家？"

5.4   There came from Chu to Teng one Xu Xing, who gave out that he acted according to the words of Shennong. Coming right to his gate, he addressed the prince Wen, saying, "A man of a distant region, I have heard that you, Prince, are practising a benevolent government, and I wish to receive a site for a house, and to become one of your people." The prince Wen gave him a dwelling place. His disciples, amounting to several tens, all wore clothes of haircloth, and made sandals of hemp and wove mats for a living. *At the same time*, Chen Xiang, a disciple of Chen Liang, and his younger brother, Xin, with their plough-handles and shares on their backs, came from Song to Teng, saying, "We have heard that you, Prince, are putting into practice the government of the *ancient* sages, *showing* that you are likewise a sage. We wish to become the subjects of a sage." When Chen Xiang saw Xu Xing, he was greatly pleased with him, and abandoning entirely whatever he had learned, became his disciple. Having an interview with Mencius, he related to him with approbation the words of Xu Xing to the following effect: — "The prince of Teng is indeed a worthy prince. He has not yet heard, however, the real doctrines of *antiquity*. Now, wise and able princes should cultivate the ground, equally and along with their people, and eat *the fruit of their labor*. They should prepare their own meals, morning and evening, while at the same time they carry on their government. But now, the *prince of* Teng has his granaries, treasuries, and arsenals, which is an oppressing of the people to nourish himself. — How can he be deemed a *real* worthy prince?" Mencius said, "I suppose that Xu Xing sows grain and eats the produce. Is it not so?" "It is so," was the answer. "I suppose *also* he weaves cloth, and wears his own manufacture. Is it not so?" "No. Xu wears clothes of haircloth." "Does he wear a cap?" "He wears a cap." "What kind of cap?" "A plain cap." "Is it woven by himself?" "No. He gets it in exchange for grain." "Why does Xu not weave it himself?" "That would injure his husbandry." "Does Xu cook his food in boilers and earthen-ware pans, and does he plough with an iron share?" "Yes." "Does he make those articles himself?" "No. He gets them in exchange for grain." *Mencius then said,* "The getting those various articles in exchange for grain, is not oppressive to the potter and the founder, and the potter and the founder in their turn, in exchanging their various articles for grain, are not oppressive to the husbandman. How should such a thing be supposed? And moreover, why does not Xu act the potter and founder, supplying himself with the articles which he uses solely from his own establishment? Why does he go confusedly dealing and exchanging with the handicraftsmen? Why does he not spare himself so much trouble?" Xu Xing replied, "The business of the handicraftsman can by no means be carried on along with the business of husbandry." *Mencius resumed,* "Then, is it the government of the empire which alone can be carried on along with the practice of husbandry? Great men have their proper business, and little men have their proper business. Moreover, in the case of any single individual, *whatever articles he can require* are ready to his hand, being produced by the various handicraftsmen. If he must first make them for his own use, this way of doing would keep the whole empire running about upon the roads. Hence, there is the saying, 'Some labor with their minds, and some labor with their strength. Those who labor with their minds govern others; those who labor with their strength are governed by others. Those who are governed by others support them; those who govern others are supported by them.' This is a principle universally recognized. In the time of Yao, when the world had not yet been perfectly reduced to order, the vast waters, flowing out of their channels, made a universal inundation. Vegetation was luxuriant, and birds and beasts swarmed. The various kinds of grain could not be grown. The birds and beasts pressed upon men. The paths marked by the feet of beasts and prints of birds crossed one another throughout the Middle Kingdom. To Yao alone this caused anxious sorrow. He raised Shun to office, and measures to regulate the disorder were set forth. Shun committed to Yi the direction of the fire to be employed, and Yi set fire to, and consumed, *the forests and vegetation on* the mountains and in the marshes, so that the birds and beasts fled away to hide themselves. Yu separated the nine streams, cleared the courses of the Ji and Ta, and led them all to the sea. He opened a vent also for the Ru and Han, and regulated the course of the Huai and Si that they all flowed into the Changjiang. When this was done, it became possible for the people of the Middle Kingdom *to cultivate the ground and* get food for themselves. During that time, Yu was eight years away from his home, and though he thrice passed the door of it, he did not enter. Although he had wished to cultivate the ground, could he have done so? The Minister of agriculture taught the people to sow and reap, cultivating the five kinds of grain. When the five kinds of grain were brought to maturity, the people all enjoyed a comfortable subsistence. Now men possess a moral nature; but if they are well fed, warmly clad, and comfortably lodged, without being taught at the same time, they become almost like the beasts. This was subject of anxious solicitude to the sage *Shun*, and he appointed Xie to be the Minister of Instruction, to teach the relations of humanity: — how, between father and son, there should be affection; between sovereign and minister, righteousness; between husband and wife, attention to their separate functions; between old and young, a proper order; and between friends, fidelity. The highly meritorious emperor said to him, 'Encourage them; lead them on; rectify them; straighten them; help them; give them wings; — thus causing them to become possessors of themselves. Then follow this up by stimulating them, and conferring benefits on them.' When the sages were exercising their solicitude for the people in this way, had they leisure to cultivate the ground? What Yao felt giving him anxiety, was the not getting Shun. What Shun felt giving him anxiety was the not getting Yu and Gaoyao. But he whose anxiety is about his hundred *mu* not being properly cultivated, is a *mere* husbandman. The imparting by a man to others of his wealth, is called 'a kindness'. The teaching others what is good, is called 'the exercise of fidelity'. The finding a man who shall benefit the empire, is called 'benevolence'. Hence to give the empire to another man would be easy, to find a man who shall benefit the empire is difficult. Confucius said, 'Great indeed was Yao as a sovereign. It is only heaven that is great, and only Yao corresponded to it. How vast was his virtue. The people could find no name for it. Princely indeed was Shun! How majestic was he, having possession of the empire, and yet seeming as if it were nothing to him!' In their governing the empire, were there no subjects on which Yao and Shun employed their minds? There were subjects, only they did not employ their minds on the cultivation of the ground. I have heard of men using *the doctrines of* our great land to change barbarians, but I have never yet heard of any being changed by barbarians. Chen Liang was a native of Chu. Pleased with the doctrines of Zhougong and Zhongni, he came northwards to the Middle Kingdom and studied them. Among the scholars of the northern regions, there was perhaps no one who excelled him. He was what you call a scholar of high and distinguished qualities. You and your brother followed him some tens of years, and when your master died, you have forthwith turned away from him. Formerly, when Confucius died, after three years had elapsed, his disciples collected their baggage, and prepared to return to their several homes. But on entering to take their leave of Zigong, as they looked towards one another, they wailed, till they all lost their voices. After this they returned to their homes, but Zigong went back, and built a house for himself on the altar-ground, where he lived alone other three years before he returned home. On another occasion, Zixia, Zizhang, and Ziyou, thinking that You Ruo resembled the sage, wished to render to him the same observances which they had rendered to Confucius. They tried to force the disciple Zeng to join with them, but he said, 'This may not be done. What has been washed in the waters of the Jiang and Han, and bleached in the autumn sun: — how glistening is it! Nothing can be added to it.' Now here is this shrike-tongued barbarian of the south, whose doctrines are not those of the ancient kings. You turn away from your master and become his disciple. Your conduct is different indeed from that of the philosopher Zeng. I have heard of *birds* leaving dark valleys to remove to lofty trees, but I have not heard of their descending from lofty trees to enter into dark valleys. In the *Praise-songs of Lu*, it is said: — 'He smote the barbarians of the west and the north, he punished Jing and Shu.' Thus Zhougong would be sure to smite them, and you become their disciple again; it appears that your change is not good." *Chen Xiang* said, "If Xu's doctrines were followed, then there would not be two prices in the market, nor any deceit in the kingdom. If a boy of five cubits were sent to the market, no one would impose on him; linen and silk of the same length would be of the same price. So it would be with *bundles of* hemp and silk, being of the same weight; with the different kinds of grain, being the same in quantity; and with shoes which were of the same size." *Mencius* replied, "It is the nature of things to be of unequal quality. Some are twice, some five times, some ten times, some a hundred times, some a thousand times, some ten thousand times as valuable as others. If you reduce them all to the same standard, that must throw the empire into confusion. If large shoes and small shoes were of the same price, who would make them? For people to follow the doctrines of Xu, would be for them to lead one another on to practice deceit. How can they avail for the government of a state?"

5.5 墨者夷之因徐辟而求见孟子。孟子曰："吾固愿见，今吾尚病，病愈，我且往见，夷子不来！"他日，又求见孟子。孟子曰："吾今则可以见矣。不直，则道不见；我且直之。吾闻夷子墨者。墨之治丧也，以薄为其道也；夷子思以易天下，岂以为非是而不贵也；然而夷子葬其亲厚，则是以所贱事亲也。"徐子以告夷子。夷子曰："儒者之道，古之人若保赤子，此言何谓也？之则以为爱无差等，施由亲始。"徐子以告孟子。孟子曰："夫夷子，信以为人之亲其兄之子，为若亲其邻之赤子乎？彼有取尔也。赤子匍匐将入井，非赤子之罪也。且天之生物也，使之一本，而夷子二本故也。盖上世尝有不葬其亲者，其亲死，则举而委之于壑。他日过之，狐狸食之，蝇蚋姑嘬之。其颡有泚，睨而不视。夫泚也，非为人泚，中心达于面目。盖归反蘽梩而掩之。掩之诚是也，则孝子仁人之掩其亲，亦必有道矣。"徐子以告夷子。夷子怃然为间曰："命之矣。"

5.5 The Mohist, Yi Zhi, sought, through Xu Pi, to see Mencius. Mencius said, "I indeed wish to see him, but at present I am still unwell. When I am better, I will myself go and see him. Yi need not come here *again*." Next day, Yi Zhi again sought to see Mencius. Mencius said, "Today I am able to see him. But if I do not correct his errors, the *true* principles will not be fully evident.

Let me first correct him. I have heard that this Yi is a Mohist. Now Mo considers that in the regulation of funeral matters a spare simplicity should be the rule. Yi thinks with *Mo's doctrines* to change *the customs of the empire.* — How does he regard them as if they were wrong, and not honor them? Notwithstanding his views, Yi buried his parents in a sumptuous manner, and so he served them in the way which his *doctrines* discountenance." The disciple Xu informed Yi of these remarks. Yi said, "Even according to the principles of the learned, we find that the ancients *acted towards the people,* 'as if they were watching over an infant'. What does this expression mean? To me it sounds that we are to love all without difference of degree; but the manifestation *of love* must begin with our parents." Xu reported this reply to Mencius, who said, "Now, does Yi really think that a man's affection for the child of his brother is *merely* like his affection for the infant of a neighbor? What is to be laid hold of in that *expression* is simply this — that if an infant crawling about is about to fall into a well, it is no crime in the infant. Moreover, Heaven gives birth to creatures in such a way that they have one root, and Yi makes them to have two roots. This is the cause *of his error.* And, in the most ancient times, there were some who did not inter their parents. When their parents died, they took them up and threw them into some water-channel. Afterwards, when passing by them, *they saw* foxes and wild-cats devouring them, and flies and gnats biting at them. The perspiration started out upon their foreheads, and they looked away, unable to bear the sight. It was not on account of other people that this perspiration flowed. The emotions of their hearts affected their faces and eyes, and instantly they went home, and came back with baskets and spades and covered the bodies. If *the covering them thus* was indeed right, you may see that the filial son and virtuous man, in interring *in a handsome manner* their parents, act according to a proper rule." The disciple Xu informed Yi of what Mencius had said. Yi was thoughtful for a short time, and then said, "He has instructed me."

卷六　滕文公章句下
BOOK VI　TENG WEN GONG　PART II

6.1　陈代曰："不见诸侯，宜若小然；今一见之，大则以王，小则以霸。且《志》曰：'枉尺而直寻'，宜若可为也。"孟子曰："昔齐景公田，招虞人以旌，不至，将杀之。志士不忘在沟壑，勇士不忘丧其元。孔子奚取焉？取非其招不往也。如不待其招而往，何哉？且夫枉尺而直寻者，以利言也。如以利，则枉寻直尺而利，亦可为与？昔者赵简子使王良与嬖奚乘，终日而不获一禽。嬖奚反命曰：'天下之贱工也。'或以告王良，良曰：'请复之。'强而后可，一朝而获十禽。嬖奚反命曰：'天下之良工也。'简子曰：'我使掌与女乘。'谓王良。良不可，曰：'吾为之范我驰驱，终日不获一；为之诡遇，一朝而获十。《诗》云："不失其驰，舍矢如破。"我不贯与小人乘，请辞。'御者且羞与射者比；比而得禽兽，虽若丘陵，弗为也。如枉道而从彼，何也？且子过矣：枉己者，未有能直人者也。"

6.1　Chen Dai said to *Mencius*, "In not *going to* wait upon any of the princes, you seem to me to be standing on a small point. If now you were once to wait upon them, the result might be so great that you would make one of them emperor, or, if smaller, that you would make one of them chief of all the other princes. Moreover, the *History* says, 'By bending *only* one cubit, you make

eight cubits straight.' It appears to me like a thing might be done."
Mencius said, "Formerly, the prince Jing of Qi once when was
hunting, called his forester to him by a flag. *The forester* would not
come, *and the prince* was going to kill him. *With reference to this
incident, Confucius said*, 'The determined officer never forgets
that his end may be in a ditch or a stream; the brave officer never
forgets that he may lose his head.' What was it *in the forester* that
Confucius thus approved? He approved his not going *to the prince*,
when summoned by the article which was not appropriate to him.
If one *go to see the princes* without waiting to be invited, what can
be thought of him? Moreover, *that sentence*, 'By bending only one
cubit, you make eight cubits straight,' is spoken with reference
to the gain *that may be got*. If gain be the object, then, if it can
be got by bending eight cubits to make one cubit straight, may
we likewise do that? Formerly, the officer Zhao Jian made Wang
Liang set as charioteer for his favorite Xi, when, in the course of a
whole day, they did not get a single bird. The favorite Xi reported
this result, saying, 'He is the poorest charioteer in the world.'
Some one told this to Wang Liang, who said, 'I beg leave to try
again.' By dint of pressing, this was accorded to him, when in one
morning they got ten birds. The favorite, reporting this result,
said, 'He is the best charioteer in the world.' Jian said, 'I will make
him always drive your carriage for you.' When he told Wang
Liang so, *however*, Liang refused, saying, '*I drove* for him, strictly
observing the proper rules for driving, and in the whole day he
did not get one *bird*. I *drove* for him so as deceitfully to intercept
the *birds*, and in one morning he got ten. It is said in the *Book of*

Poetry: "There is no failure in the management of their horses; the arrows are discharged surely, like the blows of an ax." I am not accustomed to drive for a mean man. I beg leave to decline the office.' Thus this charioteer even was ashamed to bend improperly to the will of *such an* archer. Though, by bending to it, they would have caught birds and animals enough to form a hill, he would not do so. If I were to bend my principles and follow those princes, of what kind would my conduct be? And you are wrong. Never has a man who has bent himself been able to make others straight."

6.2 景春曰："公孙衍、张仪岂不诚大丈夫哉？一怒而诸侯惧，安居而天下熄。"孟子曰："是焉得为大丈夫乎？子未学礼乎？丈夫之冠也，父命之；女子之嫁也，母命之，往送之门，戒之曰：'往之女家，必敬必戒，无违夫子！'以顺为正者，妾妇之道也。居天下之广居，立天下之正位，行天下之大道；得志，与民由之；不得志，独行其道。富贵不能淫，贫贱不能移，威武不能屈，此之谓大丈夫。"

6.2 Jing Chun said to *Mencius*, "Are not Gongsun Yan and Zhang Yi really great men? Let them once be angry, and all the princes are afraid. Let them live quietly, and the flames of trouble are extinguished throughout the empire." Mencius said, "How can such men be great men? Have you not read the Ritual *Usages*? — At the capping of a young man, his father admonishes him. At the marrying away of a young woman, her mother admonishes her, accompanying her to the door on her leaving, and cautioning her with these words, 'You are going to your home. You must be respectful; you must be careful. Do not disobey your husband.' *Thus*, to look upon compliance as their correct course is the rule for women. To dwell in the wide house of the world, to stand in the correct seat of the world, and to walk in the great path of the world; when he obtains his desire *for office*, to practice his principles for the good of the people; and when that desire is disappointed, to practice them alone; to be above the power of riches and honors to make dissipated, of poverty and mean condition to make swerve from principle, and of power and force to make bend: — these characteristics constitute the great man."

6.3 周霄问曰:"古之君子仕乎?"孟子曰:"仕,《传》曰:'孔子三月无君,则皇皇如也,出疆必载质。'公明仪曰:'古之人三月无君,则吊。'""三月无君则吊,不以急乎?"曰:"士之失位也,犹诸侯之失国家也。《礼》曰:'诸侯耕助,以供粢盛;夫人蚕缫,以为衣服。牺牲不成,粢盛不洁,衣服不备,不敢以祭。惟士无田,则亦不祭。'牲杀、器皿、衣服不备,不敢以祭,则不敢以宴,亦不足吊乎?""出疆必载质,何也?"曰:"士之仕也,犹农夫之耕也;农夫岂为出疆舍其耒耜哉?"曰:"晋国亦仕国也,未尝闻仕如此其急。仕如此其急也,君子之难仕,何也?"曰:"丈夫生而愿为之有室,女子生而愿为之有家;父母之心,人皆有之。不待父母之命、媒妁之言,钻穴隙相窥，逾墙相从，则父母国人皆贱之。古之人未尝不欲仕也，又恶不由其道。不由其道而往者，与钻穴隙之类也。"

6.3 Zhou Xiao asked *Mencius*, saying, "Did superior men of old time take office?" Mencius replied, "They did. The *Record* says, 'If Confucius was three months without *being employed by some* sovereign, he looked anxious and unhappy. When he passed from the boundary of a state, he was sure to carry with him his proper gift of introduction.' Gongming Yi said, 'Among the ancients, if an officer was three months unemployed by a sovereign, he was condoled with.' " *Xiao said*, "Did not this condoling, on being three months unemployed by a sovereign, show a too great urgency?" *Mencius* answered, "The loss of his place to an officer is like the loss of his kingdom to a prince. It is said in the *Book of Rites*, 'A prince ploughs himself, and is assisted *by the people*, to supply the millet *for sacrifice*. His wife keeps silkworms, and unwinds their cocoons, to make the garments *for sacrifice*. If the victims be not perfect, the millet not pure, and the dress not complete, he does not presume to sacrifice. And the scholar who, *out of office*, has no holy field, in the same way, does not sacrifice.' The victims for slaughter, the vessels, and the garments, not being all complete, he does not presume to sacrifice and then neither may he dare to feel happy. Is there not here sufficient ground also for condolence?" *Xiao again asked*, "What was the meaning of *Confucius*, always carrying his proper gift of introduction with him, when he passed over the boundaries *of the State where he had been*?" "An officer's being in office," was the reply, "is like the ploughing of a husbandman. Does a husbandman part with his plough, because he goes from one state to another?" *Xiao* pursued, "The kingdom of Jin is one, as well as others, of official employments, but I have not heard of any being thus earnest about being in office. If there should be this urgency about being in office, why does a superior man make any difficulty about taking it?" *Mencius* answered, "When a son is born, what is desired for him is that he may have a wife; when a daughter is born, what is desired for her is that she may have a husband. This feeling of the parents is possessed by all men. If *the young people*, without waiting for the orders of their parents, and the arrangements of the go-betweens, shall bore holes to steal a sight of each other, or get over the wall to be with each other, then their parents and all other people will despise them. The ancients did indeed always desire to be in office, but they also hated being so by any improper way. To go *to get office* by an improper way is of a class with *young people's* boring holes."

6.4　彭更问曰：“后车数十乘，从者数百人，以传食于诸侯，不以泰乎？”孟子曰：“非其道，则一箪食不可受于人；如其道，则舜受尧之天下，不以为泰——子以为泰乎？”曰：“否，士无事而食，不可也。”曰：“子不通功易事，以羡补不足，则农有馀粟，女有馀布；子如通之，则梓匠轮舆皆得食于子。于此有人焉，入则孝，出则悌，守先王之道，以待后之学者，而不得食于子；子何尊梓匠轮舆而轻为仁义者哉？”曰：“梓匠轮舆，其志将以求食也；君子之为道也，其志亦将以求食与？”曰：

"子何以其志为哉？其有功于子，可食而食之矣。且子食志乎？食功乎？"曰："食志。"曰："有人于此，毁瓦画墁，其志将以求食也，则子食之乎？"曰："否。"曰："然则子非食志也，食功也。"

6.4　Peng Geng asked *Mencius*, saying, "Is it not an extravagant procedure to go from one prince to another and live upon them, followed by several tens of carriages, and attended by several hundred men?" Mencius replied, "If there be not a proper ground *for taking it*, a single bamboo-cup of rice may not be received from a man. If there be such a proper ground, then Shun's receiving the empire from Yao is not to be considered excessive. Do you think it was excessive?" *Geng* said, "No. But for a scholar *performing* no service to receive his support notwithstanding, is improper." *Mencius* answered, "If you do not have an intercommunication of the productions of labor, and an interchange of *men's* services, so that *one from his* overplus may supply the deficiency of another, then husbandmen will have a superfluity of grain, and women will have a superfluity of cloth. If you have such an interchange, carpenters and carriage-wrights may all get their food from you. Here now is a man, who, at home, is filial, and abroad, respectful to his elders; who watches over the principles of the ancient kings, awaiting *the rise of future* learners: — and yet you will refuse to support him. How is it that you give honor to the carpenter and carriage-wright, and slight him who practices benevolence and righteousness?" *Peng Geng* said, "The aim of the carpenter and carriage-wright is *by their trades* to seek for a living. Is it also the aim of the superior man in his practice of principles thereby to seek for a living?" "What have you to do," returned *Mencius*, "with his purpose? He is of service to you. He deserves to be supported and should be supported. And *let me ask*, — Do you remunerate a man's intention, or do you remunerate his service?" *To this Geng* replied, "I remunerate his intention." *Mencius* said, "There is a man here, who breaks your tiles, and draws *unsightly* figures on your walls: — his purpose may be thereby to seek for his living, but will you indeed remunerate him?" "No," said Geng. *Mencius then* concluded, "That being the case, it is not the purpose which you remunerate, but the work done."

6.5　万章问曰："宋，小国也；今将行王政，齐楚恶而伐之，则如之何？"孟子曰："汤居亳，与葛为邻，葛伯放而不祀。汤使人问之曰：'何为不祀？'曰：'无以供牺牲也。'汤使遗之牛羊。葛伯食之，又不以祀。汤又使人问之曰：'何为不祀？'曰：'无以供粢盛也。'汤使亳众往为之耕，老弱馈食。葛伯率其民，要其有酒食黍稻者夺之，不授者杀之。有童子以黍肉饷，杀而夺之。《书》曰：'葛伯仇饷。'此之谓也。为其杀是童子而征之，四海之内皆曰：'非富天下也，为匹夫匹妇复雠也。''汤始征，自葛载，'十一征而无敌于天下。东面而征，西夷怨；南面而征，北狄怨，曰：'奚为后我？'民之望之，若大旱之望雨也。归市者弗止，芸者不变，诛其君，吊其民，如时雨降。民大悦，《书》曰：'徯我后，后来其无罚！''有攸不惟臣，东

征，绥厥士女，篚厥玄黄，绍我周王见休，惟臣附于大邑周。'

其君子实玄黄于篚，以迎其君子，其小人箪食壶浆，以迎其小

人；救民于水火之中，取其残而已矣。《太誓》曰：'我武惟扬，

侵于之疆，则取于残，杀伐用张，于汤有光。'不行王政云尔；

苟行王政，四海之内皆举首而望之，欲以为君；齐楚虽大，何

畏焉？"

6.5   Wan Zhang asked *Mencius*, saying, "Song is a small state. *Its ruler* is now setting about to practice the *true* royal government, and Qi and Chu hate and attack him. What in this case is to be done?" *Mencius* replied, "When Tang dwelt in Bo, he adjoined to the *state of* Ge, the chief of which was living in a dissolute state and neglecting *his proper* sacrifices. Tang sent messengers to inquire why he did not sacrifice. He replied, 'I have no means of supplying the necessary victims.' *On this*, Tang caused oxen and sheep to be sent to him, but he ate them, and still continued not to sacrifice. Tang again sent messengers to ask him the same question as before, then he replied, 'I have no means of obtaining the necessary millet.' *On this*, Tang sent the mass of the people of Bo to go and till the ground for him, while the old and feeble carried their food to them. The chief of Ge led his people to intercept those who were thus charged with wine, cooked rice, millet, and paddy, and took their stores from them, while they killed those who refused to give them up. There was a boy who had some millet and flesh for the laborers, who was thus slain and robbed. What is said in the *Book of History*, 'The chief of Ge behaved as an enemy to the provision-carriers,' has reference to this. Because of his murder of this boy, *Tang* proceeded to punish him. All within the four seas said, 'It is not because he desires the riches of the empire, but to avenge a common man and woman.' When Tang began his work of executing justice, he commenced with Ge, and though he punished eleven *princes*, he had not an enemy in the empire. When he pursued his work in the east, the rude tribes in the west murmured. So did those on the north, when he was engaged in the south. Their cry was 'Why does he make us last?' *Thus*, the people's longing for him was like their longing for rain in a time of great drought. The frequenters of the markets stopped not. Those engaged in weeding *in the fields* made no change *in their operations*. While he punished their rulers, he consoled the people. *His progress* was like the falling of opportune rain, and the people were delighted. It is said in the *Book of History*, 'We have waited for our prince. When our prince comes, we may escape from the punishments *under which we suffer*.' 'There being some who would not become the subjects of *Zhou*, *King Wu* proceeded to punish them on the east. He gave tranquillity to their people, who *welcomed him* with baskets full of their black and yellow silks, *saying* — From henceforth we shall serve the sovereign of *our dynasty of* Zhou, that we may be made happy by him.' So they joined themselves, as subjects, to the great city of Zhou. Thus, the men of station of Shang took baskets full of black and yellow *silks* to meet the men of station of Zhou, and the lower classes of the one met those of the other with baskets of rice and vessels of congee. *Wu* saved the people from the midst of fire and water, seizing only their oppressors, *and destroying them.* In the *Great Declaration* it is said, 'My power shall be put forth, and invading the territories of *Yu*, I will seize the oppressor. I will put him to death to punish him, — so shall the greatness of my work appear, more glorious than that of Tang.' *Song* is not as you say, practicing *true* royal government, and so forth. If it were practicing royal government, all within the four seas would be lifting up their heads, and looking for *its prince*, wishing to have him for their sovereign. Great as Qi and Chu are what would there be to fear from them?"

6.6　孟子谓戴不胜曰：“子欲子之王之善与？我明告子。有楚大夫于此，欲其子之齐语也，则使齐人傅诸？使楚人傅诸？”曰：“使齐人傅之。”曰：“一齐人傅之，众楚人咻之，虽日挞而求其齐也，不可得矣；引而置之庄岳之间数年，虽日挞而求其楚，亦不可得矣。子谓薛居州，善士也。使之居于王所。在于王所者，长幼卑尊皆薛居州也，王谁与为不善？在王所者，长幼卑尊皆非薛居州也，王谁与为善？一薛居州，独如宋王何？”

6.6　Mencius said to Dai Busheng, "I see that you are desiring your king to be virtuous, and will plainly tell you *how he may be made so.* Suppose that there is a great officer of Chu here, who wishes his son to learn the speech of Qi. Will he in that case employ a man of Qi as his tutor, or a man of Chu?" "He will employ a man of Qi to teach him," said *Busheng. Mencius* went on, "If *but* one man of Qi be teaching him, and there be a multitude of men of Chu continually shouting out about him, although *his father* beat him every day, wishing him to learn the speech of Qi, it will be impossible for him to do so. But in the same way, if he were to be taken and placed for several years in Zhuang or Yue, though *his father* should beat him, wishing him to speak the language of Chu, it would be impossible for him to do so. You supposed that Xue Juzhou was a scholar of virtue and you have got him placed in attendance on the king. Suppose that all in attendance on the king, old and young, high and low, were Xue Juzhous whom would the king have to do evil with? And suppose that all in attendance on the king, old and young, high and low, are not Xue Juzhous whom will the king gave to do good with? What can one Xue Juzhou do alone for the king of Song?"

6.7　公孙丑问曰："不见诸侯何义？"孟子曰："古者不为臣不见。段干木逾垣而辟之，泄柳闭门而不纳，是皆已甚；迫，斯可以见矣。阳货欲见孔子而恶无礼，大夫有赐于士，不得受于其家，则往拜其门。阳货瞰孔子之亡也，而馈孔子蒸豚；孔子亦瞰其亡也，而往拜之。当是时，阳货先，岂得不见？曾子曰：'胁肩谄笑，病于夏畦。'子路曰：'未同而言，观其色赧赧然，非由之所知也。'由是观之，则君子之所养，可知已矣。"

6.7　Gongsun Chou asked *Mencius*, saying, "What is the point of righteousness involved in your not going to see the princes?" *Mencius* replied, "Among the ancients, if one had not been a minister in a *state*, he did not go to *see the sovereign*. Duan Gan Mu leaped over his wall to avoid the prince. Xie Liu shut his door, and would not admit the prince. These two, however, *carried their scrupulosity* to excess. When a prince is urgent, it is not improper to see him. Yang Huo wished to get Confucius to go to see him, but disliked doing so by any want of propriety. *As it is the rule, therefore, that* when a great officer sends a gift to a scholar, if the latter be not at home to receive it, he must go to the *officer's* to pay his respects, Yang Huo watched when Confucius was out, and sent him a roasted pig. Confucius, in his turn, watched when He was out, and went to pay his respects to him. At that time, Yang Huo had taken the initiative; — how could Confucius decline going to see him? The philosopher Zeng said, 'They who shrug up their shoulders, and laugh in a flattering way, toil harder than the summer *laborer in the fields.*' Zilu said, 'There are those who talk with people with whom they have no *great* community *of feeling*. If you look at their countenances, they are full of blushes. I do not desire to know such persons.' By considering these remarks, the *spirit* which the superior man nourishes may be known."

6.8　戴盈之曰：“什一，去关市之征，今兹未能，请轻之，以待来年，然后已，何如？”孟子曰：“今有人日攘其邻之鸡者，或告之曰：‘是非君子之道。’曰：‘请损之，月攘一鸡，以待来年，然后已。’——如知其非义，斯速已矣，何待来年？”

6.8　Dai Yingzhi said to *Mencius*, "I am not able at present and immediately to do with the levying of a tithe *only*, and abolishing the duties charged at the passes and in the markets. With your leave I will lighten, however, both the tax and the duties, until next year, and will then make an end of them. What do you think of such a course?" Mencius said, "Here is a man, who every day appropriates some of his neighbor's strayed fowls. Some one says to him, 'Such is not the way of a good man;' and he replies, 'With your leave I will diminish my appropriations, and will take only one fowl a month, until next year, when I will make an end of the practice.' If you know that the thing is unrighteous, then use all dispatch in putting an end to it: — why wait till next year?"

6.9　公都子曰："外人皆称夫子好辩，敢问何也？"孟子曰："予岂好辩哉？予不得已也。天下之生久矣，一治一乱。当尧之时，水逆行，泛滥于中国，蛇龙居之，民无所定；下者为巢，上者为营窟。《书》曰：'洚水警余。'洚水者，洪水也。使禹治之。禹掘地而注之海，驱蛇龙而放之菹；水由地中行，江、淮、河、汉是也。险阻既远，鸟兽之害人者消，然后人得平土而居之。尧舜既没，圣人之道衰，暴君代作，坏宫室以为污池，民无所安息；弃田以为园囿，使民不得衣食。邪说暴行又作，园囿、污池、沛泽多而禽兽至。及纣之身，天下又大乱。周公相武王诛纣，伐奄三年讨其君，驱飞廉于海隅而戮之，灭国者五十，驱虎、豹、犀、象而远之，天下大悦。《书》曰：'丕显哉，文王谟！丕承哉，武王烈！佑启我后人，咸以正无缺。'世衰道微，邪说暴行有作，臣弑其君者有之，子弑其父者有之。孔子惧，作《春秋》。《春秋》，天子之事也；是故孔子曰：'知我者其惟《春秋》乎！罪我者其惟《春秋》乎！'圣王不作，诸侯放恣，处士横议，杨朱、墨翟之言盈天下。天下之言不归杨，则归墨。杨氏为我，是无君也；墨氏兼爱，是无父也。无父无君，是禽兽也。公明仪曰：'庖有肥肉，厩有肥马；民有饥色，野有饿莩，此率兽而食人也。'杨墨之道不息，孔子之道不著，是邪说诬民，充塞仁义也。仁义充塞，则率兽食人，人将相食。吾为此惧。闲先圣之道，距杨墨，放淫辞，邪说者不得作。作于其心，害于其事；作于其事，害于其政。圣人复起，不易吾言矣。昔者禹抑洪水而天下平，周公兼夷狄，驱猛兽而百姓宁。孔子成《春秋》而乱臣贼子惧。《诗》云：'戎狄是膺，荆舒是惩，则莫我敢承。'无父无君，是周公所膺也。我亦欲正人心，息邪说，距诐行，放淫辞，以承三圣者；岂好辩哉？予不得已也。能言距杨墨者，圣人之徒也。"

6.9　The disciple Gongdu said to *Mencius*, "Master, the people beyond *our school* all speak of you as being fond of disputing. I venture to ask whether it be so." *Mencius* replied, "Indeed, I am not fond of disputing, but I am compelled to do it. A long time has elapsed since this world *of men* received its being, and there has been *along its history* now a period of good order, and now a period of confusion. In the time of Yao, the waters, flowing out of their channels, inundated the Middle Kingdom. Snakes and dragons, occupied it, and the people had no place where they could settle themselves. In the low grounds they made nests for themselves, and in the high grounds they made caves. It is said in the *Book of History*: 'The waters in their wild course warned me.' Those 'waters in their wild course' were the waters of the great inundation. *Shun* employed Yu to reduce the waters to order. Yu dug open *their obstructed channels*, and conducted them to the sea. He drove away the snakes and dragons, and forced them into the grassy marshes. *On this*, the waters pursued their course through the country, even the waters of the Jiang, the Huai, the He, and the Han, and the dangers and obstructions which they had occasioned were removed. The birds and beasts which had injured the people *also* disappeared, and after this men found the plains *available for them*, and occupied them. After the death of Yao and Shun, the principles that mark sages fell into decay. Oppressive sovereigns arose one after another, who pulled down houses to make ponds and lakes, so that the people knew not where they could rest in quiet, and threw fields out of cultivation to form gardens and parks, so that the people could not get clothes and food. *Afterwards*, corrupt speakings and oppressive deeds became more rife; gardens and parks, ponds and lakes, thickets and marshes, became more numerous, and birds and beasts swarmed. By the time of Zhou of Yin, the empire was again in a state of great confusion. Zhougong assisted King Wu, and destroyed Zhou of Yin. He smote Yan, and after three years put its sovereign to death. He drove Feilian to a corner by the sea, and slew him. The states which he extinguished amounted to fifty. He drove far away also the tigers, leopards, rhinoceroses, and elephants; — and the empire was greatly delighted. It is said in the *Book of History*, 'Great and splendid were the plans of King Wen! Greatly were they carried out by the energy of King Wu! They are for the assistance and instruction of us who are of an after day. They are all in principle correct, and deficient in nothing.' *Again* the world fell into decay, and principles faded away. Perverse speakings and oppressive deeds waxed rife again. There were instances of ministers who murdered their sovereigns, and of sons who murdered their fathers. Confucius was afraid, and made the *Spring and Autumn*. What the *Spring and Autumn* contains are matters proper to the emperor. On this account Confucius said, 'Yes? It is the *Spring and Autumn* which will make men know me, and it is the *Spring and Autumn* which will make men condemn me!' *Once more*, sage emperors cease to arise, and the princes of the states give the reins to their lusts. Unemployed scholars indulge in unreasonable discussions. The words of Yang Zhu and Mo Di fill the empire. *If you listen to* people's discourses throughout it, *you will find that* they have adopted the views either of Yang or of Mo. Now, Yang's principle is — 'each one for himself,' which does not acknowledge *the claims of* the sovereign. Mo's principle is — 'to love all equally,' which does not acknowledge *the peculiar affection due to* a father. But to acknowledge neither king nor father is to be in the state of a beast. Gongming Yi said, 'In their kitchens, there is fat meat. In their stables, there are fat horses. But their people have the look of hunger, and on the wilds there are those who have died of famine. This is leading on beasts to devour men.' If the principles of Yang and Mo be not stopped, and the principles of Confucius not set forth, then those perverse speakings will delude the people, and stop up *the path of* benevolence and righteousness. When benevolence and righteousness are stopped up, beasts will be led on to devour men, and men will devour one another. I am alarmed by these things, and address myself to the defence of the doctrines of the former sages, and to oppose Yang and Mo. I drive away their licentious expressions, so that such perverse speakers may not be able to show themselves. Their delusions spring up in men's minds, and do injury to their practice of affairs. Shown in their practice of affairs, they are pernicious to their government. When sages shall rise up again, they will not change my words. In former times, Yu repressed the vast waters *of the inundation*, and the empire was reduced to order. Zhougong's achievements extended even to the barbarous tribes of the east and north, and he drove away all ferocious animals, and the people enjoyed repose. Confucius completed the *Spring and Autumn*, and rebellious ministers and villainous sons were struck with terror. It is said in the *Book of Poetry*, 'He smote the barbarians of the west and the north, he punished Jing and Shu; and no one dared to resist us.' These father deniers and king deniers would have been smitten by Zhougong. I also wish to rectify men's hearts, and to put an end to those perverse doctrines, to oppose their one-sided actions and banish away their licentious expressions; — and thus to carry on the work of the three sages. Do I do so because I am fond of disputing? I am compelled to do it. Whoever is able to oppose Yang and Mo is a disciple of the sages."

6.10　匡章曰："陈仲子岂不诚廉士哉？居於陵，三日不食，耳无闻，目无见也。井上有李，螬食实者过半矣，匍匐往，将食之；三咽，然后耳有闻，目有见。"孟子曰："于齐国之士，吾必以仲子为巨擘焉。虽然，仲子恶能廉？充仲子之操，则蚓而后可者也。夫蚓，上食槁壤，下饮黄泉。仲子所居之室，伯夷之所筑与？抑亦盗跖之所筑与？所食之粟，伯夷之所树与？抑亦盗跖之所树与？是未可知也。"曰："是何伤哉？彼身织屦，妻辟纑，以易之也。"曰："仲子，齐之世家也；兄戴、盖禄万钟；以兄之禄为不义之禄而不食也，以兄之室为不义之室而不居也，辟兄离母，处于於陵。他日归，则有馈其兄生鹅者，已频顣曰：'恶用是鶃鶃者为哉？'他日，其母杀是鹅也，与之食之。其兄自外至，曰：'是鶃鶃之肉也。'出而哇之。以母则不食，以妻则食之；以兄之室则弗居，以於陵则居之，是尚为能充其类也乎？若仲子者，蚓而后充其操者也。"

6.10　Kuang Zhang said *to Mencius*, "Is not Chen Zhong a man of true self-denying purity? He was living in Wuling, and for three days was without food, till he could neither hear, nor see. Over a well there grew a plum tree, the fruit of which had been more than half-eaten by worms. He crawled to it, and tried to eat *some of the fruit*, when, after swallowing three mouthfuls, he recovered his sight and hearing." Mencius replied, "Among the scholars of Qi, I must regard Zhong as the thumb *among the fingers*. But still, where is the self-denying purity *he pretends to*? To carry out the principles which he holds, one must become an earth-worm, for so only can it be done. Now, an earth-worm eats the dry mould above, and drinks the yellow spring below. Was the house in which Zhong dwells built by a Boyi? Or was it built by a robber like Zhi? Was the millet which he eats planted by a Boyi? Or was it planted by a robber like Zhi? These are things which cannot be known." "But," said *Zhang*, "what does that matter? He himself weaves sandals of hemp, and his wife twists hempen threads, to barter them." Mencius rejoined, "Zhong belongs to an ancient and noble family of Qi. His elder brother Dai received from Gai a revenue of 10,000 *zhong*, but he considered his brother's emolument to be unrighteous, and would not eat of it, and in the same way he considered his brother's house to be unrighteous, and would not dwell in it. Avoiding his brother and leaving his mother, he went and dwelt in Wuling. One day afterwards, he returned to their house, when it happened that some one sent his brother a present of a live goose. He, knitting his eye-brows, said, 'What are you going to use that cackling thing for?' By-and-by his mother killed the goose, and gave him some of it to eat. Just then his brother came into the house, and said, 'It's the flesh of that cackling thing,' upon which he went out and vomited it. Thus what his mother gave him he would not eat but what his wife gives him he eats. He will not dwell in his brother's house, but he dwells in Wuling. How can he in such circumstances complete the style of life which he professes? With such principles as Zhong holds, a man must be an earth-worm, and then he can carry them out."

卷七　离娄章句上

BOOK VII　LI LOU　PART I

7.1　孟子曰："离娄之明，公输子之巧，不以规矩，不能成方员；师旷之聪，不以六律，不能正五音；尧舜之道，不以仁政，不能平治天下。今有仁心仁闻而民不被其泽，不可法于后世者，不行先王之道也。故曰，徒善不足以为政，徒法不能以自行。《诗》云：'不愆不忘，率由旧章。'遵先王之法而过者，未之有也。圣人既竭目力焉，继之以规矩准绳，以为方员平直，不可胜用也；既竭耳力焉，继之以六律正五音，不可胜用也；既竭心思焉，继之以不忍人之政，而仁覆天下矣。故曰，为高必因丘陵，为下必因川泽；为政不因先王之道，可谓智乎？是以惟仁者宜在高位。不仁而在高位，是播其恶于众也。上无道揆也，下无法守也，朝不信道，工不信度，君子犯义，小人犯刑，国之所存者幸也。故曰，城郭不完，兵甲不多，非国之灾也；田野不辟，货财不聚，非国之害也。上无礼，下无学，贼民兴，丧无日矣。《诗》曰：'天之方蹶，无然泄泄。'泄泄犹沓沓也。事君无义，进退无礼，言则非先王之道者，犹沓沓也。故曰：责难于君谓之恭，陈善闭邪谓之敬，吾君不能谓之贼。"

7.1　Mencius said, "The power of vision of Li Lou, and skill of hand of Gongshu, without the compass and square, could not form squares and circles. The acute ear of the music-master

Kuang, without the pitch-tubes, could not determine correctly the five notes. The principles of Yao and Shun, without a benevolent government, could not secure the tranquil order of the empire. There are now *princes* who have benevolent hearts and a reputation for benevolence, while yet the people do not receive any benefits from them, nor will they leave any example to future ages; — all because they do not put into practice the ways of the ancient kings. Hence we have the saying: — Virtue alone is not sufficient for the exercise of government; laws alone cannot carry themselves into practice. It is said in the *Book of Poetry*, 'Without transgression, without forgetfulness, following the ancient canons.' Never has any one fallen into error, who followed the laws of the ancient kings. When the sages had used the vigor of their eyes, they called in to their aid the compass, the square, the level, and the line, to make things square, round, level, and straight: — the use of the *instruments* is inexhaustible. When they had used their power of hearing to the utmost, they called in the pitch-tubes to their aid to determine the five notes: — the use of these *tubes* is inexhaustible. When they had exerted to the utmost the thoughts of their hearts, they called in to their aid a government that could not endure to witness the sufferings of men: — and their benevolence overspread the empire. Hence we have the saying — To raise a thing high, we must begin from *the top of* a mound or a hill; to dig to a *great* depth, we must commence in *the low ground of* a stream or a marsh. Can he be pronounced wise, in the exercise of government, does not proceed according to the ways of the former kings? Therefore only the benevolent ought to be in high stations. When a man destitute of benevolence is in a high station, he thereby disseminates his wickedness among all *below him.* When the prince has no principles by which he examines *his administration,* and his ministers have no laws by which they keep themselves *in the discharge of their duties*, in the court obedience is not paid to principle, and in the office obedience is not paid to rule. Superiors violate the laws of righteousness and inferiors violate the penal laws. It is only by a fortunate chance that a kingdom in such a case is preserved. Therefore, it is said: It is not the exterior and interior walls being incomplete, and the supply of weapons offensive and defensive not being large, which constitutes the calamity of a kingdom. It is not the cultivable area not being extended, and stores and wealth not being accumulated, which occasions the ruin of a kingdom. When superiors do not observe the rules of propriety, and inferiors do not learn, then seditious people spring up, and *that kingdom* will perish in no time. It is said in the *Book of Poetry*: 'When such an overthrow of *Zhou* is being produced by Heaven, be not ye so much at your ease!' 'At your ease': — that is, dilatory. And so dilatory may *those officers* be deemed, who serve their prince without righteousness, who take office and retire from it without regard to propriety, and who in their words disown the ways of the ancient kings. Therefore it is said: To urge one's sovereign to difficult achievements may be called showing respect for him. To set before him what is good and repress his perversities, may be called showing reverence for him. *He who does not do these things, saying to himself,* — My sovereign is incompetent to this, may be said to play the thief with him."

7.2　孟子曰：“规矩，方员之至也；圣人，人伦之至也。欲为君，尽君道，欲为臣，尽臣道。二者皆法尧舜而已矣。不以舜之所以事尧事君，不敬其君者也；不以尧之所以治民治民，贼其民者也。孔子曰：‘道二，仁与不仁而已矣。’暴其民甚，则身弑国亡；不甚，则身危国削，名之曰‘幽’‘厉’，虽孝子慈孙，百世不能改也。《诗》云：‘殷鉴不远，在夏后之世。’此之谓也。”

7.2　Mencius said, "The compass and square produce perfect circles and squares. By the sages, the human relations are perfectly exhibited. He who a sovereign would perfectly discharge the duties of a sovereign, and he who as a minister would perfectly discharge the duties of a minister, have only to imitate — the one Yao, and the other Shun. He who does not serve his sovereign as Shun served Yao, does not respect his sovereign, and he who does not rule his people as Yao ruled his, injures his people. Confucius said, 'There are but two courses, which can be pursued, that of virtue and its opposite.' *A sovereign who* carries the oppression of his people to the highest pitch, will himself be slain, and his kingdom will perish. If one stop short of the highest pitch, his life will *notwithstanding* be in danger, and his kingdom will be weakened. He will be styled 'The Dark' or 'The Cruel', and though he may have filial sons and affectionate grandsons, they will not be able in a hundred generations to change *the designation*. This is what is intended in the words of the *Book of Poetry*: 'The beacon of Yin was not remote, it was in the time of the sovereign of Xia.'"

7.3　孟子曰："三代之得天下也以仁，其失天下也以不仁。国之所以废兴存亡者亦然。天子不仁，不保四海；诸侯不仁，不保社稷；卿大夫不仁，不保宗庙；士庶人不仁，不保四体。今恶死亡而乐不仁，是犹恶醉而强酒。"

7.3 Mencius said, "It was by benevolence that the three dynasties gained the empire, and by not being benevolent that they lost it. It is by the same means that the decaying and flourishing, the preservation and perishing of states, are determined. If the emperor be not benevolent, he cannot preserve the empire *from passing from him*. If the sovereign of a state be not benevolent, he cannot preserve his kingdom. If a high noble or great officer be not benevolent, he cannot preserve his ancestral temple. If a scholar or common man be not benevolent, he cannot preserve his body. Now they hate death and ruin, and yet delight in being not benevolent, — this is like hating to be drunk, and yet being strong to *drink wine*."

7.4　孟子曰："爱人不亲，反其仁；治人不治，反其智；礼人不答，反其敬——行有不得者皆反求诸己，其身正而天下归之。《诗》云：'永言配命，自求多福。'"

7.4 Mencius said, "If a man love others, and no responsive attachment is shown to him, let him turn inwards and examine his own benevolence. If he *is trying to* rule others, and his government is unsuccessful, let him turn inwards and examine his wisdom. If he treats others politely, and they do not return his politeness, let him turn inwards and examine his own *feeling of* respect. When we do not, by what we do, realize what we desire, we must turn inwards and examine ourselves in every point. When a man's person is correct, the whole empire will turn to him *with recognition and submission*. It is said in the *Book of Poetry*: 'Be always studious to be in harmony with the ordinances *of God*, and you will obtain much happiness.' "

7.5　孟子曰: "人有恒言, 皆曰, '天下国家'。天下之本在国, 国之本在家, 家之本在身。"

7.5　Mencius said, "People have this common saying, —'The empire, the state, the family.' The root of the empire is in the state. The root of the state is in the family. The root of the family is in the person *of its head*."

7.6　孟子曰: "为政不难, 不得罪于巨室。巨室之所慕, 一国慕之; 一国之所慕, 天下慕之; 故沛然德教溢乎四海。"

7.6　Mencius said, "The administration of government is not difficult; — it lies in not offending the great families. He whom the great families affect, will be affected by the whole state, and he whom any one state affects, will be affected by the whole empire. When this is the case, such an one's virtue and teachings will spread over all within *the four seas* like the rush of water."

7.7　孟子曰: "天下有道, 小德役大德, 小贤役大贤; 天下无道,小役大，弱役强。斯二者，天也。顺天者存，逆天者亡。齐景公曰：'既不能令，又不受命，是绝物也。'涕出而女于吴。今也小国师大国而耻受命焉，是犹弟子而耻受命于先师也。如耻之，莫若师文王。师文王，大国五年，小国七年，必为政于天下矣。《诗》云：'商之孙子，其丽不亿。上帝既命，侯于周服。侯服于周，天命靡常。殷士肤敏，裸将于京。'孔子曰：'仁不可为众也。夫国君好仁，天下无敌。'今也欲无敌于天下而不以仁，是犹执热而不以濯也。《诗》云：'谁能执热，逝不以濯？'"

7.7 Mencius said, "When right government prevails in the empire, *princes of* little virtue are submissive to *those of* great, and those of little worth, to those of great. When bad government prevails in the empire, *princes of* small power are submissive to those of great, and the weak to the strong. Both these cases are *the rule of* Heaven. They who accord with Heaven are preserved, and they who rebel against Heaven perish. The duke Jing of Qi said, 'Not to be able to command others, and at the same time to refuse to receive their commands, is to cut one's-self off from all intercourse with others.' His tears flowed forth while he gave his daughter to be married to *the prince of Wu*. Now the small states imitate the large, and yet are ashamed to receive their commands. This is like a scholar's being ashamed to receive the commands of his master. For a prince who is ashamed of this, the best plan is to imitate King Wen. Let one imitate King Wen, and in five years, if his state be large, or in seven years, if it be small, he will be sure to give laws to the empire. It is said in the

Book of Poetry: 'The descendants of *the Emperors of* the Shang Dynasty, are in number more than hundreds of thousands; but, God having passed His decree, they are all submissive to Zhou. They are submissive to Zhou, because the decree of Heaven is not unchanging. The officers of Yin, admirable and alert, pour out the libations, and assist in the capital *of Zhou*.' Confucius said, '*As against* so benevolent *a sovereign*, they could not be deemed a multitude. Thus, if the prince of a state love benevolence, he will have no opponent in all the empire.' Now they wish to have no opponent in all the empire, but they *do* not *seek to attain* this by being benevolent. This is like a man laying hold of a heated substance, and not having *first* wetted *his hands*. It is said in the Book of Poetry: 'Who can take up a heated substance, without wetting *his hands*?' "

7.8　孟子曰："不仁者可与言哉？安其危而利其菑，乐其所以亡者。不仁而可与言，则何亡国败家之有？有孺子歌曰：'沧浪之水清兮，可以濯我缨；沧浪之水浊兮，可以濯我足。'孔子曰：'小子听之！清斯濯缨，浊斯濯足矣，自取之也。'夫人必自侮，然后人侮之；家必自毁，而后人毁之；国必自伐，而后人伐之。《太甲》曰：'天作孽，犹可违；自作孽，不可活。'此之谓也。"

7.8　Mencius said, "How is it possible to speak with those *princes* who are not benevolent? Their perils they count safety, their calamities they count profitable, and they have pleasure in the things by which they perish. If it were possible to talk with them who so violate benevolence, how could we have such destruction of kingdoms and ruin of families? There was a boy singing: 'When the water of the Canglang is clear, it does to wash the strings of my cap; when the water of the Canglang is muddy, it does to wash my feet.' Confucius said, 'Hear what he sings, my children. When clear, then he will wash his cap-strings, and when muddy, he will wash his feet with it. This *different application* is brought *by the water* on itself.' A man must first despise himself, and then others will despise him. A family must first destroy itself, and then others will destroy it. A kingdom must first smite itself, and then others will smite it. This is illustrated in the passage of the *Tai Jia*: 'When Heaven sends down calamities, it is still possible to escape them. When we occasion the calamities ourselves, it is not possible any longer to live.' "

7.9　孟子曰：“桀纣之失天下也，失其民也；失其民者，失其心也。得天下有道：得其民，斯得天下矣；得其民有道：得其心，斯得民矣；得其心有道：所欲与之聚之，所恶勿施，尔也。民之归仁也，犹水之就下、兽之走圹也。故为渊驱鱼者，獭也；为丛驱爵者，鹯也；为汤武驱民者，桀与纣也。今天下之君有好仁者，则诸侯皆为之驱矣。虽欲无王，不可得已。今之欲王者，犹七年之病求三年之艾也。苟为不畜，终身不得。苟不志于仁，终身忧辱，以陷于死亡。《诗》云：‘其何能淑，载胥及溺。’此之谓也。”

7.9   Mencius said, "Jie and Zhou's losing the empire, arose from their losing the people, and to lose the people means to lose their hearts. There is a way to get the empire; — get the people, and the empire is got. There is a way to get the people; — get their hearts, and the people are got. There is a way to get their hearts; — it is simply to collect for them what they like, and not to lay on them what they dislike. The people turn to a benevolent rule as water flows downwards, and as wild beasts fly to the wilderness. Accordingly, *as* the otter aids the deep waters, driving the fish into them, and the hawk aids the thickets, driving the little birds to them, *so* Jie and Zhou aided Tang and Wu, driving the people to them. If among the present sovereign of the empire, there were one who loved benevolence, all the *other* princes would aid him by driving *the people to him*. Although he wished not to become emperor, he could not avoid becoming so. The case of *one of* the present princes wishing to become emperor, is like the having to seek mugwort, three years old, to cure a seven years' sickness. If it have not been kept in store, the patient may all his life not get it. If the princes do not set their wills on benevolence, all their days will be in sorrow and disgrace, and they will be involved in death and ruin. This is illustrated by what is said in the *Book of Poetry*: 'How *otherwise* can you improve *the empire*? You will only with it go to ruin.' "

7.10   孟子曰："自暴者，不可与有言也；自弃者，不可与有为也。言非礼义，谓之自暴也；吾身不能居仁由义，谓之自弃也。仁，人之安宅也；义，人之正路也。旷安宅而弗居，舍正路而不由，哀哉！"

孟子 THE WORKS OF MENCIUS

134

7.10 Mencius said, "With those who do violence to themselves, it is impossible to speak. With those who throw themselves away, it is impossible to do anything. To disown in his conversation propriety and righteousness, is what we mean by doing violence to one's self. *To say* — 'I am not able to dwell in benevolence or pursue the path of righteousness,' is what we mean by throwing one's self away. Benevolence is the tranquil habitation of man, and righteousness is his straight path. Alas for them, who leave the tranquil dwelling empty, and do not reside in it, and who abandon the right path and do not pursue it!"

7.11 孟子曰："道在迩而求诸远，事在易而求之难：人人亲其亲，长其长，而天下平。"

7. 11 Mencius said, "The path *of duty* lies in what is near, and men seek for it in what is remote. The work *of duty* lies in what is easy and men seek for it in what is difficult. If each man would love his parents and show the due respect to his elders, the whole empire would enjoy tranquillity."

7.12 孟子曰："居下位而不获于上，民不可得而治也。获于上有道；不信于友，弗获于上矣。信于友有道，事亲弗悦，弗信于友矣。悦亲有道：反身不诚，不悦于亲矣。诚身有道，不明乎善，不诚其身矣。是故诚者，天之道也；思诚者，人之道也。至诚而不动者，未之有也；不诚，未有能动者也。"

7.12 Mencius said, "When those occupying inferior situations do not obtain the confidence of the sovereign, they cannot succeed in governing the people. There is a way to obtain the confidence of the sovereign: — if one is not trusted by his friends, he will not obtain the confidence of his sovereign. There is a way of being trusted by one's friend: — if one do not serve his parents so as to make them pleased, he will not be trusted by his friends. There is a way to make one's parents pleased: — if one, on turning his thoughts inwards finds a want of sincerity, he will not give pleasure to his parents. There is a way to the attainment of sincerity in one's self: — if a man do not understand what is good, he will not attain sincerity in himself. Therefore, sincerity is the way of Heaven. To think how to be sincere is the way of man. Never has there been one possessed of complete sincerity, who did not move others. Never has there been one who had not sincerity who was able to move others."

7.13　孟子曰：“伯夷辟纣，居北海之滨，闻文王作，兴曰：‘盍归乎来！吾闻西伯善养老者。’太公辟纣，居东海之滨，闻文王作，兴曰：‘盍归乎来！吾闻西伯善养老者。’二老者，天下之大老也，而归之，是天下之父归之也。天下之父归之，其子焉往？诸侯有行文王之政者，七年之内，必为政于天下矣。”

7.13　Mencius said, "Boyi, that he might avoid Zhou, was dwelling on the coast of the northern sea. When he heard of the rise of King Wen, he roused himself, and said, 'Why should I not go and follow him? I have heard that the chief of the West knows well how to nourish the old.' Taigong, that he might avoid Zhou, was dwelling on the coast of the eastern sea. When he heard of the rise of King Wen, he roused himself, and said, 'Why should I not go and follow him? I have heard that the chief of the West knows well how to nourish the old.' Those two old men were the greatest old men of the empire. When they came to follow King Wen, it was the fathers of the empire coming to follow him. When the fathers of the empire joined him, how could the sons go *to any others*? Were any of the princes to practice the government of King Wen, within seven years, he would be sure to be giving laws to the empire."

7.14　孟子曰："求也为季氏宰，无能改于其德，而赋粟倍他日。孔子曰：'求非我徒也，小子鸣鼓而攻之可也。'由此观之，君不行仁政而富之，皆弃于孔子者也，况于为之强战？争地以战，杀人盈野；争城以战，杀人盈城：此所谓率土地而食人肉，罪不容于死。故善战者服上刑，连诸侯者次之，辟草莱、任土地者次之。"

7.14　Mencius said, "Qiu acted as manager of the Ji family, whose *evil* ways he was unable to change, while he exacted from the people double the grain formerly paid. Confucius said, 'He is no disciple of mine. Little children, beat the drum and assail him.' Looking at the subject from the case, *we perceive that* when a prince was not practicing benevolent government, all *his ministers* who enriched him were rejected by Confucius. — How much more *would he have rejected* those who are vehement to fight for their *prince*? When contentions about territory are the ground on which they fight, they slaughter men, till the fields are filled with them. When some struggle for a city is the ground on which they fight, they slaughter men till the city is filled with them. This is what is called 'leading on the land to devour human flesh.' Death is not enough for such a crime. Therefore, those who are skilful to fight should suffer the highest punishment. Next to them *should be punished* those who unite the princes in leagues; and next to them, those who take in grassy commons, imposing the cultivation of the ground *on the people.*"

7.15 孟子曰："存乎人者，莫良于眸子。眸子不能掩其恶。胸中正，则眸子了焉，胸中不正，则眸子眊焉。听其言也，观其眸子，人焉廋哉？"

7.15 Mencius said, "Of all the parts of a man's body there is none more excellent than the pupil of the eye. The pupil cannot *be used to* hide a man's wickedness. If within the breast all be correct, the pupil is bright. If within the breast all be not correct, the pupil is dull. Listen to a man's words and look at the pupil of his eye. How can a man conceal his character?"

7.16 孟子曰："恭者不侮人，俭者不夺人。侮夺人之君，惟恐不顺焉，恶得为恭俭？恭俭岂可以声音笑貌为哉？"

7.16 Mencius said, "The respectful do not despise others. The economical do not plunder others. The prince who treats men with despite and plunders them, is only afraid that they may not prove obedient to him, how can he be regarded as respectful or economical? How can respectfulness and economy be made out of tones of the voice, and a smiling manner?' "

7.17　淳于髡曰："男女授受不亲，礼与？"孟子曰："礼也。"曰："嫂溺，则援之以手乎？"曰："嫂溺不援，是豺狼也。男女授受不亲，礼也；嫂溺，援之以手者，权也。"曰："今天下溺矣，夫子之不援，何也？"曰："天下溺，援之以道；嫂溺，援之以手——子欲手援天下乎？"

7.17　Chunyu Kun said, "Is it the rule that males and females shall not allow their hands to touch in giving or receiving anything?" Mencius replied, "It is the rule." *Kun* asked, "If a man's sister-in-law be drowning, shall he rescue her with his hand?" The reply was, "He who would not so rescue a drowning woman is a wolf. For males and females not to allow their hands to touch in giving and receiving is the *general* rule; when a sister-in-law is drowning, to rescue her with the hand is a peculiar exigency." *Kun* said, "The whole empire is drowning. How strange it is that you will not rescue it!" *Mencius* answered, "A drowning empire must be rescued with right principles, as a drowning sister-in-law has to be rescued with the hand. Do you wish me to rescue the empire with my hand?"

7.18　公孙丑曰："君子之不教子，何也？"孟子曰："势不行也。教者必以正；以正不行，继之以怒。继之以怒，则反夷矣。'夫子教我以正，夫子未出于正也。'则是父子相夷也。父子相夷，则恶矣。古者易子而教之。父子之间不责善。责善则离，离则不祥莫大焉。"

7.18 Gongsun Chou said, "Why is it that the superior man does not himself teach his son?" Mencius replied, "The circumstances of the case forbid its being done. The teacher must inculcate what is correct. When he inculcates what is correct, and his lessons are not practiced he follows them up with being angry. When he follows them up with being angry, then, contrary to what should be, he is offended with his son. *At the same time, the pupil says*, 'My master inculcates on me what is correct, and he himself does not proceed in a correct path.' The result of this is, that father and son are offended with each other. When father and son come to be offended with each other, the case is evil. The ancients exchanged sons, and one taught the son of another. Between father and son, there should be no reproving admonitions to what is good. Such reproofs lead to alienation, and than alienation there is nothing more inauspicious."

7.19 孟子曰："事孰为大？事亲为大；守孰为大？守身为大。不失其身而能事其亲者，吾闻之矣；失其身而能事其亲者，吾未之闻也。孰不为事？事亲，事之本也；孰不为守？守身，守之本也。曾子养曾皙，必有酒肉；将彻，必请所与；问有馀，必曰，'有。'曾皙死，曾元养曾子，必有酒肉；将彻，不请所与；问有馀，曰，'亡矣。'——将以复进也。此所谓养口体者也。若曾子，则可谓养志也。事亲若曾子者，可也。"

7.19 Mencius said, "Of services which is the greatest? The service of parents is the greatest. Of charges which is the greatest? The charge of one's self is the greatest. That those who do not fail to keep themselves are able to serve their parents is what I have heard. But I have never heard of any, who, having failed to keep themselves, were able *notwithstanding* to serve their parents. There are many services, but the service of parents is the root of all others. There are many charges, but the charge of one's self is the root of all others. The philosopher Zeng, in nourishing Zeng Zhe, was always sure to have wine and flesh provided. And when they were being removed, he would ask respectfully to whom he should give *what was left*. If *his father* asked whether there was anything left, he was sure to say, 'There is.' After the death of Zeng Zhe, when Zeng Yuan came to nourish *the philosopher Zeng*, he was always sure to have wine and flesh provided. But when the things were being removed, he did not ask to whom he should give *what was left*, and if *his father* asked whether there was anything left, he would answer 'No', — intending to bring them in again. This was what is called — 'nourishing the mouth and body.' We may call the philosopher Zeng's practice — 'nourishing the will.' To serve one's parents as the philosopher Zeng served his, may be accepted as filial piety."

7.20 孟子曰："人不足与適也，政不足间也；惟大人为能格君心之非。君仁，莫不仁；君义，莫不义；君正，莫不正。一正君而国定矣。"

7.20 Mencius said, "It is not enough to remonstrate with a *sovereign on account of the mal-employment* of ministers, nor to blame *errors of* government. It is only the great man who can rectify what is wrong in sovereign's mind. Let the prince be benevolent, there will be no one who is not benevolent. Let the prince be righteous, there will be no one who is not righteous. Let the prince be correct, there will be no one who is not correct. Once rectify the prince, and the kingdom will be firmly settled."

7.21 孟子曰：“有不虞之誉，有求全之毁。”

7.21 Mencius said, "There are cases of praise which could not be expected, and of reproach when the parties have been seeking to be perfect."

7.22 孟子曰：“人之易其言也，无责耳矣。”

7.22 Mencius said, "Men's being ready with their tongues arises simply from their not having been reproved."

7.23 孟子曰：“人之患在好为人师。”

7.23 Mencius said, "The evil of men is that they like to be the teachers of others."

7.24 乐正子从于子敖之齐。乐正子见孟子。孟子曰：“子亦来见我乎？”曰：“先生何为出此言也？”曰：“子来几日矣？”曰：“昔者。”曰：“昔者，则我出此言也，不亦宜乎？”曰：“舍馆未定。”曰：“子闻之也，舍馆定，然后求见长者乎？”曰：“克有罪。”

7.24   The disciple Yuezheng went in the train of Zi-ao to Qi. He came to see Mencius. Mencius said to him, "Are you also come to see me?" Yuezheng replied, "Master, why do you speak such words?" "How many days have you been here?" asked Mencius. "I came yesterday." "Yesterday! Is it not with reason then that I thus speak?" "My lodging-house was not arranged." "Have you heard that *a scholar's* lodging-house must be arranged before he visit his elder?" *Yuezheng* said, "I have done wrong."

7.25   孟子谓乐正子曰："子之从于子敖来，徒铺啜也。我不意子学古之道而以铺啜也。"

7.25   Mencius, addressing the disciple Yuezheng, said to him, "Your coming here in the train of Zi-ao was only because of the food and the drink. I could not have thought that you, having learned the doctrine of the ancients, would have acted with a view to eating and drinking."

7.26   孟子曰："不孝有三，无后为大。舜不告而娶，为无后也，君子以为犹告也。"

7.26   Mencius said, "There are three things which are unfilial, and to have no posterity is the greatest of them. Shun married, without informing his parents, because of this, *lest he should have* no posterity. Superior men consider that his doing so was the same as if he had informed them."

7.27   孟子曰："仁之实，事亲是也；义之实，从兄是也；智之实，知斯二者弗去是也；礼之实，节文斯二者是也；乐之实，乐斯二者，乐则生矣；生则恶可已也，恶可已，则不知足之蹈之、手之舞之。"

7.27 Mencius said, "The richest fruit of benevolence is this — the service of one's parents. The richest fruit of righteousness is this, — the obeying one's elder brother. The richest fruit of wisdom is this: — the knowing those two things, and not departing from them. The richest fruit of propriety is this, — the ordering and adorning those two things. The richest fruit of music is this, — the rejoicing in those two things. When they are rejoiced in, they grow. Growing, how can they be repressed? When they come to this state that they cannot be repressed, then unconsciously the feet begin to dance and the hands to move."

7.28 孟子曰："天下大悦而将归己，视天下悦而归己，犹草芥也，惟舜为然。不得乎亲，不可以为人；不顺乎亲，不可以为子。舜尽事亲之道而瞽瞍厎豫，瞽瞍厎豫而天下化，瞽瞍厎豫而天下之为父子者定，此之谓大孝。"

7.28 Mencius said, "Suppose the case of the whole empire turning in great delight to an individual to submit to him. — To regard the whole empire *thus* turning to him in great delight but as a bundle of grass; — only Shun was capable of this. *He considered* that if one could not get *the hearts of* his parents, he could not be considered *a man*; and that if he could not get to an entire accord with his parents, he could not be considered a son.

By Shun's completely fulfilling everything by which a parent could be served. Gusou was brought to find delight *in what was good*. When Gusou was brought to find that delight, the whole empire was transformed. When Gusou was brought to find that delight, all fathers and sons in the empire were established *in their respective duties*. This is called great filial piety."

8.1　孟子曰：“舜生于诸冯，迁于负夏，卒于鸣条，东夷之人也。文王生于岐周，卒于毕郢，西夷之人也。地之相去也，千有馀里；世之相后也，千有馀岁。得志行乎中国，若合符节，先圣后圣，其揆一也。”

8.1　Mencius said, "Shun was born in Zhufeng, removed to Fuxia, and died in Mingtiao; — a man near the wild tribes on the east. King Wen was born in Zhou by *mount* Qi, and died in Biying; — a man near the wild tribes on the west. Those regions were distant from one another more than a thousand *li*, and the age of the one sage was posterior to that of the other more than a thousand years. But when they got their wish, and carried their principles into practice throughout the Middle Kingdom, it was like uniting the two halves of a seal. *When we examine* the sages — both the earlier and the later, — their principles are found to be the same."

8.2　子产听郑国之政，以其乘舆济人于溱洧。孟子曰：“惠而不知为政。岁十一月，徒杠成；十二月，舆梁成，民未病涉也。君子平其政，行辟人可也，焉得人人而济之？故为政者，每人而悦之，日亦不足矣。”

8.2　When Zichan was chief minister of the state of Zheng, he would convey people across the Zhen and Wei in his own carriage. Mencius said, "It was kind, but showed that he did not understand the practice of government. When in the eleventh month of the year, the foot-bridges are completed, and the carriage-bridges in the twelfth month, the people have not the trouble of wading. Let a governor conduct his rule on principles of equal justice, and when he goes abroad, he may cause people to be removed out of his path. But how can he convey everybody across the rivers? It follows that if a governor will *try to* please everybody, he will find the days not sufficient *for his work*."

8.3 孟子告齐宣王曰:"君之视臣如手足;则臣视君如腹心;君之视臣如犬马,则臣视君如国人;君之视臣如土芥,则臣视君如寇雠。"王曰:"礼,为旧君有服,何如斯可为服矣?"曰:"谏行言听,膏泽下于民,有故而去,则君使人导之出疆,又先于其所往;去三年不反,然后收其田里。此之谓三有礼焉。如此,则为之服矣。今也为臣。谏则不行,言则不听;膏泽不下于民;有故而去,则君搏执之,又极之于其所往;去之日,遂收其田里。此之谓寇雠。寇雠,何服之有?"

8.3 Mencius said to the king Xuan of Qi, "When the prince regards his ministers as his hands and feet, his ministers regard their prince as their belly and heart; when he regards them as his dogs and horses, they regard him as any other man; when he regards them as the ground or as grass, they regard him as a robber and an enemy." The king said, "According to the rules of propriety, a minister wears mourning when he has left the service of a prince. How must *a prince* behave that his *old ministers* may thus go into mourning?" Mencius replied, "The admonitions *of a minister* having been followed, and his advice listened to, so that blessings have descended on the people, if for some cause, he leaves *the country*, the prince sends an escort to conduct him beyond the boundaries. He also anticipates *with recommendatory intimations* his arrival in the country to which he is proceeding. When he has been gone three years and does not return, *only* then at length does he take back his fields and residence. This treatment is what is called 'a thrice-repeated display of consideration.' When a prince acts thus, mourning will be worn on leaving his service. Nowadays, the remonstrances of a minister are not followed, and his advice is not listened to, so that no blessings descend on the people. When for any cause he leaves the country, the prince tries to seize him and hold him a prisoner. He also pushes him to extremity in the country to which he has gone, and on the very day of his departure, he takes back his fields and residence. This treatment shows him to be what we call 'a robber and an enemy.' What mourning can be worn for a robber and an enemy?"

8.4 孟子曰："无罪而杀士，则大夫可以去；无罪而戮民，则士可以徙。"

8.4 Mencius said, "When scholars are put to death without any crime, the great officers may *leave the country*. When the people are slaughtered without any crime, the scholars may remove."

8.5　孟子曰：“君仁，莫不仁；君义；莫不义。”

8.5　Mencius said, "If the sovereign be benevolent, all will be benevolent. If the sovereign be righteous, all will be righteous."

8.6　孟子曰：“非礼之礼，非义之义，大人弗为。”

8.6　Mencius said, "Acts of propriety which are not *really* proper, and acts of righteousness, which are not *really* righteous, the great man does not do."

8.7　孟子曰:“中也养不中，才也养不才，故人乐有贤父兄也。如中也弃不中，才也弃不才，则贤不肖之相去，其间不能以寸。”

8.7　Mencius said, "Those who keep the Mean, train up those who do not, and those who have abilities, train up those who have not, and hence men rejoice in having fathers and elder brothers who are possessed of virtue and talent. If they who keep the Mean spurn those who do not, and they who have abilities spurn those who have not, then the space between them — those so gifted and the ungifted — will not admit an inch."

8.8　孟子曰：“人有不为也，而后可以有为。”

8.8　Mencius said, "Men must be decided on what they will not do, and then they are able to act with vigour *in what they ought to do.*"

8.9　孟子曰：“言人之不善，当如后患何？”

8.9　Mencius said, "What future misery have they and ought they to endure, who talk of what is not good in others!"

8.10　孟子曰："仲尼不为已甚者。"

8.10　Mencius said, "Zhongni did not do extraordinary things."

8.11　孟子曰："大人者，言不必信，行不必果，惟义所在。"

8.11　Mencius said, "The great man does not think beforehand of his words that they may be sincere, nor of his actions that they may be resolute; — he simply *speaks and does* what is right."

8.12　孟子曰："大人者，不失其赤子之心者也。"

8.12　Mencius said, "The great man is he who does not lose his child's heart."

8.13　孟子曰："养生者不足以当大事，惟送死可以当大事。"

8.13　Mencius said, "The nourishment of *parents when* living is not sufficient to be accounted the great thing. It is only in the performing their obsequies when dead, that we have what can be considered the great thing."

8.14　孟子曰："君子深造之以道，欲其自得之也。自得之，则居之安；居之安，则资之深；资之深，则取之左右逢其原，故君子欲其自得之也。"

8.14　Mencius said, "The superior man makes his advances *in what he is learning* with deep earnestness and by the proper course, wishing to get hold of it as in himself. Having got hold of it in himself, he abides in it calmly and firmly. Abiding in it calmly and firmly, he reposes reliance on it. Reposing a deep reliance on it, he seizes it on the left and right, meeting everywhere with it as a fountain *from which things flow*. It is on this account that the superior man wishes to get hold of what he is learning as in himself."

8.15 孟子曰："博学而详说之，将以反说约也。"

8.15 Mencius said, "In learning extensively and discussing minutely what is learned, the object *of the superior man* is that he may be able to go back and set forth in brief what is essential."

8.16 孟子曰："以善服人者，未有能服人者也；以善养人，然后能服天下。天下不心服而王者，未之有也。"

8.16 Mencius said, "Never has he who would by his excellence subdue men been able to subdue them. *Let a prince* seek by his excellence to nourish men, and he will be able to subdue the whole empire. It is impossible that any one should become ruler of the empire to whom it has not yielded the subjection of the heart."

8.17 孟子曰："言无实不祥。不祥之实，蔽贤者当之。"

8.17 Mencius said, "Words which are not true are inauspicious, and the words which are most truly obnoxious to the name of inauspicious, are those which throw into the shade men of talents and virtue."

8.18　徐子曰："仲尼亟称于水，曰'水哉，水哉！'何取于水也？"孟子曰："源泉混混，不舍昼夜。盈科而后进，放乎四海。有本者如是，是之取尔。苟为无本，七八月之间雨集，沟浍皆盈；其涸也，可立而待也。故声闻过情，君子耻之。"

8.18　The disciple Xu said, "Zhongni often praised water, saying, 'O water! O water!' What did he find in water *to praise*?" Mencius replied, "There is a spring of water; how it gushes out! It rests not day nor night. It fills up every hole, and then advances, flowing on to the four seas. Such is water having a spring! It was this which he found in it to praise. But suppose that the water has no spring. — In the seventh and eighth months when the rain falls abundantly, the channels in the fields are all filled, but their being dried up again may be expected in a short time. So a superior man is ashamed of a reputation beyond his merits."

8.19　孟子曰："人之所以异于禽兽者几希，庶民去之，君子存之。舜明于庶物，察于人伦，由仁义行，非行仁义也。"

8.19　Mencius said, "That whereby man differs from the lower animals is but small. The mass of people cast it away, while superior men preserve it. Shun clearly understood the multitude of things, and closely observed the relations of humanity. He walked along the path of benevolence and righteousness; he did not *need to* pursue benevolence and righteousness."

8.20　孟子曰："禹恶旨酒而好善言。汤执中，立贤无方。文王视民如伤，望道而未之见。武王不泄迩，不忘远。周公思兼

三王，以施四事；其有不合者，仰而思之，夜以继日；幸而得
之，坐以待旦。"

8.20　Mencius said, "Yu hated the pleasant wine, and loved good words. Tang held fast the Mean, and employed men of talents and virtue without regard to where they came from. King Wen looked on the people *as he would on a man who was* wounded, and he looked towards the right path as if he could not see it. King Wu did not slight the near, and did not forget the distant. The duke of Zhou desired to unite in himself *the virtues* of those kings, *those founders of the three dynasties*, that he might display in his practice the four things *which they did*. If he saw any thing in them not suited *to his time*, he looked up and thought about it, from daytime into the night, and when he was fortunate enough to master the difficulty, he sat waiting for the morning."

8.21　孟子曰："王者之迹熄而《诗》亡，《诗》亡然后《春秋》作。晋之《乘》，楚之《梼杌》，鲁之《春秋》，一也；其事则齐桓、晋文，其文则史。孔子曰：'其义则丘窃取之矣。'"

8.21　Mencius said, "The traces of imperial rule were extinguished, and the *imperial* odes ceased to be made. When those odes ceased to be made, then the *Spring and Autumn* was produced. The *Sheng* of Jin, the *Taowu* of Chu, and the *Spring and Autumn* of Lu, were books of the same character. The subject of the *Spring and Autumn* was the affairs of Huan of Qi and Wen of Jin, and its style was the historical. Confucius said, 'Its *righteous* decisions I ventured to make.'"

8.22　孟子曰："君子之泽五世而斩，小人之泽五世而斩。予未得为孔子徒也，予私淑诸人也。"

8.22　Mencius said, "The influence of a sovereign sage terminates in the fifth generation. The influence of a mere sage does the same. Although I could not be a disciple of Confucius himself, I have endeavored to cultivate my virtue by means of others *who were*."

8.23　孟子曰："可以取，可以无取，取伤廉；可以与，可以无与，与伤惠；可以死，可以无死，死伤勇。"

8.23　Mencius said, "When it appears proper to take a thing, and *afterwards* not proper, to take it is contrary to moderation. When it appears proper to give a thing and *afterwards* not proper, to give it is contrary to kindness. When it appears proper to sacrifice one's life, and *afterwards* not proper, to sacrifice it is contrary to bravery."

8.24　逢蒙学射于羿，尽羿之道，思天下惟羿为愈己，于是杀羿。孟子曰："是亦羿有罪焉。"公明仪曰："宜若无罪焉。"曰："薄乎云尔，恶得无罪？郑人使子濯孺子侵卫，卫使庚公之斯追之，子濯孺子曰：'今日我疾作，不可以执弓，吾死矣夫！'问其仆曰：'追我者谁也？'其仆曰：'庚公之斯也。'曰：'吾生矣。'其仆曰：'庚公之斯，卫之善射者也；夫子曰吾生，何谓也？'曰：'庚公之斯学射于尹公之他，尹公之他学射于我。夫尹公之他，端

人也，其取友必端矣。'庾公之斯至，曰：'夫子何为不执弓？'
曰：'今日我疾作，不可以执弓。'曰：'小人学射于尹公之他，
尹公之他学射于夫子。我不忍以夫子之道反害夫子。虽然，今
日之事，君事也，我不敢废。'抽矢，扣轮，去其金，发乘矢
而后反。"

8.24　Pang Meng learned archery of Yi. When he had acquired completely all the science of Yi, he thought that in all the empire only Yi was superior to himself, and so he slew him. Mencius said, "In this case Yi also was to blame." Gongming Yi *indeed* said, "It would appear as if he were not to be blamed." Mencius said, "But he thereby only meant that his blame was slight. How can he be held without any blame? The people of Zheng sent Zizhuo Ru to make a stealthy attack on Wei, which sent Yugong Zhisi to pursue him. Zizhuo Ru said, 'Today I feel unwell, so that I cannot hold my bow. I am a dead man!' *At the same time* he asked his driver, 'Who is it that is pursuing me?' The driver said, 'It is Yugong Zhisi,' *on which* he exclaimed, 'I shall live.' The driver said, 'Yugong Zhisi is the best archer of Wei, what do you mean by saying: I shall live?' *Ru* replied, "Yugong Zhisi learned archery from Yingong Zhita who again learned it from me. Now, Yingong Zhita is an upright man, and the friends of his selection must be upright *also*.' When Yugong Zhisi came up, he said, 'Master, why are you not holding your bow?' Ru answered him, 'Today I am feeling unwell, and cannot hold my bow.' *On this Zhisi* said, 'I learned archery from Yingong Zhita who again learned it from you. I cannot bear to injure you with your own science. The business of today, however, is the prince's business, which I dare not neglect.' He then took his arrows, knocked off their steel-points against the carriage-wheel, discharged four of them, and returned."

8.25　孟子曰："西子蒙不洁，则人皆掩鼻而过之；虽有恶人，齐戒沐浴，则可以祀上帝。"

8.25　Mencius said, "If the lady Xi had been covered with a filthy *head-dress*, all people would have stopped their noses in passing her. Though a man may be wicked, yet if he adjust his thoughts, fast, and bathe, he may sacrifice to God."

8.26　孟子曰："天下之言性也，则故而已矣。故者以利为本。所恶于智者，为其凿也。如智者若禹之行水也，则无恶于智矣。禹之行水也，行其所无事也。如智者亦行其所无事，则智亦大矣。天之高也，星辰之远也，苟求其故，千岁之日至，可坐而致也。"

8.26　Mencius said, "All who speak about the natures *of things*, have in fact only their phenomena, *to reason from*, and the value of a phenomenon is in its being natural. What I dislike in your wise men is their boring out *their conclusions*. If those wise men would only act as Yu did when he conveyed away the waters, there would be nothing to dislike in their wisdom. The manner in which Yu conveyed away the waters was by doing what gave him no trouble. If your wise men would also do that which gave them no trouble, their knowledge would also be great. There is heaven so high, there are the stars so distant. If we have investigated their phenomena, we may, while sitting *in our places*, go back to the solstice of a thousand years *ago*."

8.27 公行子有子之丧，右师往吊。入门，有进而与右师言者，有就右师之位而与右师言者。孟子不与右师言，右师不悦曰："诸君子皆与驩言，孟子独不与驩言，是简驩也。"孟子闻之，曰："礼，朝廷不历位而相与言，不逾阶而相揖也。我欲行礼，子敖以我为简，不亦异乎？"

8.27 The officer Gonghang having on hand the funeral of one of his sons, the Master of the Right went to condole with him. When *this noble* entered the door, some called him to them and spoke with him, and some went to his place and spoke with him. Mencius did not speak with him, so that he was displeased, and said, "All the gentlemen have spoken with me. There is only Mencius who does not speak to me, thereby slighting me." Mencius, having heard of this remark, said, "According to the prescribed rules, in the court, individuals may not change their places to speak with one another, nor may they pass from their ranks to bow to one another. I was wishing to observe this rule, and Zi-ao understands it that I was slighting him: — is not this strange?"

8.28 孟子曰："君子所以异于人者，以其存心也。君子以仁存心，以礼存心。仁者爱人，有礼者敬人。爱人者，人恒爱之；敬人者，人恒敬之。有人于此，其待我以横逆，则君子必

自反也：'我必不仁也，必无礼也，此物奚宜至哉?'其自反
而仁矣，自反而有礼矣，其横逆由是也，君子必自反也：'我
必不忠。'自反而忠矣，其横逆由是也，君子曰：'此亦妄人也
已矣。如此，则与禽兽奚择哉？于禽兽又何难焉?'是故君子
有终身之忧，无一朝之患也。乃若所忧则有之：舜，人也；我，
亦人也。舜为法于天下，可传于后世，我由未免为乡人也，是
则可忧也。忧之如何？如舜而已矣。若夫君子所患则亡矣。非
仁无为也，非礼无行也。如有一朝之患，则君子不患矣。"

8.28 Mencius said, "That whereby the superior man is distinguished from other men is what he preserves in his heart, — namely, benevolence and propriety. The benevolent man loves others. The man of propriety shows respect to others. He who loves others is constantly loved by them. He who respects others is constantly respected by them. Here is a man, who treats me in a perverse and unreasonable manner. The superior man in such a case will turn round upon himself — 'I must have been wanting in benevolence; I must have been wanting in propriety; — how should this have happened to me?' He examines himself, and is *specially* benevolent. He turns round upon himself, and is *specially* observant of propriety. The perversity and unreasonableness of the other, *however*, are still the same. The superior man will *again* turn round on himself, — 'I must have been failing to do my utmost.' He turns round upon himself, and proceeds to do his utmost, but still the perversity and unreasonableness of the other are repeated. *On this* the superior man says, 'This is a man utterly lost indeed! Since he conducts himself so, what is there to choose between him and a brute? Why should I go to contend with a brute? Thus it is that the superior man has a life-long anxiety and not one morning's calamity. As to what is matter of anxiety to him, that he has. — *He says*, 'Shun was a man, and I also am a man. *But* Shun became an example to the empire, and *his conduct* was worthy to be handed down to after ages, while I am nothing better than a villager.' This indeed is proper matter of anxiety to him. And in what way is he anxious about it? Just that he may be like Shun: — then only will he stop. As to what the superior man would feel to be a calamity, there is no such thing. He does nothing which is not according to benevolence, and, nor acts any which is not according to propriety. If there should befall him one morning's calamity, the superior man does not account it a calamity."

8.29　禹、稷当平世，三过其门而不入，孔子贤之。颜子当乱世，居于陋巷，一箪食，一瓢饮，人不堪其忧，颜子不改其乐，孔子贤之。孟子曰："禹、稷、颜回同道。禹思天下有溺者，由己溺之也；稷思天下有饥者，由己饥之也，是以如是其急也。禹、稷、颜子易地则皆然。今有同室之人斗者，救之，虽被发缨冠而救之，可也；乡邻有斗者，被发缨冠而往救之，则惑也；虽闭户可也。"

8.29　Yu and Ji, in an age of transquilizing government, thrice passed their doors without entering them. Confucius praised them. The disciple Yan, in an age of confusion, dwelt in a mean narrow lane, having his single bamboo-cup of rice, and his single gourd-dish of water; other men could not have endured the distress, but he did not allow his joy to be affected by it. Confucius praised him. Mencius said, "Yu, Ji, and Yan Hui agreed in the principle of their conduct. Yu thought that if any one in the empire were drowned, it was as if he drowned him. Ji thought that if any one in the empire suffered hunger, it was as if he famished him. It was on this account that they were so earnest. If Yu and Ji, and the philosopher Yan, had exchanged places, each would have done what the other did. Here now in the same apartment with you are people fighting: — *you ought to* part them. Though you part them with your cap simply tied over your unbound hair, your conduct will be allowable. If the fighting be *only* in the village or neighborhood, if you go to put an end to it with your cap tied over your hair unbound, you will be in error. Although you should shut your door *in such a case*, your conduct would be allowable."

8.30　公都子曰："匡章，通国皆称不孝焉。夫子与之游，又从而礼貌之，敢问何也?"孟子曰："世俗所谓不孝者五：惰其四支，不顾父母之养，一不孝也；博弈好饮酒，不顾父母之养，二不孝也；好货财，私妻子，不顾父母之养，三不孝也；从耳目之欲，以为父母戮，四不孝也；好勇斗很，以危父母，五不孝也。章子有一于是乎? 夫章子，子父责善而不相遇也。责善，朋友之道也；父子责善，贼恩之大者。夫章子，岂不欲有夫妻子母之属哉? 为得罪于父, 不得近。出妻屏子, 终身不养焉。其设心以为不若是, 是则罪之大者, 是则章子而已矣。"

8.30 The disciple Gongdu said, "Throughout the whole kingdom everybody pronounces Kuangzhang unfilial. But you, Master, keep company with him, and moreover treat him with politeness. I venture to ask why you do so." Mencius replied, "There are five things which are said in the common practice of the age to be unfilial. The first is laziness in the use of one's four limbs, without attending to the nourishment of his parents. The second is gambling and chess-playing, and being fond of wine, without attending to the nourishment of his parents. The third is being fond of goods and money, and selfishly attached to his wife and children, without attending to the nourishment of his parents. The fourth is following the desires of one's ears and eyes, so as to bring his parents to disgrace. The fifth is being fond of bravery, fighting and quarrelling so as to endanger his parents. Is Zhang guilty of any one of these things? Now between Zhang and his father there arose disagreement, he, the son, reproving his father, to urge him to what was good. To urge one another to what is good by reproofs is the way of friends. But such urging between father and son is the greatest injury to the kindness *which should prevail between them*. Moreover, did not Zhang wish to have *in his family* the relationships of husband and wife, child and mother? But because he had offended his father, and was not permitted to approach him, he sent away his wife, and drove forth his son, and all his life receives no cherishing attention from them. He settled it in his mind that if he did not act in this way, his would be one of the greatest of crimes. — Such and nothing more is the case of Zhang."

8.31　曾子居武城，有越寇，或曰："寇至，盍去诸？"曰："无寓人于我室，毁伤其薪木。"寇退，则曰："修我墙屋，我将反。"寇退，曾子反。左右曰："待先生如此其忠且敬也，寇至，则先去以为民望；寇退，则反，殆于不可。"沈犹行曰："是非汝所知也。昔沈犹有负刍之祸，从先生者七十人，未有与焉。"子思居于卫，有齐寇。或曰："寇至，盍去诸？"子思曰："如伋去，君谁与守？"孟子曰："曾子、子思同道。曾子，师也，父兄也；子思，臣也，微也。曾子、子思易地则皆然。"

8.31　When the philosopher Zeng dwelt in Wucheng, there came a band from Yue to plunder it. Some one said *to him*, "The plunderers are coming: — why not leave this?" Zeng *on this left the city*, saying *to the man in charge of the house*, "Do not lodge any persons in my house, lest they break and injure the plants and trees." When the plunderers withdrew, he sent word to him, saying, "Repair the walls of my house. I am about to return." When the plunderers retired, the philosopher Zeng returned *accordingly*. His disciples said, "Since our master was treated with so much sincerity and respect, for him to be the first to go away on the arrival of the plunderers, so as to be observed by the people, and then to return on their retiring, appears to us to be improper." Shenyou Xing said, "You do not understand this matter. Formerly, when Shenyou was exposed to the outbreak of the grass-carriers, there were seventy disciples in our master's following, and none of them took part in the matter." When Zisi was living in Wei, there came a band from Qi to plunder. Some one said to him, "The plunderers are coming, — why not leave this?" Zisi said, "If I go away, whom will the prince have to guard *the state* with?" Mencius said, "The philosopher Zeng and *Zisi* agreed in the principle of their conduct. Zeng was a teacher: — in the place of a father or elder brother. *Zisi* was a minister: — in a meaner place. If the philosopher Zeng and Zisi had exchanged places, the one would have done what the other did."

8.32   储子曰:"王使人瞯夫子,果有以异于人乎?"孟子曰:"何以异于人哉? 尧舜与人同耳。"

8.32   The officer Chu said to *Mencius*, "Master, the king sent persons to spy out whether you were really different from other men." Mencius said, "How should I be different from other men! Yao and Shun were just the same as other men."

8.33   齐人有一妻一妾而处室者,其良人出,则必餍酒肉而后反。其妻问所与饮食者,则尽富贵也。其妻告其妾曰:"良人出,则必餍酒肉而后反;问其与饮食者,尽富贵也,而未尝有显者来,吾将瞯良人之所之也。"蚤起,施从良人之所之,遍国中无与立谈者。卒之东郭墦间,之祭者,乞其馀;不足,又顾而之他——此其为餍足之道也。其妻归,告其妾,曰:"良人者,所仰望而终身也,今若此——"与其妾讪其良人,而相泣于中庭,而良人未之知也，施施从外来，骄其妻妾。由君子观之，则人之所以求富贵利达者，其妻妾不羞也，而不相泣者，几希矣。

8.33　A man of Qi had a wife and a concubine, and lived together with them in his house. When their husband went out, he would get himself well filled with wine and flesh, and then return, and, on his wife's asking him with whom he ate and drank, they were sure to be all wealthy and honorable people. The wife informed the concubine, saying, "When our good man goes out, he is sure to come back having partaken plentifully of wine and flesh. I asked with whom he ate and drank, and they are all, it seems, wealthy and honorable people. And yet no people of distinction ever come here. I will spy out where our good man goes." *Accordingly*, she got up early in the morning, and privately followed wherever her husband went. Throughout the whole city, there was no one who stood or talked with him. At last, he came to those who were sacrificing among the tombs beyond the outer wall on the east, and begged what they had over. Not being satisfied, he looked about, and went to another party: — and this was the way in which he got himself satiated. His wife returned, and informed the concubine, saying, "It was to our husband that we looked up in hopeful contemplation, with whom our lot is cast for life; — and now these are his ways!" On this, along with the concubine she reviled their husband, and they wept together in the middle hall. In the mean time the husband, knowing nothing of all this, came in with a jaunty air, carrying himself proudly to his wife and concubine. In the view of a superior man, as to the ways by which men seek for riches, honors, gain, and advancement, there are few of their wives and concubines who would not be ashamed and weep together *on account of them.*

9.1　万章问曰："舜往于田，号泣于旻天，何为其号泣也?"孟子曰："怨慕也。"万章曰："'父母爱之，喜而不忘；父母恶之，劳而不怨。'然则舜怨乎?"曰："长息问于公明高曰:'舜往于田，则吾既得闻命矣,号泣于旻天,于父母,则吾不知也。'公明高曰:'是非尔所知也。'夫公明高以孝子之心，为不若是恝，我竭力耕田，共为子职而已矣，父母之不我爱，于我何哉? 帝使其子九男二女，百官牛羊仓廪备，以事舜于畎亩之中，天下之士多就之者，帝将胥天下而迁之焉。为不顺于父母，如穷人无所归。天下之士悦之，人之所欲也，而不足以解忧；好色，人之所欲，妻帝之二女，而不足以解忧；富，人之所欲，富有天下，而不足以解忧；贵，人之所欲，贵为天子，而不足以解忧。人悦之、好色、富贵，无足以解忧者，惟顺于父母可以解忧。人少，则慕父母；知好色，则慕少艾；有妻子，则慕妻子；仕则慕君，不得于君则热中。大孝终身慕父母。五十而慕者，予于大舜见之矣。"

9.1 Wan Zhang asked *Mencius*, saying, "*When* Shun went into the fields, he cried out and wept towards the pitying heavens. Why did he cry out and weep?" Mencius replied, "He was dissatisfied, and full of earnest desire." Wan Zhang said, "When his parents love him, a son rejoices and forgets them not. When his parents hate him, though they punish him, he does not murmur. Was Shun then murmuring *against his parents*?" Mencius answered, "Chang Xi asked Gongming Gao, saying, 'As to Shun's going into the fields, I have received your instructions, but I do not know about his weeping and crying out to the pitying heavens and to his parents.' Gongming Gao answered him, 'You do not understand that matter.' Now, Gongming Gao supposed that the heart of the filial son could not be so free of sorrow. *Shun would say*, 'I exert my strength to cultivate the fields, but I am there by only discharging my office as a son. What can there be in me that my parents do not love me?' The emperor caused his own children, nine sons and two daughters, the various officers, oxen and sheep, store-houses and granaries, *all* to be prepared, to serve Shun amid the channeled fields. Of the scholars of the empire there were multitudes who flocked to him. The emperor designed that *Shun* should superintend the empire along with him, and then to transfer it to him entirely. But because his parents were not in accord with him, he felt like a poor man who has nowhere to turn to. To be delighted in by the scholars of the empire, is what men desire, but it was not sufficient to remove the sorrow of *Shun*. The possession of beauty is what men desire, and *Shun* had for his wives the two daughters of the emperor, but this was not sufficient to remove his sorrow. Riches are what men desire, and the empire was the rich property of *Shun*, but this was not sufficient to remove his sorrow. Honors are what men desire, and *Shun* had the dignity of being emperor, but this was not sufficient to remove his sorrow. The reason why the being the object of men's delight, the possession of beauty, riches, and honors, were not sufficient to remove his sorrow, was that it could be removed only by his getting his parents to be in accord with him. The desire of the child is towards his father and mother. When he becomes conscious of the attractions of beauty, his desire is towards young and beautiful women. When he comes to have a wife and children, his desire is towards them. When he obtains office, his desire is towards his sovereign, — if he cannot get the regard of his sovereign, he burns within. *But* the man of great filial piety, to the end of his life, has his desire towards his parents. In the great Shun, I see the case of one whose desire at fifty years was towards them."

9.2　　万章问曰："《诗》云,'娶妻如之何? 必告父母。'信斯言也, 宜莫如舜。舜之不告而娶, 何也?"孟子曰："告则不得娶。男女居室, 人之大伦也。如告, 则废人之大伦, 以怼父母, 是以不告也。"万章曰："舜之不告而娶, 则吾既得闻命矣; 帝之妻舜而不告, 何也?"曰："帝亦知告焉则不得妻也。"万章曰："父母使舜完廪, 捐阶, 瞽瞍焚廪。使浚井, 出, 从而揜之。象曰:'谟盖都君咸我绩, 牛羊父母, 仓廪父母, 干戈朕, 琴朕, 弤朕, 二嫂使治朕栖。'象往入舜宫, 舜在床琴。象曰:'郁陶思君尔。'忸怩。舜曰:'惟兹臣庶, 汝其于予治。'不识舜不知象之将杀已与?"曰："奚而不知也? 象忧亦忧, 象喜亦喜。"曰:

"然则舜伪喜者与?"曰:"否;昔者有馈生鱼于郑子产,子产使校人畜之池。校人烹之,反命曰:'始舍之,圉圉焉;少则洋洋焉;攸然而逝。'子产曰'得其所哉! 得其所哉!'校人出,曰:'孰谓子产智?予既烹而食之,曰:得其所哉,得其所哉。'故君子可欺以其方,难罔以非其道。彼以爱兄之道来,故诚信而喜之,奚伪焉?"

9.2   Wan Zhang asked *Mencius*, saying, "It is said in the *Book of Poetry*, 'In marrying a wife, how ought a man to proceed? He must inform his parents.' If the rule be indeed as here expressed, no man ought to have illustrated it so well as Shun. How was it that Shun's marriage took place without his informing *his parents*?' " Mencius replied, "If he had informed them, he would not have been able to marry. That male and female should dwell together, is the greatest of human relations. If *Shun* had informed his parents, he must have made void this greatest of human relations, thereby incurring their resentment. On this account, he did not inform them." Wan Zhang said, "As to Shun's marrying without informing his parents, I have heard your instructions; but how was it that the emperor gave him his daughters as wives without informing *Shun's parents*?" *Mencius* said, "The emperor also knew that if he informed them, he could not marry his daughters to him." Wan Zhang said, "His parents set Shun to repair a granary, to which, the ladder having been removed, Gusou set fire. They *also* made him dig a well. He got out, but they, *not knowing that*, proceeded to cover him up. Xiang said, 'Of the scheme to cover up the city-forming prince the merit is all mine. Let my parents have his oxen and sheep. Let them have his storehouse and granaries. His shield and spear shall be mine. His lute shall be mine. His bow shall be mine. His two wives I shall make attend for me to my bed.' Xiang then went away into Shun's palace, and there was Shun on his couch playing on his lute. Xiang said, 'I am coming simply because I was thinking anxiously about you.' *At the same time*, he blushed deeply. Shun said to him, 'There are all my officers, — do you undertake the government of them for me.' I do not know whether Shun was ignorant of Xiang's wishing to kill him." *Mencius* answered, "How could he be ignorant of that? But when Xiang was sorrowful, he was also sorrowful; when Xiang was joyful, he was also joyful." *Zhang* said, "In that case, then, did not Shun rejoice hypocritically?" Mencius replied, "No. Formerly, some one sent a present of a live fish to Zichan of Zheng. Zichan ordered his pond-keeper to keep it in the pond, but that officer cooked it, and reported the execution of his commission, saying, 'When I first let it go, it appeared embarrassed. In a little, it seemed to be somewhat at ease, and then it swam away joyfully.' Zichan observed, 'It had got into its element! It had got into its element!' The pond-keeper then went out and said, 'Who calls Zichan a wise man? After I had cooked and eaten the fish, he said, — 'It had got into its element! It had got into its element!' Thus a superior man may be imposed on by what seems to be as it ought to be, but he cannot be entrapped by what is contrary to right principle. Xiang came in the way in which the love of his elder brother would have made him come, therefore, *Shun* sincerely believed him, and rejoiced. What hypocrisy was there?"

9.3 万章问曰："象日以杀舜为事，立为天子则放之，何也？"

孟子曰："封之也；或曰，放焉。"万章曰："舜流共工于幽州，放驩兜于崇山，杀三苗于三危，殛鲧于羽山，四罪而天下咸服，诛不仁也。象至不仁，封之有庳。有庳之人奚罪焉？仁人固如是乎——在他人则诛之，在弟则封之？"曰："仁人之于弟也，不藏怒焉，不宿怨焉，亲爱之而已矣。亲之，欲其贵也；爱之，欲其富也。封之有庳，富贵之也。身为天子，弟为匹夫，可谓亲爱之乎？""敢问或曰放者，何谓也？"曰："象不得有为于其国，天子使吏治其国而纳其贡税焉，故谓之放，岂得暴彼民哉？虽然，欲常常而见之，故源源而来，'不及贡，以政接于有庳。'此之谓也。"

9.3　Wan Zhang said, "Xiang made it his daily business to slay Shun. When *Shun* was made emperor, how was it that he *only* banished him?" Mencius said, "He raised him to be a prince. Some supposed that it was banishing him." Wan Zhang said, "Shun banished the superintendent of works to Youzhou; he sent away Huandou to the mountain Chong; he slew *the prince of* San Miao in Sanwei; and he imprisoned Gun on the mountain Yu. When the crimes of those four were thus punished, the whole empire acquiesced: — It was a cutting off of men who were destitute of benevolence. But Xiang was *of all men* the most destitute of benevolence, and *Shun* raised him to be the prince of Youbi; — Of what crimes had the people of Youbi been guilty? Does a benevolent man really act thus? In the case of other men, he cut them off; in the case of his brother, he raised him to be a prince."

Mencius replied, "A benevolent man does not lay up anger, nor cherish resentment against his brother but only regards him with affection and love. Regarding him with affection, he wishes him to be honorable; regarding him with love, he wishes him to be rich. The appointment of *Xiang* to be the prince of Youbi was to enrich and ennoble him. If while Shun himself was emperor, his brother had been a common man, could he have been said to regard him with affection and love?" *Wan Zhang* said, "I venture to ask what you mean by saying that some supposed that it was a banishing of Xiang?" *Mencius* replied, "Xiang could do nothing in his state. The emperor appointed an officer to administer its government, and to pay over its revenues to him. This treatment of him led to its being said that he was banished. How *indeed* could he be allowed the means of oppressing the people? Nevertheless, *Shun* wished to be continually seeing him, and, by this arrangement, he came incessantly *to court*, as is signified in that expression — 'He did not wait for the rendering of tribute, or affairs of government, to receive the prince of Youbi.'"

9.4 　咸丘蒙问曰："语云：'盛德之士，君不得而臣，父不得而子。'舜南面而立，尧帅诸侯北面而朝之，瞽瞍亦北面而朝之。舜见瞽瞍，其容有蹙。孔子曰：'于斯时也，天下殆哉，岌岌乎！'不识此语诚然乎哉？"孟子曰："否；此非君子之言，齐东野人之语也。尧老而舜摄也。《尧典》曰，'二十有八载，放勋乃徂落，百姓如丧考妣，三年，四海遏密八音。'孔子曰：'天无二日，民无二王。'舜既为天子矣，又帅天下诸侯以为尧三年丧，

是二天子矣。"咸丘蒙曰："舜之不臣尧,则吾既得闻命矣。《诗》
云:'普天之下,莫非王土;率土之滨,莫非王臣。'而舜既为
天子矣,敢问瞽瞍之非臣,如何?"曰:"是诗也,非是之谓
也;劳于王事而不得养父母也。曰:'此莫非王事,我独贤劳也。'
故说《诗》者,不以文害辞,不以辞害志。以意逆志,是为得
之。如以辞而已矣,《云汉》之诗曰:'周馀黎民,靡有孑遗。'
信斯言也,是周无遗民也。孝子之至,莫大乎尊亲;尊亲之至,
莫大乎以天下养。为天子父,尊之至也;以天下养,养之至也。
《诗》曰:'永言孝思,孝思维则。'此之谓也。《书》曰:'祗
载见瞽瞍,夔夔齐栗,瞽瞍亦允若。'是为父不得而子也?"

9.4 Xianqiu Meng asked *Mencius*, saying, "There is the saying,
— 'A scholar of complete virtue may not be employed as a
minister by his sovereign, nor treated as a son by his father.
Shun stood with his face to the south, and Yao, at the head of all
the princes, appeared before him at court with his face to the
north. Gusou also did the same. When Shun saw Gusou, his
countenance became discomposed. Confucius said, '*At this time,
in what a perilous condition was the empire! Its state was indeed
unsettled.*' — I do not know whether what is here said really
took place." Mencius replied, "No. These are not the words of a
superior man. They are the sayings of an uncultivated person of
the east of Qi. When Yao was old, Shun was associated with him
in the government. It is said in the *Canon of Yao*, 'After twenty
and eight years, the highly meritorious one deceased. The people
acted as if they were mourning for a father or mother for three

years, and up to *the borders of the* four seas every sound of music was hushed.' Confucius said, 'There are not two suns in the sky, nor two sovereigns over the people.' Shun having been emperor, and, moreover, leading on all the princes to observe the three years' mourning for Yao, there would have been in this case two emperors." Xianqiu Meng said, "On the point of Shun's not treating Yao as a minister, I have received your instructions. But it is said in the *Book of Poetry:* 'Under the whole heaven, every spot is the sovereign's ground; to the borders of the land, every individual is the sovereign's minister.' — And Shun had become emperor. I venture to ask how it was that Gusou was not one of his ministers." *Mencius* answered, "That ode is not to be understood in that way: — It speaks of being laboriously engaged in the sovereign's business, so as not to be able to nourish one's parents; *as if the author* said, 'This is all the sovereign's business, and *how is it that* I alone am supposed to have ability, and am made to toil in it?' Therefore, those who explain the odes, may not insist on one term so as to do violence to a sentence, nor on a sentence so as to do violence to the general scope. They must try with their thoughts to meet that scope, and then we shall apprehend it. If we simply take single sentences, there is that in the ode called *the Milky Way,* — 'Of the black haired people of the remnant of Zhou, there is not half a one left.' If it had been really as thus expressed, then not an individual of the people of Zhou was left. Of all which a filial son can attain to, there is nothing greater than his honoring his parents. And of what can be attained to in the honoring one's parents, there is nothing greater than the nourishing them with the whole empire. Gusou was the father of the emperor — this was the height of honor. *Shun* nourished him with the whole empire: — this was the height of nourishing. In this was verified the sentiment in the *Book of Poetry*: 'Ever cherishing filial thoughts, those filial thoughts became an example *to after ages.*' It is said in the *Book of History*, 'Reverently performing his duties, he waited on Gusou, and was full of veneration and awe. Gusou also believed him and conformed to virtue.' — This is the *true* case of *the scholar of complete virtue* not being treated as a son by his father."

9.5　万章曰："尧以天下与舜，有诸？"孟子曰："否；天子不能以天下与人。""然则舜有天下也，孰与之？"曰："天与之。""天与之者，谆谆然命之乎？"曰："否；天不言，以行与事示之而已矣。"曰："以行与事示之者，如之何？"曰："天子能荐人于天，不能使天与之天下；诸侯能荐人于天子，不能使天子与之诸侯；大夫能荐人于诸侯，不能使诸侯与之大夫。昔者，尧荐舜于天，而天受之；暴之于民，而民受之；故曰：天不言，以行与事示之而已矣。"曰："敢问荐之于天，而天受之；暴之于民，而民受之，如何？"曰："使之主祭，而百神享之，是天受之；使之主事，而事治，百姓安之，是民受之也。天与之，人与之，故曰，天子不能以天下与人。舜相尧二十有八载，非人之所能为也，天也。尧崩，三年之丧毕，舜避尧之子于南河之南，天下诸侯朝觐者，不之尧之子而之舜；讼狱者，不之尧之子而之舜；讴歌者，不讴歌尧之子而讴歌舜，故曰，天也。夫然后之中国，践天子位焉。而居尧之宫，逼尧之子，是篡也，非天与也。《泰誓》曰，'天视自我民视，天听自我民听，'此之谓也。"

9.5 Wan Zhang said, "Was it the case that Yao gave the empire to Shun?" Mencius said, "No. The emperor cannot give the empire to another." "Yes; — but Shun had the empire. Who gave it to him?" "Heaven gave it to him," was the answer. " 'Heaven gave it to him', did *Heaven* confer its appointment on him with specific injunctions?" *Mencius* replied, "No. Heaven does not speak. It simply showed its will by his personal conduct, and his conduct of affairs." " 'It showed its will by his personal conduct and his conduct of affairs': how was this?" Mencius's answer was, "The emperor can present a man to Heaven, but he cannot make Heaven give that man the empire. A prince can present a man to the emperor, but he cannot cause the emperor to make that man a prince. A great officer can present a man to his prince, but he cannot cause the prince to make that man a great officer. Yao presented Shun to Heaven, and Heaven accepted him; and that he exhibited him to the people, and the people accepted him. Therefore I say, 'Heaven does not speak. It simply indicated its will by his personal conduct and his conduct of affairs.' " *Zhang* said, "I presume to ask how it was that Yao presented *Shun* to Heaven, and Heaven accepted him; and that he exhibited him to the people, and the people accepted him." *Mencius* replied, "He caused him to preside over the sacrifices, and all the spirits were well pleased with them; — thus Heaven accepted him. He caused him to preside over the conduct of affairs, and affairs were well administered, so that the people reposed under him; — thus the people accepted him. Heaven gave *the empire* to him. The people gave it to him. Therefore I said, The emperor cannot give the empire to another. Shun assisted Yao *in the government* for twenty and eight years; — this was more than man could have done, and was from Heaven. After the death of Yao, when the three years' mourning was completed, Shun withdrew from the son of Yao to the south of South River. The princes of the empire, however, repairing to court, went not to the son of Yao, but they went to Shun. Litigants went not to the son of Yao, but they went to Shun. Singers sang not the son of Yao, but they sang Shun. Therefore I said, *'Heaven gave him the empire.'* It was after these things that he went to the Middle Kingdom, and occupied the emperor's seat. If he had, *before these things*, taken up his residence in the palace of Yao, and had applied pressure to the son of Yao, it would have been an act of usurpation, and not the gift of Heaven. This sentiment is expressed in the words of the *Great Declaration*, — 'Heaven sees according as my people see; Heaven hears according as my people hear.'"

9.6 万章问曰:"人有言,'至于禹而德衰,不传于贤,而传于子。'有诸?"孟子曰:"否,不然也;天与贤,则与贤;天与子,则与子。昔者,舜荐禹于天,十有七年,舜崩,三年之丧毕,禹避舜之子于阳城,天下之民从之,若尧崩之后不从尧之子而从舜也。禹荐益于天，七年，禹崩。三年之丧毕，益避禹之子于箕山之阴。朝觐讼狱者不之益而之启，曰：'吾君之子也。'讴歌者不讴歌益而讴歌启，曰：'吾君之子也。'丹朱之不肖，舜之子亦不肖。舜之相尧，禹之相舜也，历年多，施泽于民久。启贤，能敬承继禹之道。益之相禹也，历年少，施泽于民未久。舜、禹、益相去久远，其子之贤不肖，皆天也，非人之所能为也。莫之为而为者，天也；莫之致而至者，命也。匹夫而有天下者，德必若舜禹，而又有天子荐之者，故仲尼不有天下。继世以有天下，天之所废，必若桀纣者也，故益、伊尹、周公不有天下。伊尹相汤以王于天下。汤崩，太丁未立，外丙二年，仲壬四年。太甲颠覆汤之典刑，伊尹放之于桐，三年，太甲悔过，自怨自艾，于桐处仁迁义，三年，以听伊尹之训己也，复归于亳。周公之不有天下，犹益之于夏，伊尹之于殷也。孔子曰：'唐虞禅，夏后殷周继，其义一也。'"

9.6 Wan Zhang asked *Mencius*, saying, "People say, 'When *the disposal of the empire* came to Yu, his virtue was inferior *to that of Yao and Shun*, and he transmitted it not to the worthiest but to his son.' Was it so?" Mencius replied, "No; it was not so. When Heaven gave the empire to the worthiest, it was given to the worthiest. When Heaven gave it to the son *of the preceding emperor*, it was given to him. Shun presented Yu to Heaven. Seventeen years elapsed, and Shun died. When the three years' mourning was expired, Yu withdrew from the son of Shun to Yang Cheng. The people of the empire followed him just as after the death of Yao, instead of following his son, they had followed Shun. Yu presented Yi to Heaven, seven years elapsed, and Yu died. When the three years' mourning was expired, Yi withdrew from the son of Yu to the north of mount Ji. *The princes*, repairing to court, went not to Yi, but they went to Qi, *son of Yu. Litigants did not go to Yi, but they went to* Qi, saying, 'He is the son of our sovereign'; the singers did not sing Yi, but they sang Qi, saying, 'He is the son of our sovereign.' That Danzhu was not equal *to his father Yao*, and Shun's son not equal to him; that Shun assisted Yao, and Yu assisted Shun, for many years, conferring benefits on the people for a long time; but Qi, a man of virtue and talents, being able to adopt Yu's principle reverently; and moreover, Yi assisted Yu for not many years conferring benefits on the people for a short time; that *thus* the length of time during which Shun, Yu, and Yi, *assisted in the government* was so different; and that the sons of the emperors were — the one a man of talents and virtue, and the other two inferior to their fathers — all this was from Heaven, and what could not be produced by man. That which is done without man's doing it is from Heaven. That which happens without man's causing it to happen is from the ordinance *of Heaven*. In the case of a private individual obtaining the empire, there must be in him virtue equal to that of Shun or Yu, and moreover there must be the presenting of him *to Heaven* by the *preceding* emperor. It was on this account that Confucius did not obtain the empire. When the empire is possessed by *natural* succession, the emperor who is displaced by Heaven must be like Jie of Xia and Zhou of Shang. It was on this account that Yi,

Yi Yin, and Zhougong did not obtain the empire. Yi Yin assisted Tang so that he became sovereign over the empire. After the demise of Tang, Taiding having died before he could be appointed emperor, Waibing reigned two years, and Zhongren four. Tai Jia was then turning upside down the statutes of Tang, when Yi Yin placed him in Tong, for three years. *There* Tai Jia repented of his errors, was contrite, and reformed himself. In Tong he came to dwell in benevolence and moved towards righteousness, during those three years, listening to the lessons given to him by *Yi Yin*. Then *Yi Yin* again returned *with him* to Bo. Zhougong's not getting the empire was like the case of Yi and *the throne of* Xia, or like that of Yi Yin and *the throne of* Yin. Confucius said, 'Tang and Yu resigned the throne *to their worthy ministers*. The sovereign of Xia and *those of* Yin and Zhou transmitted it to their sons. The principle of righteousness was the same *in all the* cases.'"

9.7 万章问曰:"人有言,'伊尹以割烹要汤',有诸?"孟子曰:"否,不然,伊尹耕于有莘之野,而乐尧舜之道焉。非其义也,非其道也,禄之以天下,弗顾也;系马千驷,弗视也。非其义也,非其道也,一介不以与人,一介不以取诸人。汤使人以币聘之,嚣嚣然曰:'我何以汤之聘币为哉?我岂若处畎亩之中,由是以乐尧舜之道哉?'汤三使往聘之,既而幡然改曰:'与我处畎亩之中,由是以乐尧舜之道,吾岂若使是君为尧舜之君哉?吾岂若使是民为尧舜之民哉?吾岂若于吾身亲见之哉?天之生此民也,使先知觉后知,使先觉觉后觉也。予,天民之先

觉者也；予将以斯道觉斯民也。非予觉之，而谁也?'思天下
之民匹夫匹妇有不被尧舜之泽者，若已推而内之沟中。其自任
以天下之重如此，故就汤而说之以伐夏救民。吾未闻枉己而正
人者也，况辱己以正天下者乎？圣人之行不同也，或远，或
近；或去，或不去；归洁其身而已矣。吾闻其以尧舜之道要汤，
未闻以割烹也。《伊训》曰：'天诛造攻自牧宫，朕载自亳。'"

9.7　Wan Zhang asked Mencius, saying, "People say that Yi Yin
sought an introduction to Tang by his knowledge of cookery. Was
it so?" Mencius replied, "No, it was not so. Yi Yin was a farmer
in the lands of the prince of You Xin, delighting in the principles
of Yao and Shun. In any matter contrary to the righteousness
which they prescribed, or contrary to their principles, though
he had been offered the empire, he would not have regarded
it; though there had been yoked for him a thousand teams of
horses, he would not have looked at them. In any matter contrary
to the righteousness which they prescribed, or contrary to their
principles, he would neither have given nor taken a single straw.
Tang sent persons with presents of silk to entreat him to enter
his service. With an air of indifference and self-satisfaction he
said, 'What can I do with those silks with which Tang invites
me? Is it not best for me to abide in the channeled fields, and so
delight myself with the principles of Yao and Shun?' Tang thrice
sent messengers to invite him. After this, with the change of
resolution displayed in his countenance, he spoke in a different
style, — 'Instead of abiding in the channeled fields and thereby
delighting myself with the principles of Yao and Shun, had I not

better make this prince a prince like Yao or Shun, and this people like the people of Yao or Shun? Had I not better in my own person see these things for myself? Heaven's plan in the production of mankind is this: — that they who are first informed should instruct those who are later in being informed, and they who first apprehend principles should instruct those who are slower to do so. I am one of Heaven's people who have first apprehended; — I will take these principles and instruct this people in them. If I do not instruct them, who will do so? He thought that among all the people of the empire, even the private men and women, if there were any who did not enjoy such benefits as Yao and Shun conferred, it was as if he himself pushed them into a ditch. He took upon himself the heavy charge of the empire in this way, and therefore he went to Tang and pressed upon him the subject of attacking Xia and saving the people. I have not heard of one who bent himself, and at the same time made others straight; — how much less could one disgrace himself, and thereby rectify the whole empire? The actions of the sages have been different. Some have kept remote *from court*; and some have drawn near *to them*; some have left their offices; and some have not done so: — That to which those different courses all turn is simply the keeping of their persons pure. I have heard that Yi Yin sought an introduction to Tang by the doctrines of Yao and Shun. I have not heard that he did so by his knowledge of cookery. In the *Instructions of Yi*, it is said, 'Heaven destroying Jie of Xia commenced attacking him in the palace of Mu. I commenced in Bo.' "

9.8　万章问曰："或谓孔子于卫主痈疽，于齐主侍人瘠环，有诸乎？"孟子曰："否，不然也；好事者为之也。于卫主颜雠由。弥子之妻与子路之妻，兄弟也。弥子谓子路曰：'孔子主我，卫卿可得也。'子路以告。孔子曰：'有命。'孔子进以礼，退以义，得之不得曰'有命'。而主痈疽与侍人瘠环，是无义无命也。孔子不悦于鲁卫，遭宋桓司马将要而杀之，微服而过宋。是时孔子当阨，主司城贞子，为陈侯周臣。吾闻观近臣，以其所为主；观远臣，以其所主。若孔子主痈疽与侍人瘠环，何以为孔子？"

9.8　Wan Zhang asked *Mencius*, saying, "Some say that Confucius, when he was in Wei, lived with the ulcer-doctor, and when he was in Qi, with the attendant, Ji Huan; — was it so?" Mencius replied, "No; it was not so. Those are the inventions of men fond of strange things. When he was in Wei, he lived with Yan Chouyou. The wives of the officers Mi and Zilu were sisters, and Mi told Zilu, 'If Confucius will lodge with me, he may attain to the dignity of a high noble of Wei.' Zilu informed Confucius of this, and he said, 'That is as ordered *by Heaven*.' Confucius went into office according to propriety, and retired from it according to righteousness. In regard to his obtaining office or not obtaining it, he said, 'That is as ordered.' But if he had lodged with the ulcer-doctor, and with the attendant Ji Huan, that would neither have been according to righteousness, nor any ordering *of Heaven*. When Confucius, being dissatisfied in Lu and Wei, *had left those states*, he met with the attempt of Huan, the Master of the horse, of Song, to intercept and kill him. Consequently he crossed Song in disguise. At that time, though he was in circumstances of distress, he lodged with the city master Zheng, who was then a minister of Zhou, the prince of Chen. I have heard that *the characters of* ministers about court may be discerned from those whom they entertain, and those of stranger officers, from those with whom they lodge. If Confucius had lodged with the ulcer-doctor, and with the attendant Ji Huan, how could he have been Confucius?"

9.9 万章问曰："或曰，'百里奚自鬻于秦养牲者，五羊之皮，食牛，以要秦穆公。'信乎？"孟子曰："否，不然；好事者为之也。百里奚，虞人也。晋人以垂棘之璧与屈产之乘，假道于虞以伐虢。宫之奇谏，百里奚不谏。知虞公之不可谏而去之秦，年已七十矣，曾不知以食牛干秦穆公之为污也，可谓智乎？不可谏而不谏，可谓不智乎？知虞公之将亡而先去之，不可谓不智也。时举于秦，知穆公之可与有行也而相之，可谓不智乎？相秦而显其君于天下，可传于后世，不贤而能之乎？自鬻以成其君，乡党自好者不为，而谓贤者为之乎？"

9.9 Wan Zhang asked *Mencius*, "Some say that Baili Xi sold himself to a cattle-keeper of Qin, for the skins of five sheep and fed his oxen, in order to find an introduction to the prince Mu of Qin; — was this the case?" Mencius said, "No, it was not so. This story was invented by men fond of strange things. Baili Xi was a man of Yu. The people of Jin, by the inducement of gem of Chuiji, and four horses of the Qu breed, borrowed a passage through Yu to attack Guo. *On that occasion*, Gong Zhiqi remonstrated *against granting their request*, and Baili Xi did not remonstrate. When he knew that the prince of Yu was not to be remonstrated with, and, leaving that State, went to Qin, he had reached the age of seventy. If by that time he did not know that it would be a mean thing to seek an introduction to the prince Mu of Qin by feeding oxen, could he be called wise? But not remonstrating where it was of no use to remonstrate, could he be said to be wise? Knowing that the prince of Yu would be ruined, and leaving him before that event, he cannot be said not to have been wise. Being then advanced in Qin, he knew that the prince Mu was one with whom he would enjoy a field for action, and became minister to him; — could he, *acting thus*, be said not to be wise? Having become chief minister of Qin, he made his prince distinguished throughout the empire, and worthy of being handed down to future ages, — could he have done this, if he had not been a man of talents and virtue? As to selling himself in order to accomplish all the aims of his prince, even a villager who had a regard for himself would not do such a thing, and shall we say that a man of talents and virtue did it?"

万章章句上 WAN ZHANG PART I

185

10.1　孟子曰:"伯夷,目不视恶色,耳不听恶声。非其君,不事;非其民,不使。治则进,乱则退。横政之所出,横民之所止,不忍居也。思与乡人处,如以朝衣朝冠坐于涂炭也。当纣之时,居北海之滨,以待天下之清也。故闻伯夷之风者,顽夫廉,懦夫有立志。伊尹曰:'何事非君?何使非民?'治亦进,乱亦进,曰:'天之生斯民也,使先知觉后知,使先觉觉后觉。予,天民之先觉者也。予将以此道觉此民也。'思天下之民匹夫匹妇有不与被尧舜之泽者,若己推而内之沟中——其自任以天下之重也。柳下惠不羞污君,不辞小官。进不隐贤,必以其道。遗佚而不怨,阨穷而不悯。与乡人处,由由然不忍去也。'尔为尔,我为我,虽袒裼裸裎于我侧,尔焉能浼我哉?'故闻柳下惠之风者,鄙夫宽,薄夫敦。孔子之去齐,接淅而行;去鲁,曰,'迟迟吾行也,去父母国之道也。'可以速而速,可以久而久,可以处而处,可以仕而仕,孔子也。"孟子曰:"伯夷,圣之清者也;伊尹,圣之任者也;柳下惠,圣之和者也;孔子,圣之时者也。孔子之谓集大成。集大成也者,金声而玉振之也。金声也者,始条理也;玉振之也者,终条理也。始条理者,智之事也;终条理者,圣之事也。智,譬则巧也;圣,譬则力也。由射于百步之外也，其至，尔力也；其中，非尔力也。"

10.1 Mencius said, "Boyi would not allow his eyes to look on a bad sight, nor his ears to listen to a bad sound. He would not serve a prince whom he did not approve, nor command a people whom he did not esteem. In a time of good government he took office, and on the occurrence of confusion he retired. He could not bear to dwell either in *a court* from which a lawless government emanated, or among lawless people. He considered his being in the same place with a villager, as if he were to sit amid mud and coals with his court robes and court cap. In the time of Zhou, he dwelt on the shores of the north sea, waiting the purification of the empire. Therefore when men *now* hear the character of Boyi, the corrupt become pure, and the weak acquire determination. Yi Yin said, 'Whom may I not serve? My serving him makes him my sovereign. What people may I not command? My commanding them makes them my people.' In a time of good government he took office, and when confusion prevailed, he also took office. He said, 'Heaven's plan in the production of mankind is this: — that they who are first informed should instruct those who are later in being informed, and they who first apprehend principles should instruct those who are slower in doing so. I am the one of Heaven's people who has first apprehended. — I will take these principles and instruct the people in them.' He thought that among all the people of the empire, even the common men and women, if there were any who did not share in the enjoyment of such benefits as Yao and Shun conferred, it was as if he himself pushed them into a ditch; — for he took upon himself the heavy charge of the empire. Hui of Liuxia was not ashamed to serve an impure prince, nor did he think it low to be an inferior officer. When advanced to employment, he did not conceal his virtue, *but* made it a point to carry out his principles. When dismissed and left without office, he yet did not murmur. When straitened by poverty, he yet did not grieve. When thrown into the company of village people, he was quite at ease and could not bear to leave them. *He had a saying*, 'You are you, and I am I. Although you stand by my side with breast and arms bare, or with your body naked, how can you defile me?' Therefore when men now hear the character of Hui of Liuxia, the mean become generous, and the niggardly become liberal. When Confucius was leaving Qi, he strained off with his hand the water in which his rice was being rinsed, *took the rice*, and went away. When he left Lu, he said, 'I will set out by and by: — it was right he should leave the country of his parents in this way.' When it was proper to go away quickly, he did so; when it was proper to delay, he did so; when it was proper to keep in retirement, he did so; when it was proper to go into office, he did so; — this was Confucius." Mencius said, "Boyi among the sages was the pure one; Yi Yin was the one most inclined to take office; Hui of Liuxia was the accommodating one; and Confucius was the timeous one. In Confucius we have what is called a complete concert. A complete concert is when the *large* bell, proclaims the *commencement of the music*, and the ringing stone proclaims its close. The metal sound commences the blended harmony of all the instruments, and the winding up with the stone terminates that blended harmony. The commencing that harmony is the work of wisdom. The terminating it is the work of sageness. As a comparison for wisdom, we may liken it to skill, and as a comparison for sageness, we may liken it to strength; — as in the case of shooting at a mark a hundred paces distant. That you reach it is owing to your strength, but that you hit the mark is not owing to your strength."

10.2　北宫锜问曰："周室班爵禄也，如之何？"孟子曰："其详不可得闻也，诸侯恶其害己也，而皆去其籍；然而轲也尝闻其略也。天子一位，公一位，侯一位，伯一位，子、男同一位，凡五等也。君一位，卿一位，大夫一位，上士一位，中士一位，下士一位，凡六等。天子之制，地方千里，公侯皆方百里，伯七十里，子、男五十里，凡四等。不能五十里，不达于天子，附于诸侯，曰附庸。天子之卿受地视侯，大夫受地视伯，元士受地视子、男。大国地方百里，君十卿禄，卿禄四大夫，大夫倍上士，上士倍中士，中士倍下士，下士与庶人在官者同禄，禄足以代其耕也。次国地方七十里，君十卿禄，卿禄三大夫，大夫倍上士，上士倍中士，中士倍下士，下士与庶人在官者同禄，禄足以代其耕也。小国地方五十里，君十卿禄，卿禄二大夫，大夫倍上士，上士倍中士，中士倍下士，下士与庶人在官者同禄，禄足以代其耕也。耕者之所获，一夫百亩；百亩之粪，上农夫食九人，上次食八人，中食七人，中次食六人，下食五人。庶人在官者，其禄以是为差。"

10.2 Beigong Qi asked *Mencius*, saying, "What was the arrangement of dignities and emoluments determined by the house of Zhou?" Mencius replied, "The particulars of that arrangement cannot be learned, for the princes, disliking them as injurious to themselves, have all made away with the records of them. Still I have learned the general outline of them. The Emperor constituted one dignity; the Gong one; the Hou one; the Bo one; and the Zi and the Nan each one of equal rank: — altogether making five degrees of dignity. The sovereign again constituted one dignity; the chief minister one; the great officer one; the scholars of the first class one; those of the middle class one; and those of the lowest class one, — altogether making six degrees of dignity. To the emperor there was allotted a territory of a thousand *li* square. A Gong and a Hou each a hundred *li* square. A Bo had seventy *li*, and a Zi and a Nan had each fifty *li*. The assignments altogether were of four amounts. Where the territory did not amount to fifty *li*, the chief could not have access himself to the emperor. His land was attached to some Hou-ship, and was called a Fuyong. The chief ministers of the emperor received an amount of territory equal to that of a Hou; a great officer received as much as a Bo; and a scholar of the first class as much as a Zi or a Nan. In a great state, where the territory was a hundred *li* square, the sovereign had ten times as much income as the chief ministers; a chief minister four times as much as a great officer; a great officer twice as much as a scholar of the first class; a scholar of the first class twice as much as one of the middle; a scholar of the middle class twice as much as one of the lowest; the scholars of the lowest class, and such of the common people as were employed about the government offices, had the same emolument; — as much, namely, as was equal to what they would have made by tilling the fields. In a state of the next order, where the territory was seventy *li* square, the sovereign had ten times as much revenue as the chief minister; a chief minister three times as much as a great officer; a great officer twice as much as a scholar of the first class; a scholar of the first class twice as much as one of the middle; a scholar of the middle class twice as much as one of the lowest; the scholars of the lowest class, and such of the common people as were employed about the government offices, had the same emolument, — as much, namely, as was equal to what they would have made by tilling the fields. In a small state, where the territory was fifty *li* square, the sovereign had ten times as much revenue as the chief minister; a chief minister had twice as much as a great officer; a great officer twice as much as a scholar of the highest class; a scholar of the highest class twice as much as one of the middle; a scholar of the middle class twice as much as one of the lowest; the scholars of the lowest class, and such of the common people as were employed about the government offices, had the same emolument; — as much, namely, as was equal to what they would have made by tilling the fields. As to those who tilled the fields, each husbandman received a hundred *mu*. When those *mu* were manured, the best husbandmen of the highest class supported nine individuals, and those ranking next to them supported eight. The best husbandmen of the second class supported seven individuals, and those ranking next to them supported six; while husbandmen of the lowest class only supported five. The salaries of the common people who were employed about the government offices were regulated according to these differences."

10.3 万章问曰："敢问友。"孟子曰："不挟长，不挟贵，不挟兄弟而友。友也者，友其德也，不可以有挟也。孟献子，百乘之家也，有友五人焉：乐正裘、牧仲，其三人，则予忘之矣。献子之与此五人者友也，无献子之家者也。此五人者，亦有献子之家，则不与之友矣。非惟百乘之家为然也，虽小国之君亦有之。费惠公曰：'吾于子思，则师之矣；吾于颜般，则友之矣；王顺、长息则事我者也。'非惟小国之君为然也，虽大国之君亦有之。晋平公之于亥唐也，入云则入，坐云则坐，食云则食；虽蔬食菜羹，未尝不饱，盖不敢不饱也。然终于此而已矣。弗与共天位也，弗与治天职也，弗与食天禄也，士之尊贤者也，非王公之尊贤也。舜尚见帝，帝馆甥于贰室，亦飨舜，迭为宾主，是天子而友匹夫也。用下敬上，谓之贵贵；用上敬下，谓之尊贤。贵贵尊贤，其义一也。"

10.3 Wan Zhang asked *Mencius*, saying, "I venture to *ask the principles* of friendship." Mencius replied, "Friendship should be maintained without any presumption on the ground of one's superior age, or station, or *the circumstances of his* relatives. Friendship *with a man* is friendship with his virtue, and does not admit of assumptions of superiority. There was Meng Xian, *chief of* a family of a hundred chariots. He had five friends, namely Yuezheng Qiu, Mu Zhong, and three others *whose names* I have forgotten. With those five men Xian maintained a friendship, because they thought nothing about his family. If they had thought about his family, he would not have maintained his friendship with them. Not only has the *chief of* a family of a hundred chariots acted thus. The same thing was exemplified by the sovereign of a small state. The prince Hui of Bi said, 'I treat Zisi as my master, and Yan Ban as my friend. As to Wang Shun and Chang Xi, they serve me.' Not only has the sovereign of a small state acted thus. The same thing has been exemplified by the sovereign of a large state. There was the prince Ping of Jin with Hai Tang: — when *Tang* told him to come into his house, he came; when he told him to be seated, he sat; when he told him to eat, he ate. There might only be coarse rice and soup of vegetables, but he always ate his fill, not daring to do otherwise. Here, however, he stopped, and went no farther. He did not call him to share any of Heaven's places, or to govern any of Heaven's offices, or to partake of any of Heaven's emoluments. His conduct was but a scholar's honoring virtue and talents, not the honoring them proper to a king or a prince. Shun went up to court and saw the emperor, who lodged him as his son-in-law in the second palace. The emperor also enjoyed there Shun's hospitality. Alternately he was host and guest. Here was the emperor maintaining friendship with a private man. Respect shown by inferiors to superiors is called giving to the noble the observance due to rank. Respect shown by superiors to inferiors is called giving honor to talents and virtue.

The rightness in each case is the same."

10.4　万章问曰:"敢问交际何心也?"孟子曰:"恭也。"曰:"'却之却之为不恭,'何哉?"曰:"尊者赐之,曰,'其所取之者义乎,不义乎?'而后受之,以是为不恭,故弗却也。"曰:"请无以辞却之,以心却之,曰,'其取诸民之不义也,'而以他辞无受,不可乎?"曰:"其交也以道,其接也以礼,斯孔子受之矣。"万章曰:"今有御人于国门之外者,其交也以道,其馈也以礼,斯可受御与?"曰:"不可;《康诰》曰:'杀越人于货,闵不畏死,凡民罔不谮。'是不待教而诛者也。殷受夏、周受殷,所不辞也,于今为烈,如之何其受之?"曰:"今之诸侯取之于民也,犹御也。苟善其礼际矣,斯君子受之,敢问何说也?"曰:"子以为有王者作,将比今之诸侯而诛之乎?其教之不改而后诛之乎?夫谓非其有而取之者盗也,充类至义之尽也。孔子之仕于鲁也,鲁人猎较,孔子亦猎较。猎较犹可,而况受其赐乎?"曰:"然则孔子之仕也,非事道与?"曰:"事道也。""事道奚猎较也?"曰:"孔子先簿正祭器,不以四方之食供簿正。"曰:"奚不去也?"曰:"为之兆也。兆足以行矣,而不行,而后去,是以未尝有所终三年淹也。孔子有见行可之仕,有际可之仕,有公养之仕。于季桓子,见行可之仕也;于卫灵公,际可之仕也;于卫孝公,公养之仕也。"

10.4　Wan Zhang asked *Mencius*, saying, "I venture to ask what *feeling of the* mind is expressed in the presents of friendship."

Mencius replied, "*The feeling of* respect." "How is it," pursued *Zhang*, "that 'the declining a present is accounted disrespectful'?" The answer was, "When one of honorable rank presents a gift, to say *in the mind*, 'Was the way in which he got this righteous or not?' I must know this before I can receive it; — this is deemed disrespectful, and therefore presents are not declined." *Wan Zhang* asked *again*, "When one does not take on him in so many express words to refuse the gift, but having declined it in his heart, saying, 'It was taken by him unrighteously from the people,' and then assigns some other reason for not receiving it; — is not this a proper course?" *Mencius said*, "When the donor offers it on a ground of reason, and his manner of doing so is according to propriety, — in such a case Confucius would have received it." Wan Zhang said, "Here now is one who stops and robs people outside the gates of the city. He offers his gift on a ground of reason, and does so in a manner according to propriety; — would the reception of it so acquired by robbery be proper?" Mencius replied, "It would not be proper. In the *Announcement to Kang*, it is said, 'When men kill others, and roll over their bodies to take their property, being reckless and fearless of death, among all the people there are none but detest them.' — Thus, such characters are to be put to death, without waiting to give them warning. Yin received *this rule* from Xia, and Zhou received it from Yin. It cannot be questioned, and to the present day is clearly acknowledged. How can the gift *of a robber* be received?" *Zhang* said, "The princes of the present day take from their people just as a robber despoils his victim. Yet if they put a good face of propriety on their gifts, then the superior man receives them. I venture to ask how you explain this." *Mencius* answered, "Do you think that, if there should arise a truly imperial sovereign, he would collect the princes of the present day, and put them all to death? Or would he admonish them, and then on their not changing their ways, put them to death? Indeed, to call every one who takes what does not properly belong to him a robber, is pushing a point of resemblance to the utmost, and insisting on the most refined idea of righteousness. When Confucius was in office in Lu, the people struggled together for the game taken in hunting, and he also did the same. If that struggling for the captured game was proper, how much more may the gifts of the princes be received!" *Zhang* urged, "Then, are we to suppose that when Confucius held office, it was not with the view to carry his doctrines into practice?" *Mencius* replied, "It was with that view." And *Zhang rejoined,* "If the practice of his doctrines was his business, what had he to do with that struggling for the captured game?" *Mencius* said, "Confucius first rectified his vessels of sacrifice according to the registers, and did not fill them so rectified with food gathered from every quarter." "But why did he not go away?" "He wished to make a trial *of carrying his doctrines into practice.* When that trial was sufficient to show they could be practiced, and they were still not practiced, then he went away, and thus it was that he never completed in any state a residence of three years. Confucius took office when he saw that the practice *of his doctrines* was likely; he took office when his reception was proper; he took office when he was supported by the state. In the case of his relation to Ji Huan, he took office, seeing that the practice of his doctrines was likely. With the prince Ling of Wei he took office, because his reception was proper. With the prince Xiao of Wei he took office, because he was maintained by the state."

10.5 孟子曰："仕非为贫也，而有时乎为贫；娶妻非为养也，而有时乎为养。为贫者，辞尊居卑，辞富居贫。辞尊居卑，辞富居贫，恶乎宜乎？抱关击柝。孔子尝为委吏矣，曰，'会计当而已矣。'尝为乘田矣，曰，'牛羊茁壮长而已矣。'位卑而言高，罪也；立乎人之本朝，而道不行，耻也。"

10.5 Mencius said, "Office is not *sought* on account of poverty, yet there are times when one seeks office on that account. Marriage is not entered into for the sake of being attended to by the wife, yet there are times when one marries on that account. He who *takes office* on account of his poverty must decline an honorable situation and occupy a low one; he must decline riches and prefer to be poor. What office will be in harmony with this declining an honorable situation, and occupying a low one, this declining riches and preferring to be poor? *Such an one as* that of guarding the gates, or beating the watchman's stick. Confucius was once keeper of stores, and he then said, 'My calculations must all be right. That is all I have to care about.' He was once in charge of the public fields, and he then said, 'That oxen and sheep must be fat and strong, and superior. That is all I have to care about.' When one is in a low situation, to speak of high matters is a crime. When a scholar stands in a prince's court, and his principles are not carried into practice, it is a shame to him."

10.6 万章曰："士之不托诸侯，何也？"孟子曰："不敢也。诸侯失国，而后托于诸侯，礼也；士之托于诸侯，非礼也。"万章曰："君馈之粟，则受之乎？"曰："受之。""受之何义也？"曰："君之于氓也，固周之。"曰："周之则受，赐之则不受，何也。"曰："不敢也。"曰："敢问其不敢何也？"曰："抱关击柝者皆有常职以食于上。无常职而赐于上者，以为不恭也。"曰："君馈之，则受之，不识可常继乎？"曰："缪公之于子思也，亟问，亟馈鼎肉。子思不悦。于卒也，摽使者出诸大门之外，北面稽首再拜而不受，曰：'今而后知君之犬马畜伋。'盖自是台无馈也。悦贤不能举，又不能养也，可谓悦贤乎？"曰："敢问国君欲养君子，如何斯可谓养矣？"曰："以君命将之，再拜稽首而受。其后廪人继粟，庖人继肉，不以君命将之。子思以为鼎肉使己仆仆尔亟拜也，非养君子之道也。尧之于舜也，使其子九男事之，二女女焉，百官牛羊仓廪备，以养舜于畎亩之中，后举而加诸上位，故曰，王公之尊贤者也。"

10.6 Wan Zhang said, "What is the reason that a scholar does not accept a stated support from a prince?" Mencius replied, "He does not presume to do so. When a prince loses his state, and then accepts a stated support from another prince, this is in accordance with propriety. But for a scholar to accept such support from any of the princes is not in accordance with propriety." Wan Zhang said, "If the prince send him a present of grain, *for instance*, does he accept it?" "He accepts it," answered Mencius. "On what principle of rightness does he accept it?" "Why — the prince ought to assist the people in their necessities." *Zhang* pursued, "Why is it that the scholar will thus accept the prince's help, but will not accept his pay?" The answer was, "He does not presume to do so." "I venture to ask why he does not presume to do so." "Even the keepers of the gates, with their watchmen's sticks, have their regular offices for which they can take their support from the prince. He who without a regular office should receive the pay of the prince must be deemed disrespectful." Zhang asked, "If the prince sends a scholar a present, he accepts it. I do not know whether this present may be constantly repeated." *Mencius* answered, "There was the conduct of the prince Mu to Zisi — He made frequent inquiries after Zisi's health, and sent him frequent presents of cooked meat. Zisi was displeased, and at last having motioned to the messenger to go outside the great door, he bowed his head to the ground with his face to the north, did obeisance twice and declined the gift, saying, 'From this time forth I shall know that the prince supports me as a dog or a horse.' And from that time a servant was no more sent with the presents. When a prince professes to be pleased with a man of talents and virtue, and can neither promote him to office, nor support him *in the proper way*, can he be said to be pleased with him?" Zhang said, "I venture to ask how the sovereign of a state, when he wishes to support a superior man, must proceed, that he may be said to do so in the proper way?" Mencius answered, "*At first*, the present must be offered with the prince's commission, and the scholar making obeisance twice with his head bowed to the ground will receive it. But after this the store-keeper will continue to send grain, and the master of the kitchen to send meat, presenting it as if without the prince's express commission. Zisi considered that the meat from the prince's caldron, giving him the annoyance of constantly doing obeisance, was not the way to support a superior man. There was Yao's conduct to Shun: — He caused his nine sons to serve him, and gave him his two daughters in marriage; he caused the various officers, oxen and sheep, storehouses and granaries, *all* to be prepared to support Shun amid the channeled fields, and then he raised him to the most exalted situation. From this we have the expression — The honouring of virtue and talents proper to a king or a prince."

10.7　万章曰："敢问不见诸侯, 何义也?" 孟子曰："在国曰市井之臣, 在野曰草莽之臣, 皆谓庶人。庶人不传质为臣, 不敢见于诸侯, 礼也。" 万章曰："庶人, 召之役, 则往役; 君欲见之, 召之, 则不往见之, 何也?" 曰："往役, 义也; 往见, 不义也。且君之欲见之也, 何为也哉?" 曰："为其多闻也, 为其贤也。" 曰："为其多闻也, 则天子不召师, 而况诸侯乎? 为其贤也, 则吾未闻欲见贤而召之也。缪公亟见于子思, 曰: '古千乘之国以友士, 何如?' 子思不悦, 曰: '古之人有言曰, 事之云乎, 岂曰友之云乎?' 子思之不悦也, 岂不曰: '以位, 则子, 君也, 我, 臣也; 何敢与君友也? 以德, 则子事我者也,美可以与我友？'千乘之君求与之友而不可得也，而况可召与？齐景公田，招虞人以旌，不至，将杀之。志士不忘在沟壑，勇士不忘丧其元。孔子奚取焉？取非其招不往也。"曰："敢问招虞人何以？"曰："以皮冠，庶人以旃，士以旂，大夫以旌。以大夫之招招虞人，虞人死不敢往；以士之招招庶人，庶人岂敢往哉？况乎以不贤人之招招贤人乎？欲见贤人而不以其道，犹欲其入而闭之门也。夫义，路也；礼，门也。惟君子能由是路，出入是门也。《诗》云，'周道如底，其直如矢；君子所履，小人所视。'"万章曰："孔子，君命召，不俟驾而行；然则孔子非与？"曰："孔子当仕有官职，而以其官召之也。"

10.7 Wan Zhang said, "I venture to ask what principle of righteousness is involved in *a scholar's* not going to see the princes." Mencius replied, "A scholar residing in the city, is called 'a minister of the market-place and well,' and one residing in the country is called 'a minister of the grass and plants.' In both cases he is a common man, and it is the rule of propriety that common men, who have not presented the introductory present and become ministers, should not presume to have interviews with the prince." Wan Zhang said, "If a common man is called to perform any service, he goes and performs it; — How is it that a scholar, when the prince, wishing to see him, calls him to his presence, refuses to go?" Mencius replied, "It is right to go and perform the service; it would not be right to go and see the prince." "And," added Mencius, "on what account is it that the prince wishes to see *the scholar*?" "Because of his extensive information, because of his talents and virtue," was the reply. "If because of his extensive information," said Mencius, "such a person is a teacher, and the emperor would not call him; — how much less may any of the princes do so? If because of his talents and virtue, then I have not heard of any one wishing to see a person with those qualities, and calling him to his presence. During the frequent interviews of the prince Mu with Zisi, he *one day* said to him, 'Anciently, princes of a thousand chariots have yet been on terms of friendship with scholars; — What do you think *of such an intercourse?*' Zisi was displeased, and said, 'The ancients have said, "*The scholar should be served*, how should they have merely said that *he should be made a friend of?*" ' When Zisi was thus displeased, did he not say within himself, — 'With regard to our stations, you are sovereign, and I am subject. How can I presume to be on terms of friendship with my sovereign? With regard to our virtue, you ought to make me your master. How may you be on terms of friendship with me?' *Thus*, when a prince of a thousand chariots sought to be on terms of friendship with a scholar, he could not obtain his wish: — how much less could he call him to his presence! The prince Jing of Qi, once, when he was hunting, called his forester to him by a flag. *The forester* would not come, and *the prince* was going to kill him. *With reference to this incident, Confucius* said, 'The determined officer never forgets that *his end may be* in a ditch or a stream; the brave officer never forgets that he may lose his head.' What was it *in the forester* that Confucius thus approved? He approved his not going *to the prince*, when summoned by the article which was not appropriate to him." Zhang said, "May I ask with what a forester should be summoned?" Mencius replied, "With a skin cap. A common man *should be summoned* with a plain banner; a scholar *who has taken office*, with one having dragons embroidered on it; and a great officer with one having feathers suspended from the top of the staff. When the forester was summoned with the article appropriate to the summoning of a great officer, he would have died rather than presume to go. If a common man were summoned with the article appropriate to the summoning of a scholar, how could he presume to go? How much more may we expect this refusal to go, when a man of talents and virtue is summoned in a way which is inappropriate to his character! When a prince wishes to see a man of talents and virtue, and does not take the proper course *to get his wish*, it is as if he wished him to enter *his palace*, and shut the door against him. Now, righteousness is the way, and propriety is the door, but it is only the superior man who can follow this way, and go out and in by this door. It is said in the *Book of Poetry*: 'The way to Zhou is level like a whetstone, and straight as an arrow. The officers tread it, and the lower people see it.' " Wan Zhang said, "When Confucius received the prince's message calling him, he went without waiting for his carriage. And so— did Confucius do wrong?" Mencius replied, "Confucius was in office, and had its appropriate duties. And moreover, he was summoned on the business of his office."

10.8　孟子谓万章曰：“一乡之善士斯友一乡之善士，一国之善士斯友一国之善士，天下之善士斯友天下之善士。以友天下之善士为未足，又尚论古之人。颂其诗，读其书，不知其人，可乎？是以论其世也。是尚友也。"

10.8　Mencius said to Wan Zhang, "The scholar whose virtue is most distinguished in a village shall make friends of all the virtuous scholars in the village. The scholar whose virtue is most distinguished throughout a state shall make friends of all the virtuous scholars of that state. The scholar whose virtue is most distinguished throughout the empire shall make friends of all the virtuous scholars of the empire. When a scholar feels that his friendship with all the virtuous scholars of the empire is not sufficient *to satisfy him*, he proceeds to ascend to consider the men of antiquity. He repeats their poems, and reads their books, and as he does not know what they were as men, to ascertain this, he considers their history. This is to ascend and make friends *of the men of antiquity*."

10.9　齐宣王问卿。孟子曰："王何卿之问也？"王曰："卿不同乎？"曰："不同；有贵戚之卿，有异姓之卿。"王曰："请问贵戚之卿。"曰："君有大过则谏；反复之而不听，则易位。"王勃然变乎色。曰："王勿异也。王问臣，臣不敢不以正对。"王色定，然后请问异姓之卿。曰："君有过则谏，反复之而不听，则去。"

10.9　The king Xuan of Qi asked about the *office of* chief ministers. Mencius said, "Which chief ministers is Your Majesty asking about?" "Are there differences among them?" inquired the king. "There are," was the reply. "There are the chief ministers who are noble and relatives *of the prince*, and there are those who are of a different surname." The king said, "I beg to ask about the chief ministers who are noble and relatives of the prince." Mencius answered, "If the prince have great faults, they ought to remonstrate with him, and if he do not listen to them after they have done so again and again, they ought to dethrone him." The king on this looked moved, and changed countenance. Mencius said, "Let not Your Majesty be offended. You asked me, and I dare not answer but according to truth." The king's countenance became composed, and he then begged to ask about chief ministers who were of a different surname *from the prince*. Mencius said, "When the prince has faults, they ought to remonstrate with him, and if he do not listen to them after they have done this again and again, they ought to leave *the state*."

卷十一　告子章句上
BOOK XI　GAO ZI　PART I

11.1　告子曰：“性犹杞柳也，义犹桮棬也；以人性为仁义，犹以杞柳为桮棬。”孟子曰：“子能顺杞柳之性而以为桮棬乎？将戕贼杞柳而后以为桮棬也？如将戕贼杞柳而以为桮棬，则亦将戕贼人以为仁义与？率天下之人而祸仁义者，必子之言夫！”

11.1　The philosopher Gao said, *"Man's* nature is like the qi willow, and righteousness is like a cup or a bowl. The fashioning benevolence and righteousness out of man's nature is like the making cups and bowls from the qi willow." Mencius replied, "Can you, leaving untouched the nature of the willow, make with it cups and bowls? You must do violence and injury to the willow, before you can make cups and bowls with it. If you must do violence and injury to the willow in order to make cups and bowls with it, *on your principles* you must in the same way do violence and injury to humanity in order to fashion from it benevolence and righteousness! Your words, alas! would certainly lead all men on to reckon benevolence and righteousness to be calamities."

11.2　告子曰：“性犹湍水也，决诸东方则东流，决诸西方则西流。人性之无分于善不善也，犹水之无分于东西也。”孟子曰：“水信无分于东西，无分于上下乎？人性之善也，犹水之就下也。

人无有不善，水无有不下。今夫水，搏而跃之，可使过额；激而行之，可使在山。是岂水之性哉？其势则然也。人之可使为不善，其性亦犹是也。"

11.2 The philosopher Gao said, *"Man's* nature is like water whirling round *in a corner.* Open a passage for it to the east, and it will flow to the east; open a passage for it to the west, and it will flow to the west. Man's nature is indifferent to good and evil, just as the water is indifferent to the east and west." Mencius replied, "Water indeed *will flow* indifferently to the east or west, but will it flow indifferently up or down? The tendency of man's nature to good is like the tendency of water to flow downwards. There are none but have this tendency to good, *just* as all water flows downwards. Now by striking water and causing it to leap up, you may make it go over your forehead, and, by damming and leading it, you may force it up a hill; — But are such movements according to the nature of water? It is the force applied which causes them. When men are made to do what is not good, their nature is dealt with in this way."

11.3 告子曰："生之谓性。"孟子曰："生之谓性也，犹白之谓白与？"曰："然。""白羽之白也，犹白雪之白；白雪之白犹白玉之白与？"曰："然。""然则犬之性犹牛之性，牛之性犹人之性与？"

11.3 The philosopher Gao said, "Life is what is to be understood by nature." Mencius asked him, "Do you say that by nature you mean life, just as you say that white is white?" "Yes, I do," was the reply. Mencius added, "Is the whiteness of a white feather like that of white snow, and the whiteness of white snow like that of white gem?" *Gao again* said, "Yes." "Very well," *pursued Mencius.* "Is the nature of a dog like the nature of an ox, and the nature of an ox like the nature of a man?"

11.4　告子曰："食色，性也。仁，内也，非外也；义，外也，非内也。"孟子曰："何以谓仁内义外也？"曰："彼长而我长之，非有长于我也；犹彼白而我白之，从其白于外也，故谓之外也。"曰："异于白马之白也，无以异于白人之白也；不识长马之长也，无以异于长人之长与？且谓长者义乎？长之者义乎？"曰："吾弟则爱之，秦人之弟则不爱也，是以我为悦者也，故谓之内。长楚人之长，亦长吾之长，是以长为悦者也，故谓之外也。"曰："耆秦人之炙，无以异于耆吾炙，夫物则亦有然者也，然则耆炙亦有外与？"

11.4　The philosopher Gao said, "*To enjoy* food and *delight in* colors is nature. Benevolence is internal and not external; righteousness is external and not internal." Mencius asked him, "What is the ground of your saying that benevolence is internal and righteousness external?" He replied, "There is a man older than I, and I give honor to his age. It is not that there is *first* in me a principle of such reverence to age. It is just as when there is a white man, and I consider him white; — according as he is so externally to me. On this account, I pronounce *of righteousness* that it is external." Mencius said, "There is no difference between our pronouncing a white horse to be white and our pronouncing a white man to be white. But is there no difference between the regard with which we acknowledge the age of an old horse and that with which we acknowledge the age of an old man? And what is it which is called righteousness? — The fact of a man's being old? Or the fact of our giving honor to his age?" Gao said, "There is my younger brother; — I love him. But the younger brother of a man of Qin I do not love; — that is the feeling is determined by myself, and therefore I say that benevolence is internal. *On the other hand*, I give honor to an old man of Chu, and I also give honor to an old man of my own *people*; that is, the feeling is determined by the age, and therefore I say that righteousness is external." *Mencius* answered him, "Our enjoyment of meat roasted by a man of Qin does not differ from our enjoyment of meat roasted by ourselves. Thus, *what you insist on* takes place also in the case of such things, and will you say likewise that our enjoyment of a roast is external?"

11.5　孟季子问公都子曰：“何以谓义内也?”曰：“行吾敬，故谓之内也。”“乡人长于伯兄一岁，则谁敬?”曰：“敬兄。”“酌则谁先?”曰：“先酌乡人。”“所敬在此，所长在彼，果在外，非由内也。”公都子不能答，以告孟子。孟子曰：“敬叔父乎? 敬弟乎? 彼将曰，‘敬叔父。’曰，‘弟为尸，则谁敬?’彼将曰，‘敬弟。’子曰，‘恶在其敬叔父也?’彼将曰，‘在位故也。’子亦曰，‘在位故也。庸敬在兄，斯须之敬在乡人。’”季子闻之，曰：

"敬叔父則敬，敬弟則敬，果在外，非由內也。"公都子曰："冬日則飲湯，夏日則飲水，然則飲食亦在外也？"

11.5 The disciple Meng Ji asked Gongdu, saying, "On what ground is it said that righteousness is internal?" Gongdu replied, "We *therein* act out our feeling of respect, and therefore it is said to be internal." *The other objected,* "Suppose the case of a villager older than your elder brother by one year, to which of them would you show the *greater respect?*" "To my brother," was the reply. "But for which of them would you first pour out wine *at a feast?*" "For the villager." *Meng Ji argued,* "Now your feeling of reverence rests on the one, and *now* the honor due to age is rendered to the other — this is certainly determined by what is without, and does not proceed from within." Gongdu was unable to reply, and told the conversation to Mencius. Mencius said, *"You should ask him,* 'Which do you respect most — your uncle, or your younger brother?' He will answer, 'My uncle.' Ask him *again,* 'If your younger brother be personating a dead ancestor, to which do you show the greater respect, — *to him or to your uncle?*' He will say, 'To my younger brother.' You can go on, 'But where is the respect due, as you said, to your uncle!' He will reply to this, '*I show the respect to my younger brother,* because of the position which he occupies,' and you can likewise say, '*So my respect to the villager is* because of the position which he occupies. Ordinarily, my respect is rendered to my elder brother; for a brief season, *on occasion,* it is rendered to the villager.'" Meng Ji heard this and observed, "When respect is due to my uncle, I respect him, and when respect is due to my younger brother, I respect him; — the thing is certainly determined by what is without, and does not proceed from within." Gongdu replied, "In winter we drink things hot, in summer we drink things cold; and so, *on your principle*, eating and drinking also depend on what is external!"

11.6 公都子曰："告子曰：'性无善无不善也。'或曰：'性可以为善，可以为不善；是故文武兴，则民好善；幽厉兴，则民好暴。'或曰：'有性善，有性不善；是故以尧为君而有象；以瞽瞍为父而有舜；以纣为兄之子，且以为君，而有微子启、王子比干。'今曰'性善'，然则彼皆非与？"孟子曰："乃若其情，则可以为善矣，乃所谓善也。若夫为不善，非才之罪也。恻隐之心，人皆有之；羞恶之心，人皆有之；恭敬之心，人皆有之；是非之心，人皆有之。恻隐之心，仁也；羞恶之心，义也；恭敬之心，礼也；是非之心，智也。仁义礼智，非由外铄我也，我固有之也，弗思耳矣。故曰，'求则得之，舍则失之。'或相倍蓰而无算者，不能尽其才者也。《诗》曰，'天生蒸民，有物有则。民之秉彝，好是懿德。'孔子曰：'为此诗者，其知道乎！故有物必有则；民之秉彝也，故好是懿德。'"

11.6 The disciple Gongdu said, "The philosopher Gao says, '*Man's* nature is neither good nor bad.' Some say, '*Man's* nature may be made to practice good, and it may be made to practice evil, and accordingly, under Wen and Wu, the people loved what was good, *while* under You and Li, they loved what was cruel.' Some say, 'The nature of some is good, and the nature of others is bad. Hence it was that under such a sovereign as Yao there yet appeared Xiang; that with such a father as Gusou there yet appeared Shun; and that with Zhou for their sovereign, and the son of their elder brother besides, there were found Qi the viscount of Wei, and the prince Bigan.' And now you say, 'The nature is good.' Then are all those wrong?" Mencius said, "From the feelings proper to it, it is constituted for the practice of what is good. This is what I mean in saying that the *nature* is good. If men do what is not good, the blame cannot be imputed to their natural powers. The feeling of commiseration belongs to all men; so does that of shame and dislike; and that of reverence and respect; and that of approving and disapproving. The feeling of commiseration *implies the principle* of benevolence; that of shame and dislike, the principle of righteousness; that of reverence and respect, the principle of propriety; and that of approving and disapproving, the principle of knowledge. Benevolence, righteousness, propriety, and knowledge, are not infused into us from without. We are certainly furnished with them. *And a different view*, is simply from want of reflection. Hence it is said: 'Seek and you will find them. Neglect and you will lose them.' Men differ from one another in regard to them; — some as much again as others, some five times as much, and some to an incalculable amount; — it is because they cannot carry out fully their *natural* powers. It is said in the *Book of Poetry*: 'Heaven in producing mankind, gave them their *various* faculties and relations with *their specific* laws. These are the invariable rules of nature for all to hold, and *all* love this admirable virtue.' Confucius said, 'The maker of this ode knew indeed the principle *of our nature!*' We may thus see that every faculty and relation must have its law, and since there are invariable rules for all to hold, they consequently love this admirable virtue."

11.7 孟子曰："富岁，子弟多赖；凶岁，子弟多暴，非天之降才尔殊也，其所以陷溺其心者然也。今夫麰麦，播种而耰之，其地同，树之时又同，浡然而生，至于日至之时，皆熟矣。虽有不同，则地有肥硗，雨露之养、人事之不齐也。故凡同类者，举相似也，何独至于人而疑之？圣人，与我同类者。故龙子曰：'不知足而为屦，我知其不为蒉也。'屦之相似，天下之足同也。口之于味，有同耆也；易牙先得我口之所耆者也。如使口之于味也，其性与人殊，若犬马之与我不同类也，则天下何耆皆从易牙之于味也？至于味，天下期于易牙，是天下之口相似也。惟耳亦然。至于声，天下期于师旷，是天下之耳相似也。惟目亦然。至于子都，天下莫不知其姣也。不知子都之姣者，无目者也。故曰，口之于味也，有同耆焉；耳之于声也，有同听焉；目之于色也，有同美焉。至于心，独无所同然乎？心之所同然者何也？谓理也，义也。圣人先得我心之所同然耳。故理义之悦我心，犹刍豢之悦我口。"

11.7 Mencius said, "In good years the children of the people are most of them good, while in bad years the most of them abandon themselves to evil. It is not owing to their natural powers conferred by Heaven that they are thus different. The abandonment is owing to the circumstances through which they allow their minds to be ensnared and drowned in *evil*. There now is barley. — Let it be sown and covered up; the ground being the same, and the time of sowing likewise the same, it grows rapidly up, and when the full time is come, it is all found to be ripe. Although there may be inequalities *of produce*, that is owing to the *difference of the* soil, as rich or poor, to the *unequal* nourishment afforded by the rains and dews, and to the different ways in which man has performed his business in *reference to* it. Thus all things which are the same in kind are like to one another; — why should we doubt in regard to man, as if he were a solitary exception to this? The sage and we are the same in kind. In accordance with this the scholar Long said, 'If a man make hempen sandals without knowing *the size of people's feet, yet* I know that he will not make *them like* baskets.' Sandals are all like one another, because all men's feet are like one another. So with the mouth and flavors. — All mouths have the same relishes. Yiya *only* apprehended before me what my mouth relishes. Suppose that his mouth in its relish for flavors differed from that of other men, as is the case with dogs or horses which are not the same in kind with us, why should all men be found following Yiya in their relishes? In the matter of tastes the whole empire models itself after Yiya; that is, the mouths of all men are like one another. And so also it is with the ear. In the matter of sounds, the whole empire models itself after the music-master Kuang; that is, the ears of all men are like one another. And so also it is with the eye. In the case of Zidu, there is no man but would recognize that he was beautiful. Any one who would not recognize the beauty of Zidu must have no eyes. Therefore I say, — *Men's* mouths agree in having the same relishes; their ears agree in enjoying the same sounds; their eyes agree in recognizing the same beauty; — shall their minds alone be without that which they similarly approve? What is it then of which they similarly approve? It is, I say, the principles *of our nature*, and the determinations of righteousness. The sages only apprehended before me that of which my mind approves along with other men. Therefore the principles of our nature and the determinations of righteousness are agreeable to my mind, just as the flesh of grass and grain-fed animals is agreeable to my mouth."

11.8　孟子曰："牛山之木尝美矣，以其郊于大国也，斧斤伐之，可以为美乎？是其日夜之所息，雨露之所润，非无萌蘖之生焉，牛羊又从而牧之，是以若彼濯濯也。人见其濯濯也，以为未尝有材焉，此岂山之性也哉？虽存乎人者，岂无仁义之心哉？其所以放其良心者，亦犹斧斤之于木也，旦旦而伐之，可以为美乎？其日夜之所息，平旦之气，其好恶与人相近也者几希，则其旦昼之所为，有梏亡之矣。梏之反覆，则其夜气不足以存；夜气不足以存，则其违禽兽不远矣。人见其禽兽也，而以为未尝有才焉者，是岂人之情也哉？故苟得其养，无物不长；苟失其养，无物不消。孔子曰：'操则存，舍则亡；出入无时，莫知其乡。'惟心之谓与？"

11.8　Mencius said, "The trees of the Niu mountain were once beautiful. Being situated, however, in the borders of a large state, they were hewn down with axes and bills, — and could they retain their beauty? Still through the activity of the vegetative life day and night, and the nourishing influence of the rain and dew, they were not without buds and sprouts springing forth, but then came the cattle and goats and browsed upon them. To these things is owing the bare and stripped appearance *of the mountain*, which when people see, they think it was never finely wooded. But is this the nature of the mountain? And so *also of* what properly belongs to man; — shall it be said that the mind *of any man* was without benevolence and righteousness? The way in which a man loses his proper goodness of mind is like the way in which the trees are denuded by axes and bills. Hewn down day after day, can it — *the mind* — retain its beauty? But there is a development of its life day and night, and in the *calm* air of the morning, just between night and day, the mind feels in a degree those desires and aversions which are proper to humanity, but the feeling is not strong, and it is fettered and destroyed by what takes place during the day. This fettering taking place again and again, the restorative influence of the night is not sufficient to preserve *the proper goodness of the mind*; and when this proves insufficient for that purpose, the nature becomes not much different from that of the irrational animals, which when people see, they think that it never had those powers *which I assert*. But does this condition represent the feelings proper to humanity? Therefore, if it receive its proper nourishment, there is nothing which will not grow. If it lose its proper nourishment, there is nothing which will not decay away. Confucius said, 'Hold it fast, and it remains with you. Let it go, and you lose it. Its outgoing and incoming cannot be defined as to time or place.' It is the mind of which this is said!"

11.9　孟子曰："无或乎王之不智也，虽有天下易生之物也，一日暴之，十日寒之，未有能生者也。吾见亦罕矣，吾退而寒之者至矣，吾如有萌焉何哉！今夫弈之为数，小数也；不专心致志，则不得也。弈秋，通国之善弈者也。使弈秋诲二人弈，其一人专心致志，惟弈秋之为听。一人虽听之，一心以为有鸿鹄将至，思援弓缴而射之，虽与之俱学，弗若之矣。为是其智弗若与？曰：非然也。"

11.9　Mencius said, "It is not to be wondered at that the king is not wise! Suppose the case of the most easily growing thing in the world; — if you let it have one day's genial heat, and then expose it for ten days to cold, it will not be able to grow. It is but seldom that I have an audience of the king, and when I retire, there come *all* those who act upon him like the cold. Though I succeed in bringing out some buds *of goodness*, of what avail is it! Now chess-playing is but a small art, but without his whole mind being given, and his will bent to it, a man cannot succeed at it. Chess Qiu is the best chess-player in all the kingdom. Suppose that he is teaching two men to play. — The one gives to the subject his whole mind and bends to it all his will, doing nothing but listening to Chess Qiu. The other, although *he seems to be* listening to him, has his whole mind running on a swan which he thinks is approaching, and wishes to bend his bow, adjust the string to the arrow, and shoot it. Although he is learning along with the other, he does not come up to him. Why? — Because his intelligence is not equal? Not so."

11.10　孟子曰："鱼，我所欲也，熊掌亦我所欲也；二者不可得兼，舍鱼而取熊掌者也。生亦我所欲也，义亦我所欲也；二者不可得兼，舍生而取义者也。生亦我所欲，所欲有甚于生者，故不为苟得也；死亦我所恶，所恶有甚于死者，故患有所不辟也。如使人之所欲莫甚于生，则凡可以得生者，何不用也？使人之所恶莫甚于死者，则凡可以辟患者，何不为也？由是则生而有不用也，由是则可以辟患而有不为也，是故所欲有甚于生者，所恶有甚于死者。非独贤者有是心也，人皆有之，贤者能勿丧耳。一箪食，一豆羹，得之则生，弗得则死，嘑尔而与之，行道之人弗受；蹴尔而与之，乞人不屑也；万钟则不辩礼义而受之。万钟于我何加焉？为宫室之美、妻妾之奉、所识穷乏者得我与？乡为身死而不受，今为宫室之美为之；乡为身死而不受，今为妻妾之奉为之；乡为身死而不受，今为所识穷乏者得我而为之，是亦不可以已乎？此之谓失其本心。"

11.10　Mencius said, "I like fish, and I also like bear's paws. If I cannot have the two together, I will let the fish go, and take the bear's paws. So, I like life, and I also like righteousness. If I cannot keep the two together, I will let life go, and choose righteousness. I like life indeed, but there is that which I like more than life, and therefore, I will not seek to possess it by any improper ways. I dislike death indeed, but there is that which I dislike more than death, and therefore there are occasions when I will not avoid danger. If among the things which man likes there were nothing which he liked more than life, why should he not use every means by which he could preserve it? If among the things which man dislikes there were nothing which he disliked more than death, why should he not do everything by which he could avoid danger? There are cases when men by a certain course might preserve life, and they do not employ it; when by certain things they might avoid danger, and they will not do them. Therefore, men have that which they like more than life, and that which they dislike more than death. They are not men of distinguished talents and virtue only who have this mental nature. All men have it; what belongs to such men is simply that they do not lose it. Here are a small basket of rice and a platter of soup, and the case is one in which the getting them will preserve life, and the want of them will be death; — if they are offered with an insulting voice, even a tramper will not receive them, or if you first tread upon them, even a beggar will not stoop to take them. *And yet* a man will accept of ten thousand *zhong*, without any consideration of propriety or righteousness. What can the ten thousand *zhong* add to him? *When he takes them*, is it not that he may obtain beautiful mansions, that he may secure the services of wives and concubines, or that the poor and needy of his acquaintance may be helped by him? In the former case *the offered bounty* was not received, though it would have saved from death, and now *the emolument* is taken for the sake of beautiful mansions. *The bounty* that would have preserved from death was not received, and *the emolument* is taken to get the service of wives and concubines. *The bounty* that would have saved from death was not received, and *the emolument* is taken that one's poor and needy acquaintances may be helped by him. Was it then not possible likewise to decline this? This is a case of what is called — 'Losing the proper nature of one's mind.'"

11.11 孟子曰："仁，人心也；义，人路也。舍其路而弗由，放其心而不知求，哀哉！人有鸡犬放，则知求之；有放心而不知求。学问之道无他，求其放心而已矣。"

11.11 Mencius said, "Benevolence is man's mind and righteousness is man's path. How lamentable is it to neglect the path and not pursue it, to lose this mind and not know to seek it again! When men's fowls and dogs are lost, they know to seek for them again, but they lose their mind, and, do not know to seek for it. The great end of learning is nothing else but to seek for the lost mind."

11.12 孟子曰："今有无名之指屈而不信，非疾痛害事也，如有能信之者，则不远秦楚之路，为指之不若人也。指不若人，则知恶之；心不若人，则不知恶，此之谓不知类也。"

11.12 Mencius said, "Here is *a man whose* fourth finger is bent and cannot be stretched out straight. It is not painful, nor does it incommode his business, and yet if there be any one who can make it straight, he will not think the way from Qin to Chu far *to go to him*; — because his finger is not like the finger of other people. When a man's finger is not like those of other people, he knows to feel dissatisfied, but if his mind be not like that of other people, he does not know to feel dissatisfaction. This is called — 'Ignorance of the relative *importance of things*.'"

11.13 孟子曰："拱把之桐梓，人苟欲生之，皆知所以养之者。至于身，而不知所以养之者，岂爱身不若桐梓哉？弗思甚也。"

11.13 Mencius said, "Anybody who wishes to cultivate the *tong* or the *zi*, which may be grasped with both hands, *perhaps* with one, knows by what means to nourish them. In the case of their own persons, men do not know by what means to nourish them. Is it to be supposed that their regard of their own persons is inferior to their regard for a *tong* or a *zi*? Their want of reflection is extreme."

11.14 孟子曰："人之于身也，兼所爱。兼所爱，则兼所养也。无尺寸之肤不爱焉，则无尺寸之肤不养也。所以考其善不善者，岂有他哉？于己取之而已矣。体有贵贱，有小大。无以小害大，无以贱害贵。养其小者为小人，养其大者为大人。今有场师，舍其梧槚，养其樲棘，则为贱场师焉。养其一指而失其肩背，而不知也，则为狼疾人也。饮食之人，则人贱之矣，为其养小以失大也。饮食之人无有失也，则口腹岂适为尺寸之肤哉？"

11.14 Mencius said, "There is no part of himself which a man does not love, and as he loves all so he must nourish all. There is not an inch of skin which he does not love, and so there is not an inch of skin which he will not nourish. For examining whether *his way of nourishing* be good or not, what other rule is there but this, that he determine by *reflecting* on himself where it should be applied? Some parts of the body are noble, and some ignoble; some great, and some small. The great must not be injured for the small, nor the noble for the ignoble. He who nourishes the little belonging to him is a little man, and he who nourishes the great is a great man. Here is a plantation keeper, who neglects his *wu* and *jia*, and cultivates his sour wild date-trees; — he is a poor plantation-keeper. He who nourishes one of his fingers, neglecting his shoulders or his back, without knowing *that he is doing so*, is a man *who resembles* a hurried wolf. A man who *only* eats and drinks is counted mean by others; because he nourishes what is little to the neglect of what is great. If a man, *fond of his* eating and drinking, were not to neglect *what is of more importance*, how should his mouth and belly be considered as no more than an inch of skin?"

11.15　公都子问曰:"钓是人也，或为大人，或为小人，何也?"孟子曰:"从其大体为大人，从其小体为小人。"曰:"钓是人也，或从其大体，或从其小体，何也?"曰:"耳目之官不思，而蔽于物。物交物，则引之而已矣。心之官则思，思则得之，不思则不得也。此天之所与我者。先立乎其大者，则其小者不能夺也。此为大人而已矣。"

11.15 The disciple Gongdu said, "All are equally men, but some are great men, and some are little men; — how is this?" Mencius replied, "Those who follow that part of themselves which is great are great men; those who follow that part which is little are little men." Gongdu pursued, "All are equally men, but some follow that part of themselves which is great, and some follow that part which is little; — how is this?" Mencius answered, "The senses of hearing and seeing do not think, and are obscured by *external* things. When one thing comes into contact with another, as a matter of course it leads it away. To the mind belongs the office of thinking. By thinking, it gets *the right view of things*; by neglecting to think, it fails to do this. These — *the senses and the mind* — are what Heaven has given to us. Let a man first stand fast in *the supremacy of the nobler part of* his constitution, and the inferior part will not be able to take it from him. It is simply this which makes the great man."

11.16 孟子曰：“有天爵者，有人爵者。仁义忠信，乐善不倦，此天爵也；公卿大夫，此人爵也。古之人修其天爵，而人爵从之。今之人修其天爵，以要人爵；既得人爵，而弃其天爵，则惑之甚者也，终亦必亡而已矣。”

11.16 Mencius said, "There is a nobility of Heaven, and there is a nobility of man. Benevolence, righteousness, self-consecration, and fidelity, with unwearied joy in *these* virtues; — these constitute the nobility of Heaven. To be a *gong*, a *qing*, or a *dafu*; — this constitutes the nobility of man. The men of antiquity cultivated their nobility of Heaven, and the nobility of man came to them in its train. The men of the present day cultivate their nobility of Heaven in order to seek for the nobility of man, and when they have obtained that, they throw away the other; — their delusion is extreme. The issue is simply this that they must lose *that nobility of man* as well."

11.17　孟子曰："欲贵者，人之同心也。人人有贵于己者，弗思耳矣。人之所贵者，非良贵也。赵孟之所贵，赵孟能贱之。《诗》云：'既醉以酒，既饱以德。'言饱乎仁义也，所以不愿人之膏粱之味也；令闻广誉施于身，所以不愿人之文绣也。"

11.17　Mencius said, "To desire to be honored is the common mind of men. And all men have in themselves that which is *truly* honorable. Only they do not think of it. The honor which men confer is not good honor. Those whom Zhao the Great ennobles he can make mean *again*. It is said in the *Book of Poetry*, 'He has filled us with his wine; he has satiated us with his goodness.' '*Satiated us with his goodness*,' that is, satiated us with benevolence and righteousness, and he who is so, consequently, does not wish for the fat meat and fine millet of men. A good reputation and far-reaching praise fall to him, and he does not desire the elegant embroidered garments of men."

11.18　孟子曰："仁之胜不仁也，犹水胜火。今之为仁者，犹以一杯水救一车薪之火也；不熄，则谓之水不胜火，此又与于不仁之甚者也，亦终必亡而已矣。"

11.18　Mencius said, "Benevolence subdues its opposite just as water subdues fire. Those, however, who nowadays practise benevolence *do it* as if with one cup of water they could save a whole waggon-load of fuel which was on fire, and when the flames were not extinguished, were to say that water cannot subdue fire. This conduct, moreover, greatly encourages those who are not benevolent. The final issue will simply be this — the loss *of that small amount of benevolence*."

11.19　孟子曰："五谷者，种之美者也；苟为不熟，不如荑稗。夫仁，亦在乎熟之而已矣。"

11.19　Mencius said, "Of all seeds the best are the five kinds of grain, yet if they be not ripe, they are not equal to the *ti* or the *bai*. So, the value of benevolence depends entirely on its being brought to maturity."

11.20　孟子曰："羿之教人射，必志于彀；学者亦必志于彀。大匠诲人必以规矩，学者亦必以规矩。"

11.20　Mencius said, "Yi, in teaching men to shoot, made it a rule to draw the bow to the full, and his pupils also did the same. A master workman, in teaching others, uses the compass and square, and his pupils do the same."

卷十二 告子章句下

BOOK XII   GAO ZI   PART II

12.1　任人有问屋庐子曰：“礼与食孰重？”曰：“礼重。”“色与礼孰重？”曰：“礼重。”曰：“以礼食，则饥而死；不以礼食，则得食，必以礼乎？亲迎，则不得妻；不亲迎，则得妻，必亲迎乎？”屋庐子不能对，明日之邹以告孟子。孟子曰：“于答是也，何有？不揣其本，而齐其末，方寸之木可使高于岑楼。金重于羽者，岂谓一钩金与一舆羽之谓哉？取食之重者与礼之轻者而比之，奚翅食重？取色之重者与礼之轻者而比之，奚翅色重？往应之曰：‘紾兄之臂而夺之食，则得食；不紾，则不得食，则将紾之乎？逾东家墙而搂其处子，则得妻，不搂，则不得妻，则将搂之乎？’”

12.1   A man of Ren asked the disciple Wulu, saying, "Is *an observance of* the rules of propriety *in regard to eating*, or the eating, the more important?" The answer was, "*The observance of* the rules of propriety is the more important." "Is *the gratifying* the appetite of sex, or *the doing so only* according to the rules of propriety, the more important?" The answer *again* was, "*The observance of* the rules of propriety *in the matter* is the more important." *The man* pursued, "If the result of eating only according to the rules of propriety will be death by starvation, while by disregarding those rules we may get food, must they *still* be observed *in such a case*? If according to the rule that he shall go in person to meet his wife a man cannot get married, while by disregarding that rule he may get married, must he *still observe* the rule *in such a case*?" Wulu was unable to reply to *these questions*, and the next day he went to Zou, and told them to Mencius. Mencius said, "What difficulty is there in answering these inquiries? If you do not adjust them at their lower extremities, but only put their tops on a level, a piece of wood an inch square may be made to be higher than the pointed peak of a high building. Gold is heavier than feathers; — but does that saying have reference, on the one hand, to a single clasp of gold, and, on the other, to a waggon-load of feathers? If you take a case where the eating is of the utmost importance and the observing the rules of propriety is of little importance, and compare the things together, why stop with saying merely that the eating is more important? So, taking the case where the gratifying the appetite of sex is of the utmost importance and the observing the rules of propriety is of little importance, why stop with merely saying that the gratifying the appetite is the more important? Go and answer him thus, 'If, by twisting your elder brother's arm and snatching from him what he is eating, you can get food for yourself, while, if you do not do so, you will not get anything to eat, will you so twist his arm? If by getting over your neighbor's wall, and dragging away his virgin daughter, you can get a wife, while if you do not do so, you will not be able to get a wife, will you so drag her away?'"

12.2　曹交问曰："人皆可以为尧舜,有诸?"孟子曰:"然。""交
闻文王十尺, 汤九尺, 今交九尺四寸以长, 食粟而已, 如何则
可。"曰:"奚有于是? 亦为之而已矣。有人于此, 力不能胜一
匹雏, 则为无力人矣; 今日举百钧, 则为有力人矣。然则举乌
获之任, 是亦为乌获而已矣。夫人岂以不胜为患哉? 弗为耳。
徐行后长者谓之弟, 疾行先长者谓之不弟。夫徐行者, 岂人所
不能哉? 所不为也。尧舜之道, 孝悌而已矣。子服尧之服, 诵
尧之言, 行尧之行, 是尧而已矣。子服桀之服, 诵桀之言, 行
桀之行, 是桀而已矣。"曰:"交得见于邹君, 可以假馆, 愿留
而受业于门。"曰:"夫道若大路然, 岂难知哉? 人病不求耳。
子归而求之, 有馀师。"

12.2　Jiao of Cao asked *Mencius*, saying, "*It is said*, 'All men may
be Yaos and Shuns'; is it so?" Mencius replied, "It is." *Jiao went
on*, "I have heard that King Wen was ten cubits *high*, and Tang
nine. Now I am nine cubits four inches in height. *But* I can do
nothing but eat my millet. What am I to do to realize that saying?"
Mencius answered him, "What has this — *the question of size* —
to do with the matter? It all lies simply in acting as such. Here
is a man, whose strength was not equal to lift a duckling: — he
was *then* a man of no strength. But today he says, 'I can lift 3,000
catties' weight,' and he is a man of strength. And so, he who can
lift the weight which Wu Huo lifted is just another Wu Huo. Why
should a man make a want of ability the subject of his grief? It is
only that he will not do the thing. To walk slowly, keeping behind
his elders, is to perform the part of a younger brother. To walk

quickly and precede his elders, is to violate the duty of a younger brother. Now, is it what a man cannot do — to walk slowly? It is what he does not do. The course of Yao and Shun was simply that of filial piety and fraternal duty. Wear the clothes of Yao, repeat the words of Yao, and do the actions of Yao, and you will just be a Yao. And, if you wear the clothes of Jie, repeat the words of Jie, and do the actions of Jie, you will just be a Jie." Jiao said, "I shall be having an interview with the prince of Zou, and can ask him to let me have a house to lodge in. I wish to remain here, and receive instruction at your gate." Mencius replied, "The way of truth is like a great road. It is not difficult to know it. The evil is only that men will not seek it. Do you go home and search for it, and you will have abundance of teachers."

告子章句下 GAO ZI PART II

229

12.3　公孙丑问曰："高子曰：'《小弁》，小人之诗也。'" 孟子曰："何以言之？"曰："怨。"曰："固哉，高叟之为诗也！有人于此，越人关弓而射之，则己谈笑而道之；无他，疏之也。其兄关弓而射之，则己垂涕泣而道之；无他，戚之也。《小弁》之怨，亲亲也。亲亲，仁也。固矣夫，高叟之为诗也！"曰："《凯风》何以不怨？"曰："《凯风》，亲之过小者也；《小弁》，亲之过大者也。亲之过大而不怨，是愈疏也；亲之过小而怨，是不可矶也。愈疏，不孝也；不可矶，亦不孝也。孔子曰：'舜其至孝矣，五十而慕。'"

12.3　Gongsun Chou asked *about an opinion of the scholar Gao*, saying, "Gao observed, '*The Xiao Bian* is the ode of a little man.' " Mencius asked, "Why did he say so?" "Because of the murmuring *which it expresses.*" was the reply. Mencius answered, "How stupid was that old Gao in dealing with the ode! There is a man here, and a native of Yue bends his bow to shoot him. I will advise him *not to do so*, but speaking calmly and smilingly; — for no other reason but that he is not related to me. *But* if my own brother be bending his bow to shoot the man, then I will advise him not to do so, weeping and crying the while; — for no other reason than that he is related to me. The dissatisfaction expressed in the *Xiao Bian* is the working of relative affection, and that affection shows benevolence. Stupid indeed was old Gao's criticism on the ode." *Chou then said*, "How is it that there is no dissatisfaction expressed in the *Kai Feng*?" Mencius replied, "The parent's fault referred to in the *Kai Feng* is small; that referred to in the *Xiao Bian* is great. Where the parent's fault was great, not to have murmured on account of it would have increased the want of natural affection. Where the parent's fault was small, to have murmured on account of it would have been to act like water which frets and foams about a stone that interrupts its course. To increase the want of natural affection would have been unfilial, and to fret and foam in such a manner would also have been unfilial. Confucius said, 'Shun was indeed perfectly filial! *And yet*, when he was fifty, he was full of longing desire about his parents.' "

12.4 宋轻将之楚，孟子遇于石丘，曰："先生将何之？"曰："吾闻秦楚构兵，我将见楚王说而罢之。楚王不悦，我将见秦王说而罢之。二王我将有所遇焉。"曰："轲也请无问其详，愿闻其指。说之将何如？"曰："我将言其不利也。"曰："先生之志则大矣，先生之号则不可。先生以利说秦楚之王，秦楚之王悦于利，以罢三军之师，是三军之士乐罢而悦于利也。为人臣者怀利以事其君，为人子者怀利以事其父，为人弟者怀利以事其兄，是君臣、父子、兄弟终去仁义，怀利以相接，然而不亡者，未之有也。先生以仁义说秦楚之王，秦楚之王悦于仁义，而罢三军之师，是三军之士乐罢而悦于仁义也。为人臣者怀仁义以事其君，为人子者怀仁义以事其父，为人弟者怀仁义以事其兄，是君臣、父子、兄弟去利，怀仁义以相接也，然而不王者，未之有也。何必曰利？"

12.4　Song Jian being about to go to Chu, Mencius met him in Shiqiu. "Master, where are you going?" asked *Mencius*. Jian replied, "I have heard that Qin and Chu are fighting together, and I am going to see the king of Chu and persuade him to cease hostilities. If he shall not be pleased *with my advice*, I shall go to see the king of Qin, and persuade him in the same way. Of the two kings I shall *surely* find that I can succeed with one of them." *Mencius* said, "I will not venture to ask about the particulars, but I should like to hear the scope of your plan. What course will you take to try to persuade them?" Jian answered, "I will tell them how unprofitable their course is to them." "Master," said Mencius, "your aim is great, but your argument is not good. If you, starting from the point of profit, offer your persuasive counsels to the kings of Qin and Chu, and if those kings are pleased with the consideration of profit so as to stop the movements of their armies, then all belonging to those armies will rejoice in the cessation *of war*, and find their pleasure in *the pursuit of* profit. Ministers will serve their sovereign for the profit of which they cherish the thought; sons will serve their fathers, and younger brothers will serve their elder brothers from the same consideration: — and the issue will be, that, abandoning benevolence and righteousness, sovereign and minister, father and son, younger brother and elder, will carry on all their intercourse with this thought of profit cherished in their breasts. But never has there been such a state *of society*, without ruin being the result of it. If you, starting from the ground of benevolence and righteousness, offer your counsels to the kings of Qin and Chu, and if those kings are pleased with the consideration of benevolence and righteousness so as to stop the operations of their armies, then all belonging to those armies will rejoice in the stopping *from war*, and find their pleasure in benevolence and righteousness. Ministers will serve their sovereign, cherishing the principles of benevolence and righteousness; sons will serve their fathers, and younger brothers will serve their elder brothers, in the same way; — and so, sovereign and minister, father and son, elder brother and younger, abandoning *the thought of* profit, will cherish the principles of benevolence and righteousness, and carry on all their intercourse upon them. But never has there been such a state *of society*, without the state where it prevailed rising to imperial sway. Why must you use that word 'profit'? "

12.5　孟子居邹，季任为任处守，以币交，受之而不报。处于平陆，储子为相，以币交，受之而不报。他日，由邹之任，见季子；由平陆之齐，不见储子。屋庐子喜曰："连得间矣。"问曰："夫子之任，见季子；之齐，不见储子，为其为相与？"曰："非也，《书》曰：'享多仪，仪不及物曰不享，惟不役志于享。'为其不成享也。"屋庐子悦。或问之，屋庐子曰："季子不得之邹，储子得之平陆。"

12.5　When Mencius was residing in Zou, the younger brother of the chief of Ren, who was guardian of Ren at the time, paid his respects to him by *a present of* silks, which Mencius received, not *going* to acknowledge it. When he was sojourning in Pinglu, Chu, who was prime minister of the state, sent him a similar present, which he received in the same way. Subsequently, going from Zou to Ren, he visited the guardian, but when he went from Pinglu to *the capital of* Qi, he did not visit the minister Chu. The disciple Wulu was glad, and said, "I have got an opportunity *to obtain some instruction*." He asked *accordingly*, "Master, when you went to Ren, you visited the chief's brother; and when you went to Qi, you did not visit Chu. Was it not because he is *only* the minister?" *Mencius* replied, "No. It is said in the *Book of History*, 'In presenting an offering to a superior, most depends on the demonstrations of respect. If those demonstrations are not equal to the things offered, we say there is no offering, that is, there is no act of the will in presenting the offering.' *This is* because the things so offered do not constitute an offering to a superior." Wulu was pleased, and when some one asked him *what Mencius meant*, he said, "The younger of Ren could not go to Zou, but the minister Chu might have gone to Pinglu."

12.6　淳于髡曰："先名实者，为人也；后名实者，自为也。夫子在三卿之中，名实未加于上下而去之，仁者固如此乎?"孟子曰："居下位，不以贤事不肖者，伯夷也；五就汤，五就桀者，伊尹也；不恶污君，不辞小官者，柳下惠也。三子者不同道，其趋一也。一者何也? 曰，仁也。君子亦仁而已矣，何必同?"曰："鲁缪公之时，公仪子为政，子柳、子思为臣，鲁之削也滋甚；若是乎，贤者之无益于国也!"曰："虞不用百里奚而亡，秦穆公用之而霸。不用贤则亡，削何可得与?"曰："昔者王豹处于淇，而河西善讴；绵驹处于高唐，而齐右善歌；华周杞梁之妻善哭其夫而变国俗。有诸内，必形诸外。为其事而无其功者，髡未尝睹之也。是故无贤者也；有则髡必识之。"曰："孔子为鲁司寇，不用，从而祭，燔肉不至，不税冕而行。不知者以为为肉也，其知者以为为无礼也。乃孔子则欲以微罪行，不欲为苟去。君子之所为，众人固不识也。"

12.6 Chunyu Kuan said, "He who makes fame and meritorious services his first objects, acts with a regard to others. He who makes them only secondary objects, acts with a regard to himself. You, master, were ranked among the three chief ministers *of the state*, but before your fame and services had reached either to the prince or the people, you have left your place. Is this indeed the way of the benevolent?" Mencius replied, "There was Boyi; — he abode in an inferior situation, and would not, with his virtue, serve a degenerate prince. There was Yi Yin; — he five times went to Tang, and five times went to Jie. There was Hui of Liu Xia, he did not disdain to serve a vile prince, nor did he decline a small office. The courses pursued by those three worthies were different, but their aim was one. And what was their one aim? We must answer — 'To be perfectly virtuous.' And so it is simply after this that superior men strive. Why must they all *pursue* the same course?" Kuan pursued, "In the time of the duke Mu of Lu, the government was in the hands of Gongyi, while Ziliu and Zisi were ministers. *And yet*, the dismemberment of Lu then increased exceedingly. Such was the case, a specimen how your men of virtue are of no advantage to a kingdom!" *Mencius* said, "*The prince of* Yu did not use Baili Xi, and thereby lost his state. The prince Mu of Qin used him, and became chief of all the princes. Ruin is the consequence of not employing men of virtue and talents; how can it rest with dismemberment *merely*?" Kuan urged *again*, "Formerly, when Wang Bao dwelt on the Qi, the people on the west of the *Yellow* River all became skilful at singing in *his* abrupt manner. When Mian Ju lived in Gaotang, the people in the parts of Qi on the west became skilful at singing in *his* prolonged manner. The wives of Hua Zhou and Qi Liang bewailed their husbands so skilfully, that they changed the manners of the state. When there is *the gift within*, it manifests itself without. I have never seen the man who could do the deeds *of a worthy*, and did not realize the work of one. Therefore there are *now* no men of talents and virtue. If there were, I should know them." *Mencius* answered, "When Confucius was chief minister of justice in Lu, the prince came not to follow *his counsels*. Soon after was the *solstitial* sacrifice, and when a part of the flesh presented in sacrifice was not sent to him, he went away even without taking off his cap of ceremony. Those who did not know him supposed it was on account of the flesh. Those who knew him supposed that it was on account *of the neglect* of the usual ceremony. The fact was, that Confucius wanted to go away on occasion of some small offence, not wishing to do so without some apparent cause. All men may not be expected to understand the conduct of a superior man."

12.7　孟子曰："五霸者，三王之罪人也；今之诸侯，五霸之罪人也；今之大夫，今之诸侯之罪人也。天子适诸侯曰巡狩，诸侯朝于天子曰述职。春省耕而补不足，秋省敛而助不给。入其疆，土地辟，田野治，养老尊贤，俊杰在位，则有庆，庆以地。入其疆，土地荒芜，遗老失贤，掊克在位，则有让。一不朝，则贬其爵；再不朝，则削其地；三不朝，则六师移之。是故天子讨而不伐，诸侯伐而不讨。五霸者，搂诸侯以伐诸侯者也，故曰，五霸者，三王之罪人也。五霸，桓公为盛。葵丘之会，诸侯束牲载书而不歃血。初命曰，诛不孝，无易树子，无以妾为妻。再命曰，尊贤育才，以彰有德。三命曰，敬老慈幼，无忘宾旅。四命曰，士无世官，官事无摄，取士必得，无专杀大夫。五命曰，无曲防，无遏籴，无有封而不告。曰，凡我同盟之人，既盟之后，言归于好。今之诸侯皆犯此五禁，故曰，今之诸侯，五霸之罪人也。长君之恶其罪小，逢君之恶其罪大。今之大夫皆逢君之恶，故曰，今之大夫，今之诸侯之罪人也。”

12.7   Mencius said, "The five chiefs of the princes were sinners against the three kings. The princes of the present day are sinners against the five chiefs. The great officers of the present day are sinners against the princes. The emperor visited the princes, which was called 'A tour of inspection.' The princes attended at the court of the emperor, which was called 'giving a report of office.' It was a custom in the spring to examine the ploughing, and supply any deficiency *of seed*, and in autumn to examine the reaping, and assist where there was a deficiency of the crop. When *the emperor* entered the boundaries of a state, if the *new* ground was being reclaimed, and the old fields well cultivated; if the old were nourished and the worthy honored; and if men of distinguished talents were placed in office; then *the prince* was rewarded, — rewarded with an addition to his territory. *On the other hand*, if on entering a state, the ground was found left wild or overrun with weeds; if the old were neglected and the worthy unhonored; and if the offices were filled with hard tax-gatherers; then *the prince* was reprimanded. If *a prince* once omitted his attendance at court, he was punished by degradation of rank; if he did so a second time, he was deprived of a portion of his territory; if he did so a third time, the imperial forces *were set in motion*, and he was removed *from his government*. Thus the emperor commanded the punishment, but did not himself inflict it, while the princes inflicted the punishment, but did not command it. The five chiefs, *however*, dragged the princes to punish other princes, and hence I say that they were sinners against the three kings. Of the five chiefs the most powerful was the prince Huan. At the assembly of the princes in Kuiqiu, he bound the victim and placed the writing upon it, but did not *slay it* to smear their mouths with the blood. The first injunction in their agreement was — 'Slay the unfilial; change not the son who has been appointed heir; exalt not a concubine to the rank of wife.' The second was, — 'Honor the worthy, and maintain the talented, to give distinction to the virtuous.' The third was, — 'Respect the old, and be kind to the young. Be not forgetful of strangers and travelers.' The fourth was, — 'Let not offices be hereditary, nor let officers be pluralists. In the selection of officers let the object be to get the proper men. Let not a *ruler* take it on himself to put to death a great officer.' The fifth was, — 'Follow no crooked policy in making embankments. Impose no restrictions on the sale of grain. Let there be no promotions without first announcing them *to the emperor.*' It was *then* said, 'All we who have united in this agreement shall hereafter maintain amicable relations.' The princes of the present day all violate these five prohibitions, and therefore I say that the princes of the present day are sinners against the five chiefs. The crime of him who connives at, and aids, the wickedness of his prince is small, but the crime of him who anticipates and excites that wickedness is great. The officers of the present day all go to meet their sovereigns' *wickedness*, and therefore I say that the great officers of the present day are sinners against the princes."

12.8　鲁欲使慎子为将军。孟子曰：“不教民而用之，谓之殃民。殃民者，不容于尧舜之世。一战胜齐，遂有南阳，然且不可—”慎子勃然不悦曰：“此则滑厘所不识也。”曰：“吾明告子。天子之地方千里；不千里，不足以待诸侯。诸侯之地方百里；不百里，不足以守宗庙之典籍。周公之封于鲁，为方百里也；地非不足，而俭于百里。太公之封于齐也，亦为方百里也；地非不足也，而俭于百里。今鲁方百里者五，子以为有王者作，则鲁在所损乎，在所益乎？徒取诸彼以与此，然且仁者不为，况于杀人以求之乎？君子之事君也，务引其君以当道，志于仁而已。”

12.8 *The prince of* Lu wanted to make the minister Shen commander of his army. Mencius said, "To employ an uninstructed people *in war* may be said to be destroying the people. A destroyer of the people would not have been tolerated in the times of Yao and Shun. Though by a single battle you should subdue Qi, and get possession of Nanyang, the thing ought not to be done." Shen changed countenance, and said in displeasure, "This is what I, Guli, do not understand." Mencius said, "I will lay the case plainly before you. The territory appropriated to the emperor is one thousand *li* square. Without a thousand *li*, he would not have sufficient for his entertainment of the princes. The territory appropriated to a Hou is one hundred *li* square. Without one hundred *li*, he would not have sufficient wherewith to observe the statutes kept in his ancestral temple. When Zhougong was invested with *the principalily of* Lu, it was a hundred *li* square. The territory was indeed enough, but it was not more than one hundred *li*. When Taigong was invested with the principality of Qi, it was one hundred *li* square. The territory was indeed enough, but it was not more than one hundred *li*. Now Lu is five times one hundred *li* square. If a true imperial ruler were to arise, whether do you think that Lu would be diminished or increased by him? If it were merely taking the place from the one *state* to give it to the other, a benevolent man would not do it; — how much less will he do so, when the end is to be sought by the slaughter of men! The way in which a superior man serves his prince contemplates simply the leading him in the right path, and directing his mind to benevolence."

12.9　孟子曰：“今之事君者曰，‘我能为君辟土地，充府库。’今之所谓良臣，古之所谓民贼也。君不乡道，不志于仁，而求富之，是富桀也。‘我能为君约与国，战必克。’今之所谓良臣，古之所谓民贼也。君不乡道，不志于仁，而求为之强战，是辅桀也。由今之道，无变今之俗，虽与之天下，不能一朝居也。”

12.9　Mencius said, "Those who nowadays serve their sovereigns say, 'We can for our sovereign enlarge the limits of the cultivated ground, and fill his treasuries and arsenals.' Such persons are nowadays called 'good ministers,' but anciently they were called 'robbers of the people.' If a sovereign follows not the right way, nor has his mind bent on benevolence, to seek to enrich him is to enrich a Jie. *Or they will say*, 'We can for our sovereign form alliances with other states, so that our battles must be successful.'

Such persons are nowadays called 'good ministers,' but anciently they were called 'robbers of the people.' If a sovereign follows not the right way, nor has his mind directed to benevolence, to seek to enrich him is to enrich a Jie. Although a prince, pursuing the path of the present day, and not changing its practices, were to have the empire given to him, he could not retain it for a single morning."

12.10　白圭曰：“吾欲二十而取一，何如？”孟子曰：“子之道，貉道也。万室之国，一人陶，则可乎？”曰：“不可，器不足用也。”曰：“夫貉，五谷不生，惟黍生之，无城郭、宫室、宗庙、祭祀之礼，无诸侯币帛饔飧，无百官有司，故二十取一而足也。今居中国，去人伦，无君子，如之何其可也？陶以寡，且不可以为国，况无君子乎？欲轻之于尧舜之道者，大貉小貉也；欲重之于尧舜之道者，大桀小桀也。”

12.10　Baigui said, "I want to take a twentieth *of the produce only as the tax*. What do you think of it?" Mencius said, "Your way would be that of the Mo. In a country of ten thousand families, would it do to have *only* one potter?" Gui replied, "No. The vessels would not be enough to use." *Mencius* went on, "In Mo *all* the five kinds of grain are not grown; it only produces the millet. There are no fortified cities, no edifices, no ancestral temples, no ceremonies of sacrifice; there are no princes requiring presents and entertainments; there is no system of officers with their various subordinates. On these accounts a tax of one twentieth of the produce is sufficient there. But now it is the Middle Kingdom that we live in. To banish the relationships of men, and have no superior men; — how can such a state of things be thought of? With but few potters a kingdom cannot subsist; — how much less can it subsist without men of a higher rank than others? If we wish to make the taxation lighter than the system of Yao and Shun, we shall just have a great Mo and a small Mo. If we wish to make it heavier, we shall just have the great Jie and the small Jie."

12.11　白圭曰：“丹之治水也愈于禹。”孟子曰：“子过矣。禹之治水，水之道也，是故禹以四海为壑。今吾子以邻国为壑。水逆行谓之洚水。洚水者,洪水也。仁人之所恶也。吾子过矣。”

12.11　Baigui said, "My management of the waters is superior to that of Yu." Mencius replied, "You are wrong, sir. Yu's regulation of the waters was according to the laws of water. He therefore made the four seas their receptacle, while you make the neighboring states their receptacle. Water flowing out of its channels is called an inundation. Inundating waters are a vast *waste* of water, and what a benevolent man detests. You are wrong, my good sir."

12.12　孟子曰：“君子不亮，恶乎执？”

12.12　Mencius said, "If a scholar have not faith, how shall he take a firm hold of *things*?"

12.13　鲁欲使乐正子为政。孟子曰："吾闻之，喜而不寐。"公孙丑曰："乐正子强乎？"曰："否。""有知虑乎？"曰："否。""多闻识乎？"曰："否。""然则奚为喜而不寐？"曰："其为人也好善。""好善足乎？"曰："好善优于天下，而况鲁国乎？夫苟好善，则四海之内皆将轻千里而来告之以善；夫苟不好善，则人将曰：'訑訑，予既已知之矣。'訑訑之声音颜色距人于千里之外。士止于千里之外，则谗谄面谀之人至矣。与谗谄面谀之人居，国欲治，可得乎？"

12.13 *The prince of* Lu wanting to commit the administration of his government to the disciple Yuezheng, Mencius said, "When I heard of it, I was so glad that I could not sleep." Gongsun Chou asked, "Is Yuezheng a man of vigor?" "No." "Is he wise in council?" "No." "Is he possessed of much information?" "No." "What then made you so glad that you could not sleep?" "He is a man who loves what is good." "Is the love of what is good sufficient?" "The love of what is good is more than a sufficient qualification for the government of the empire; — how much more is it so for the state of Lu! If *a minister* love what is good, all within the four seas will count one thousand *li* but a small distance, and will come and lay their good thoughts before him. If he do not love what is good, men will say, 'How self-conceited he looks? *He is saying to himself,* I know it.' The language and looks of that self-conceit will keep men off at a distance of one thousand *li*. When good men stop one thousand *li* off, calumniators, flatterers, and sycophants will make their appearance. When a minister lives among calumniators, flatterers, and sycophants, though he may wish the state to be well governed, is it possible for it to be *so*?"

12.14　陈子曰：“古之君子何如则仕？”孟子曰：“所就三，所去三。迎之致敬以有礼，言，将行其言也，则就之。礼貌未衰，言弗行也，则去之。其次，虽未行其言也，迎之致敬以有礼，则就之。礼貌衰，则去之。其下，朝不食，夕不食，饥饿不能出门户，君闻之，曰，‘吾大者不能行其道，又不能从其言也，使饥饿于我土地，吾耻之。’周之，亦可受也，免死而已矣。”

12.14　The disciple Chen said, "What were the principles on which superior men of old took office?" Mencius replied, "There were three cases in which they accepted office, and three in which they left it. If received with the utmost respect and all polite observances, and they could say *to themselves* that the prince would carry their words into practice, then they took office with him. *Afterwards*, although there might be no remission in the polite demeanor of the prince, if their words were not carried into practice, they would leave him. The second case was that in which, though *the prince could not be expected* at once to carry their words into practice, yet being received by him with the utmost respect, they took office with him. But afterwards, if there was a remission in his polite demeanor, they would leave him. The last case was that of *the superior man* who had nothing to eat, either morning or evening, and was so famished that he could not move out of his door. If the prince, on hearing of his state, said, 'I must fail in the great point, that of carrying his doctrines into practice, neither am I able to follow his words, but I am ashamed to allow him to die of want in my country'; the assistance offered in such a case might be received, but not beyond what was sufficient to avert death."

12.15　孟子曰："舜发于畎亩之中，傅说举于版筑之间，胶鬲举于鱼盐之中，管夷吾举于士，孙叔敖举于海，百里奚举于市。故天将降大任于是人也，必先苦其心志，劳其筋骨，饿其体肤，空乏其身，行拂乱其所为，所以动心忍性，曾益其所不能。人恒过，然后能改，困于心，衡于虑，而后作；徵于色，发于声，而后喻。入则无法家拂士，出则无敌国外患者，国恒亡。然后知生于忧患而死于安乐也。"

12.15　Mencius said, "Shun rose from among the channeled fields. Fu Yue was called to office from the midst of his building frames; Jiaoge from his fish and salt; Guan Yiwu from the hands of his gaoler; Sunshu Ao from *his hiding by* the seashore; and Baili Xi from the market place. Thus, when Heaven is about to confer a great office on any man, it first exercises his mind with suffering, and his sinews and bones with toil. It exposes his body to hunger, and subjects him to extreme poverty. It confounds his undertakings. By all these methods it stimulates his mind, hardens his nature, and supplies his incompetencies. Men for the most part err, and are afterwards able to reform. They are distressed in mind and perplexed in their thoughts, and then they arise to vigorous reformation. When things have been evidenced in men's looks, and set forth in their words, then they understand them. If a prince have not about his court families attached to the laws and worthy counsellors, and if abroad there are not hostile states or other external calamities, his kingdom will generally come to ruin. From these things we see how life springs from sorrow and calamity, and death from ease and pleasure."

12.16　孟子曰："教亦多术矣，予不屑之教诲也者，是亦教诲之而已矣。"

12.16　Mencius said, "There are many arts in teaching. I refuse, as inconsistent with my character, to teach a man, but I am only thereby still teaching him."

卷十三　尽心章句上
BOOK XIII　JIN XIN　PART I

13.1　孟子曰："尽其心者，知其性也。知其性，则知天矣。存其心，养其性，所以事天也。夭寿不贰，修身以俟之，所以立命也。"

13.1　Mencius said, "He who has exhausted all his mental constitution knows his nature. Knowing his nature, he knows Heaven. To preserve one's mental constitution, and nourish one's nature, is the way to serve Heaven. When neither a premature death nor long life causes a man any double-mindedness, but he waits in the cultivation of his personal character *for whatever issue*; — this is the way in which he establishes his *Heaven*-ordained being."

13.2　孟子曰："莫非命也，顺受其正；是故知命者不立乎岩墙之下。尽其道而死者，正命也；桎梏死者，非正命也。"

13.2　Mencius said, "There is an appointment for every thing. A man should receive submissively what may be correctly ascribed thereto. Therefore, he who has the true idea of what is *Heaven's* appointment will not stand beneath a precipitous wall. Death sustained in the discharge of one's duties may correctly be ascribed to the appointment *of Heaven*. Death under handcuffs and fetters cannot correctly be so ascribed."

13.3 孟子曰："求则得之，舍则失之，是求有益于得也，求在我者也。求之有道，得之有命，是求无益于得也，求在外者也。"

13.3 Mencius said, "When we get by our seeking and lose by our neglecting; — in that case seeking is of use to getting, and the things sought for are those which are in ourselves. When the seeking is according to the proper course, and the getting is *only* as appointed; — in that case the seeking is of no use to getting, and the things sought for are without ourselves."

13.4 孟子曰："万物皆备于我矣。反身而诚，乐莫大焉。强恕而行，求仁莫近焉。"

13.4 Mencius said, "All things are already complete in us. There is no greater delight than to be conscious of sincerity on self-examination. If one acts with a vigorous effort at the law of reciprocity, when he seeks for *the realization of* perfect virtue, nothing can be closer than his approximation to it."

13.5 孟子曰："行之而不著焉，习矣而不察焉，终身由之而不知其道者，众也。"

13.5 Mencius said, "To act without understanding, and to do so habitually without examination, pursuing the proper path all the life without knowing its nature, — this is the way of multitudes."

13.6 孟子曰："人不可以无耻，无耻之耻，无耻矣。"

13.6 Mencius said, "A man may not be without shame. When

one is ashamed of having been without shame, he will *afterwards* not have *occasion for* shame."

13.7　孟子曰：“耻之于人大矣，为机变之巧者，无所用耻焉。不耻不若人，何若人有？”

13.7　Mencius said, "The sense of shame is to a man of great importance. Those who form contrivances and versatile schemes distinguished for their artfulness, do not allow their sense of shame to come into action. When one differs from other men in not having this sense of shame, what will he have in common with them?"

13.8　孟子曰：“古之贤王好善而忘势；古之贤士何独不然？乐其道而忘人之势，故王公不致敬尽礼，则不得亟见之。见且由不得亟，而况得而臣之乎？”

13.8　Mencius said, "The able and virtuous monarchs of antiquity loved virtue and forgot power. And shall an exception be made of the able and virtuous scholars of antiquity, that they did not do the same? They delighted in their own principles, and were oblivious of the power of princes. Therefore, if kings and princes did not show the utmost respect, and observe all forms of ceremony, they were not permitted to come frequently and visit them. If they thus found it not in their power to pay them frequent visits, how much less could they get to employ them as ministers?"

13.9 孟子谓宋勾践曰："子好游乎？吾语子游。人知之，亦嚣嚣；人不知，亦嚣嚣。"曰："何如斯可以嚣嚣矣？"曰："尊德乐义，则可以嚣嚣矣。故士穷不失义，达不离道。穷不失义，故士得己焉；达不离道，故民不失望焉。古之人，得志，泽加于民；不得志，修身见于世。穷则独善其身，达则兼善天下。"

13.9 Mencius said to Song Goujian, "Are you fond, sir, of traveling *to the different courts*? I will tell you about such traveling. If a prince acknowledge you and follow your counsels, be perfectly satisfied. If no one do so, be the same." Goujian said, "What is to be done to secure this perfect satisfaction?" Mencius replied, "Honor virtue and delight in righteousness, and so you may *always* be perfectly satisfied. Therefore, a scholar, though poor, does not let go *his* righteousness; though prosperous, he does not leave *his own* path. Poor and not letting righteousness go; — it is thus that the scholar holds possession of himself. Prosperous and not leaving the *proper* path; — it is thus that the expectations of the people are not disappointed. When the men of antiquity realized their wishes, benefits were conferred by them on the people. If they did not realize their wishes, they cultivated their personal character, and became illustrious in the world. If poor, they attended to their own virtue in solitude; if advanced to dignity, they made the whole empire virtuous as well."

13.10 孟子曰："待文王而后兴者，凡民也。若夫豪杰之士，虽无文王犹兴。"

13.10　Mencius said, "The mass of men wait for a king Wen, and then they will receive a rousing impulse. Scholars distinguished *from the mass*, without a king Wen, rouse themselves."

13.11　孟子曰："附之以韩魏之家，如其自视欿然，则过人远矣。"

13.11　Mencius said, "Add to a man the families of Han and Wei. If he then look upon himself without being elated, he is far beyond *the mass of* men."

13.12　孟子曰："以佚道使民，虽劳不怨。以生道杀民，虽死不怨杀者。"

13.12　Mencius said, "Let the people be employed in the way which is intended to secure their ease, and though they be toiled, they will not murmur. Let them be put to death in the way which is intended to preserve their lives, and though they die, they will not murmur at him who puts them to death."

13.13　孟子曰："霸者之民，驩虞如也。王者之民，皞皞如也。杀之而不怨，利之而不庸，民日迁善而不知为之者。夫君子所过者化，所存者神，上下与天地同流，岂曰小补之哉？"

13.13　Mencius said, "Under a chief, leading all the princes, the people look brisk and cheerful. Under a true sovereign, they have an air of deep contentment. Though he slay them, they do not murmur. When he benefits them, they do not think of his merit. From day to day they make progress towards what is good, without knowing who makes them do so. Wherever the superior man passes through, transformation follows; wherever he abides, his influence is of a spiritual nature. It flows abroad, above and beneath, like that of Heaven and Earth. How can it be said that he mends society but in a small way!"

13.14　孟子曰："仁言不如仁声之入人深也。善政不如善教之得民也。善政，民畏之；善教，民爱之。善政得民财，善教得民心。"

13.14　Mencius said, "Kindly words do not enter so deeply into men as a reputation for kindness. Good government does not lay hold of the people so much as good instructions. Good government is feared by the people, while good instructions are loved by them. Good government gets the people's wealth, while good instructions get their hearts."

13.15　孟子曰："人之所不学而能者，其良能也；所不虑而知者，其良知也。孩提之童，无不知爱其亲者；及其长也，无不知敬其兄也。亲亲，仁也；敬长，义也；无他，达之天下也。"

13.15　Mencius said, "The ability possessed by men without having been acquired by learning is intuitive ability, and the knowledge possessed by them without the exercise of thought is their intuitive knowledge. Children carried in the arms all know to love their parents, and when they are grown *a little*, they all know to love their elder brothers. Filial affection for parents is *the working of* benevolence. Respect for elders is *the working of* righteousness. There is no other reason *for those feelings*; — they belong to all under Heaven."

13.16　孟子曰：“舜之居深山之中，与木石居，与鹿豕游，其所以异于深山之野人者几希；及其闻一善言，见一善行，若决江河，沛然莫之能御也。”

13.16　Mencius said, "When Shun was living amid the deep retired mountains, dwelling with the trees and rocks, and wandering among the deer and swine, the difference between him and the rude inhabitants of those remote hills appeared very small. But when he heard a single good word, or saw a single good action, he was like a stream or a river bursting its banks, and flowing out in an irresistible flood."

13.17　孟子曰：“无为其所不为，无欲其所不欲，如此而已矣。”

13.17　Mencius said, "Let a man not do what his *own sense of righteousness tells him* not to do, and let him not desire *what his sense of righteousness tells him not* to desire; — to act thus is all he has to do."

13.18　孟子曰：“人之有德慧术知者，恒存乎疢疾。独孤臣孽子，其操心也危，其虑患也深，故达。”

13.18　Mencius said, "Men who are possessed of intelligent

virtue and prudence in affairs will generally be found to have been in sickness and troubles. They are the friendless minister and concubine's son, who keep their hearts under a sense of peril, and use deep precautions against calamity. On this account they become distinguished for their intelligence."

13.19　孟子曰："有事君人者，事是君则为容悦者也；有安社稷臣者，以安社稷为悦者也；有天民者，达可行于天下而后行之者也；有大人者，正己而物正者也。"

13.19　Mencius said, "There are persons who serve the prince; they serve the prince, that is, for the sake of his countenance and favor. There are ministers who seek the tranquillity of the state, and find their pleasure in securing that tranquillity. There are those who are the people of Heaven. They, *judging that*, if they were in office, they could carry out *their principles* throughout the empire, proceed *so* to carry them out. There are those who are great men. They rectify themselves and others are rectified."

13.20　孟子曰："君子有三乐，而王天下不与存焉。父母俱存，兄弟无故，一乐也；仰不愧于天，俯不怍于人，二乐也；得天下英才而教育之，三乐也。君子有三乐，而王天下不与存焉。"

13.20　Mencius said, "The superior man has three things in which he delights, and to be ruler over the empire is not one of them. That his father and mother are both alive, and that the condition of his brothers affords no cause for anxiety; — this is one delight. That, when looking up, he has no occasion for shame before Heaven, and, below, he has no occasion to blush before men; — this is a second delight. That he can get from the whole empire the most talented individuals, and teach and nourish them; — this is the third delight. The superior man has three things in which he delights, and to be ruler over the empire is not one of them."

13.21　孟子曰："广土众民，君子欲之，所乐不存焉；中天下而立，定四海之民，君子乐之，所性不存焉。君子所性，虽大行不加焉，虽穷居不损焉，分定故也。君子所性，仁义礼智根于心，其生色也睟然，见于面，盎于背，施于四体，四体不言而喻。"

13.21　Mencius said, "Wide territory and a numerous people are desired by the superior man, but what he delights in is not here. To stand in the centre of the empire, and tranquillize the people within the four seas; — the superior man delights in this, but the highest enjoyment of his nature is not here. What belongs by his nature to the superior man cannot be increased by the largeness of his sphere of action, nor diminished by his dwelling in poverty and retirement; — for this reason that it is determinately apportioned to him *by Heaven*. What belongs by his nature to the superior man are benevolence, righteousness, propriety, and knowledge. These are rooted in his heart; their growth and manifestation are a mild harmony appearing in the countenance, a rich fullness in the back, and the character imparted to the four limbs. Those limbs understand *to arrange themselves*, without being told."

13.22　孟子曰："伯夷辟纣，居北海之滨，闻文王作，兴曰：'盍归乎来！吾闻西伯善养老者。'太公辟纣，居东海之滨，闻文王作，兴曰：'盍归乎来！吾闻西伯善养老者。'天下有善养老，则仁人以为己归矣。五亩之宅，树墙下以桑，匹妇蚕之，则老者足以衣帛矣。五母鸡，二母彘，无失其时，老者足以无失肉矣。百亩之田，匹夫耕之，八口之家足以无饥矣。所谓西伯善养老者，制其田里，教之树畜，导其妻子使养其老。五十非帛不暖，七十非肉不饱。不暖不饱，谓之冻馁。文王之民无冻馁之老者，此之谓也。"

13.22　Mencius said, "Boyi, that he might avoid Zhou, was dwelling on the coast of the northern sea. When he heard of the rise of King Wen. He roused himself and said, 'Why should I not go and follow him? I have heard that the chief of the West knows well how to nourish the old.' Taigong, to avoid Zhou, was dwelling on the coast of the eastern sea. When he heard of the rise of King Wen, he said, 'Why should I not go and follow him? I have heard that the chief of the West knows well how to nourish the old.' If there were a prince in the empire, who knew well how to nourish the old, all men of virtue would feel that he was the proper object for them to gather to. Around the homestead with its five *mu*, the space beneath the walls was planted with mulberry trees, with which the women nourished silk worms, and thus the old were able to have silk to wear. *Each family* had five brood hens and two brood sows, which were kept to their *breeding* seasons, and thus the old were able to have flesh to eat. The husbandmen cultivated their farms of one hundred *mu*, and thus their families of eight mouths were secured against want. The expression, 'The chief of the West knows well how to nourish the old,' refers to his regulation of the fields and dwellings, his teaching them to plant *the mulberry* and nourish those animals, and his instructing the wives and children, so as to make them nourish their aged. At fifty, warmth cannot be maintained without silks, and at seventy flesh is necessary to satisfy the appetite. Persons not kept warm nor supplied with food are said to be starved and famished, but among the people of King Wen, there were no aged who were starved or famished. This is the meaning of the expression in question."

13.23　孟子曰：“易其田畴，薄其税敛，民可使富也。食之以时，用之以礼，财不可胜用也。民非水火不生活，昏暮叩人之门户求水火，无弗与者，至足矣。圣人治天下，使有菽粟如水火。菽粟如水火，而民焉有不仁者乎？”

13.23　Mencius said, "Let it be seen to that their fields of grain and hemp are well cultivated, and make the taxes on them light; — so the people may be made rich. Let it be seen to that the people use their resources of food seasonably, and expend their wealth only on the prescribed ceremonies; — so their wealth will be more than can be consumed. The people cannot live without water and fire, yet if you knock at a man's door in the dusk of the evening, and ask for water and fire, there is no man who will not give them, such is the abundance of these things. A sage governs the empire so as to cause pulse and grain to be as abundant as water and fire. When pulse and grain are as abundant as water and fire, how shall the people be other than virtuous?"

13.24　孟子曰："孔子登东山而小鲁，登泰山而小天下。故观于海者难为水，游于圣人之门者难为言。观水有术，必观其澜。日月有明，容光必照焉。流水之为物也，不盈科不行；君子之志于道也，不成章不达。"

13.24　Mencius said, "Confucius ascended the eastern hill, and Lu appeared to him small. He ascended the Tai mountain, and all beneath the heavens appeared to him small. So, he who has contemplated the sea, finds it difficult to think anything of *other* waters, and he who has wandered in the gate of the sage, finds it difficult to think anything of the words of *others*. There is an art in the contemplation of water, — it is necessary to look at it as foaming in waves. The sun and moon being possessed of brilliancy, their light admitted *even* through an orifice illuminates. Flowing water is a thing which does not proceed till it has filled the hollows *in its course*. The student who has set his mind on the doctrines *of the sage*, does not advance to them but by completing one lesson after another."

13.25　孟子曰："鸡鸣而起，孳孳为善者，舜之徒也；鸡鸣而起，孳孳为利者,跖之徒也。欲知舜与跖之分,无他,利与善之间也。"

13.25　Mencius said, "He who rises at cock-crowing, and addresses himself earnestly to the practice of virtue, is a disciple of Shun. He who rises at cock-crowing, and addresses himself earnestly to the pursuit of gain, is a disciple of Zhi. If you want to know what separates Shun from Zhi, it is simply this — the interval between *the thought of* gain and *the thought of* virtue."

13.26　孟子曰:"杨子取为我,拔一毛而利天下,不为也。墨子兼爱,摩顶放踵利天下,为之。子莫执中,执中为近之。执中无权,犹执一也。所恶执一者,为其贼道也,举一而废百也。"

13.26　Mencius said, "The principle of the philosopher Yang was — 'Each one for himself.' Though he might have benefited the whole empire by plucking out a single hair, he would not have done it. The philosopher Mo loves all equally. If by rubbing *smooth* his whole body from the crown to the heel, he could have benefited the empire, he would have done it. Zimo holds a medium *between these*. By holding that medium, he is nearer the right. But by holding it without leaving room for the exigency of circumstances, it becomes like their holding their one point. The reason why I hate that holding to one point is the injury it does to the way *of right principle*. It takes up one point and disregards a hundred others."

13.27　孟子曰:"饥者甘食,渴者甘饮,是未得饮食之正也,饥渴害之也。岂惟口腹有饥渴之害? 人心亦皆有害。人能无以饥渴之害为心害，则不及人不为忧矣。"

13.27　Mencius said, "The hungry think any food sweet, and the thirsty think the same of any drink, and thus they do not get the right taste of what they eat and drink. The hunger and thirst, in fact, injure *their palate*. And is it only the mouth and belly which are injured by hunger and thirst? Men's minds are also injured by them. If a man can prevent the evils of hunger and thirst from being any evils to his mind, he need not have any sorrow about not being up with other men."

13.28　孟子曰："柳下惠不以三公易其介。"

13.28　Mencius said, "Hui of Liuxia would not for the three highest offices of state have changed his firm purpose of life."

13.29　孟子曰："有为者辟若掘井，掘井九轫而不及泉，犹为弃井也。"

13.29　Mencius said, "A man with definite aims to be accomplished may be compared to one digging a well. To dig the well to a depth of seventy-two cubits, *and stop* without reaching the spring, is after all throwing away the well."

13.30　孟子曰："尧舜，性之也；汤武，身之也；五霸，假之也。久假而不归，恶知其非有也。"

13.30　Mencius said, "Benevolence and righteousness were natural to Yao and Shun. Tang and Wu made them their own. The five chiefs of the princes feigned them. Having borrowed them long and not returned them, how could it be known they did not own them?"

13.31　公孙丑曰："伊尹曰：'予不狎于不顺，放太甲于桐，民大悦。太甲贤，又反之，民大悦。'贤者之为人臣也，其君不贤，则固可放与？"孟子曰："有伊尹之志，则可；无伊尹之志，则篡也。"

13.31　Gongsun Chou said, "Yi Yin said, 'I cannot be near *and see him so* disobedient *to reason*', and therewith he banished Tai Jia to Tong. The people were much pleased. When Tai Jia became virtuous, he brought him back, and the people were *again* much pleased.' When worthies are ministers, may they indeed banish their sovereigns *in this way*, when they are not virtuous?" Mencius replied, "If they have the same purpose as Yi Yin, they may. If they have not the same purpose, it would be usurpation."

13.32　公孙丑曰："《诗》曰：'不素餐兮'。君子之不耕而食，何也？"孟子曰："君子居是国也，其君用之，则安富尊荣；其子弟从之，则孝悌忠信。'不素餐兮'，孰大于是？"

13.32　Gongsun Chou said, "It is said, in the *Book of Poetry*, 'He will not eat the bread of idleness.' How is it that *we see* superior men eating without laboring?" Mencius replied, "When a superior man resides in a country, if its sovereign employ his counsels, he comes to tranquillity, wealth, honor, and glory. If the young in it follow his instructions, they become filial, obedient to their elders, true-hearted, and faithful. What greater example can there be than this of not eating the bread of idleness?"

13.33　王子垫问曰：“士何事？”孟子曰：“尚志。”曰：“何谓尚志？”曰：“仁义而已矣。杀一无罪非仁也，非其有而取之非义也。居恶在？仁是也，路恶在？义是也。居仁由义，大人之事备矣。”

13.33　The king's son, Dian asked *Mencius*, saying, "What is the business of the *unemployed* scholar?" Mencius replied, "To exalt his aim." *Dian asked again*, "What do you mean by exalting the aim?" The answer was, "*Setting it* simply on benevolence and righteousness. *He thinks* how to put a single innocent person to death is contrary to benevolence; how to take what one has not *a right to* is contrary to righteousness; that one's dwelling should be benevolence; and one's path should be righteousness. When benevolence is the dwelling-place *of the heart*, and righteousness the path *of the life*, the business of a great man is complete."

13.34　孟子曰：“仲子，不义与之齐国而弗受，人皆信之，是舍箪食豆羹之义也。人莫大焉亡亲戚君臣上下。以其小者信其大者，奚可哉？”

13.34　Mencius said, "Supposing that the kingdom of Qi were offered contrary to righteousness, *to Chen* Zhong, he would not receive it, and all people believe in him, *as a man of the highest worth*. But this is *only* the righteousness which declines a dish of rice or a plate of soup. A man can have no greater *crimes* than to disown his parents and relatives, and the relations of sovereign and minister, superiors and inferiors. How can it be allowed to give a man credit for the great *excellencies* because he possesses a small one?"

13.35 桃应问曰:"舜为天子,皋陶为士,瞽瞍杀人,则如之何?"孟子曰:"执之而已矣。""然则舜不禁与?"曰:"夫舜恶得而禁之? 夫有所受之也。""然则舜如之何?"曰:"舜视弃天下,犹弃敝蹝也。窃负而逃,遵海滨而处,终身䜣然,乐而忘天下。"

13.35 Tao Ying asked, saying, "Shun being emperor, and Gaoyao chief minister of justice, if Gusou had murdered a man, what would have been done in the case?" Mencius said, "Gaoyao would simply have apprehended him." "But would not Shun have forbidden such a thing?" "Indeed, how could Shun have forbidden it? Gaoyao had received *the law* from *a proper* source." "In that case what would Shun have done?" "Shun would have regarded abandoning the empire as throwing away a worn out sandal. He would privately have taken *his father* on his back, and retired into concealment, living somewhere along the sea-coast. There he would have been all his life, cheerful and happy, forgetting the empire."

13.36　孟子自范之齐，望见齐王之子，喟然叹曰：“居移气，养移体，大哉居乎！夫非尽人之子与？”孟子曰：“王子宫室、车马、衣服多与人同，而王子若彼者，其居使之然也；况居天下之广居者乎？鲁君之宋，呼于垤泽之门。守者曰：‘此非吾君也，何其声之似我君也？’此无他，居相似也。”

13.36　Mencius, going from Fan to Qi, saw the king of Qi's son at a distance, and said with a deep sigh, "One's position alters the air, *just* as the nurture affects the body. Great is the influence of position! Are not *we* all men's sons?" Mencius said, "The residence, the carriages and horses, and the dress of the king's son, are mostly the same as those of other men. That he looks so is occasioned by his position. How much more *should a peculiar air distinguish* him whose position is in the wide house of the world! When the prince of Lu went to Song, he called out at the Dieze gate, and the keeper said, 'This is not our prince. How is it that his voice is so like that of our prince?' This was occasioned by nothing but the correspondence of their positions."

13.37　孟子曰：“食而弗爱，豕交之也；爱而不敬，兽畜之也。恭敬者，币之未将者也。恭敬而无实，君子不可虚拘。”

13.37　Mencius said, "To feed *a scholar* and not love him, is to treat him as a pig. To love him and not respect him, is to keep him as a domestic animal. Honoring and respecting are what exist before any offering of gifts. If there be honoring and respecting without the reality of them, a superior man may not be retained by such empty *demonstrations*."

13.38　孟子曰："形色，天性也；惟圣人然后可以践形。"

13.38　Mencius said, "The bodily organs with their functions belong to our Heaven-conferred nature. But a man must be a sage before he can satisfy the design of his bodily organization."

13.39　齐宣王欲短丧。公孙丑曰："为期之丧，犹愈于已乎？"孟子曰："是犹或纾其兄之臂，子谓之姑徐徐云尔，亦教之孝悌而已矣。"王子有其母死者，其傅为之请数月之丧。公孙丑曰："若此者何如也？"曰："是欲终之而不可得也。虽加一日愈于已，谓夫莫之禁而弗为者也。"

13.39　The king Xuan of Qi wanted to shorten the period of mourning. Gongsun Chou said, "To have one whole year's mourning is better than doing away with it all together." Mencius said, "That is just as if there were one twisting the arm of his elder brother, and you were merely to say to him — 'Gently, gently, if you please.' Your only course should be to teach such an one filial piety and fraternal duty." *At that time*, the mother of one of the king's sons had died, and his tutor asked for him that he might be allowed to observe a few months' mourning. Gongsun Chou asked, "What do you say of this?" *Mencius* replied, "This is a case where the party wishes to complete the whole period, but finds it impossible to do so. The addition of even a single day is better than not mourning at all. I spoke of the case where there was no hindrance, and the party neglected the thing himself."

13.40　孟子曰："君子之所以教者五：有如时雨化之者，有成德者，有达财者，有答问者，有私淑艾者。此五者，君子之所以教也。"

13.40　Mencius said, "There are five ways in which the superior man effects his teaching. There are some on whom his influence descends like seasonable rain. There are some whose virtue he perfects, and some of whose talents he assists the development. There are some whose inquiries he answers. There are some who privately cultivate and correct themselves. These five ways are the methods in which the superior man effects his teaching."

13.41　公孙丑曰："道则高矣，美矣，宜若登天然，似不可及也？何不使彼为可几及而日孳孳也？"孟子曰："大匠不为拙工改废绳墨，羿不为拙射变其彀率。君子引而不发，跃如也。中道而立，能者从之。"

13.41　Gongsun Chou said, "Lofty are your principles and admirable, but *to learn them* may well be likened to ascending the heavens, something which cannot be reached. Why not *adapt your teaching so as to* cause learners to consider them attainable, and to daily exert themselves?" Mencius said, "A great artificer does not, for the sake of a stupid workman, alter or do away with the marking line. Yi did not, for the sake of a stupid archer, change his rule for drawing the bow. The superior man draws the bow, but does not discharge the arrow. *The whole thing* seems to leap *before the learner*. Such is his standing exactly in the middle of the right path. Those who are able, follow him."

13.42　孟子曰："天下有道，以道殉身；天下无道，以身殉道；未闻以道殉乎人者也。"

13.42　Mencius said, "When right principles prevail throughout the empire, one's principles must appear along with one's person. When right principles disappear from the empire, one's person must vanish along with one's principles. I have not heard of one's principles being dependent for their manifestation on other men."

13.43　公都子曰："滕更之在门也，若在所礼，而不答，何也？"
孟子曰："挟贵而问，挟贤而问，挟长而问，挟有勋劳而问，挟故而问，皆所不答也。滕更有二焉。"

13.43　The disciple Gongdu said, "When Geng of Teng made his appearance in your school, it seemed proper that a polite consideration should be paid to him, and yet you did not answer him. Why was that?" Mencius replied, "I do not answer him who questions me presuming on his nobility, nor him who presumes on his talents, nor him who presumes on his age, nor him who presumes on services performed to me, nor him who presumes on old acquaintance. Two of those things were chargeable on Geng of Teng."

13.44 孟子曰："于不可已而已者，无所不已。于所厚者薄，无所不薄也。其进锐者，其退速。"

13.44 Mencius said, "He who stops short where stopping is not allowable, will stop short in everything. He who behaves shabbily to those whom he ought to treat well, will behave shabbily to all. He who advances with precipitation will retire with speed."

13.45 孟子曰："君子之于物也，爱之而弗仁；于民也，仁之而弗亲。亲亲而仁民，仁民而爱物。"

13.45 Mencius said, "In regard to *inferior* creatures, the superior man is kind to them, but not loving. In regard to people generally, he is loving to them, but not affectionate. He is affectionate to his parents, and lovingly disposed to people *generally*. He is lovingly disposed to people *generally*, and kind to creatures."

13.46 孟子曰："知者无不知也，当务之为急；仁者无不爱也，急亲贤之为务。尧舜之知而不遍物，急先务也；尧舜之仁不遍爱人，急亲贤也。不能三年之丧，而缌、小功之察；放饭流歠，而问无齿决，是之谓不知务。"

13.46 Mencius said, "The wise embrace all knowledge, but they are most earnest about what is of the greatest importance. The benevolent embrace all in their love, but what they consider of the greatest importance is to cultivate an earnest affection for the virtuous. Even the wisdom of Yao and Shun did not extend to everything, but they attended earnestly to what was important.

Their benevolence did not show itself in acts of kindness to every man, but they earnestly cultivated an affection for the virtuous. Not to be able to keep the three years' mourning, and to be very particular about that of three months, or that of five months; to eat immoderately and swill down the soup, and at the same time to inquire about *the precept* not to tear the meat with the teeth; — such things show what I call an ignorance of what is most important."

14.1　孟子曰："不仁哉，梁惠王也！仁者以其所爱及其所不爱，不仁者以其所不爱及其所爱。"公孙丑问曰："何谓也？""梁惠王以土地之故，糜烂其民而战之。大败，将复之，恐不能胜，故驱其所爱子弟以殉之，是之谓以其所不爱及其所爱也。"

14.1　Mencius said, "The opposite indeed of benevolent was the king Hui of Liang! The benevolent, beginning with what they care for, proceed to what they do not care for. Those who are the opposite of benevolent, beginning with what they do not care for, proceed to what they care for." Gongsun Chou said, "What do you mean?" *Mencius answered*, "The king Hui of Liang, for the matter of territory, tore and destroyed his people, leading them to battle. Sustaining a great defeat, he would engage again, and afraid lest they should not be able to secure the victory, urged his son whom he loved till he sacrificed him with them. This is what I call — 'beginning with what they do not care for, and proceeding to what they care for.' "

14.2　孟子曰："春秋无义战。彼善于此，则有之矣。征者，上伐下也，敌国不相征也。"

14.2　Mencius said, "In the *Spring and Autumn* there are no righteous wars. Instances indeed there are of one war better than another. 'Correction' is when the supreme authority punishes its subjects by force of arms. Hostile states do not correct one another."

14.3   孟子曰："尽信《书》，则不如无《书》。吾于《武成》，取二三策而已矣。仁人无敌于天下，以至仁伐至不仁，而何其血之流杵也？"

14.3   Mencius said, "It would be better to be without the *Book of History* than to give entire credit to it. In the *Completion of the War*, I select two or three passages only, which I believe. The benevolent man has no enemy under Heaven. When *the prince*, the most benevolent, was engaged against him who was the most the opposite, how could the blood *of the people* have flowed till it floated the pestles of the mortars?"

14.4   孟子曰："有人曰：'我善为陈，我善为战。'大罪也。国君好仁，天下无敌焉。南面而征，北狄怨；东面而征，西夷怨。曰：'奚为后我？'武王之伐殷也，革车三百两，虎贲三千人。王曰：'无畏！宁尔也，非敌百姓也。'若崩厥角稽首。征之为言正也，各欲正己也，焉用战？"

14.4   Mencius said, "There are men who say — 'I am skilful at marshalling troops, I am skilful at conducting a battle!' — They are great criminals. If the sovereign of a state love benevolence, he will have no enemy in the empire. When *Tang* was executing his work of correction in the south, the rude tribes on the north murmured. When he was executing it in the east, the rude tribes on the west murmured. Their cry was — 'Why does he make us last?' When King Wu punished Yin, he had only three hundred chariots of war, and three thousand life-guards. The king said, 'Do not fear. Let me give you repose. I am no enemy to the people!' *On this*, they bowed their heads to the earth, like the horns of animals falling off. Imperial correction is but another word for rectifying. Each state wishing itself to be corrected, what need is there for fighting?"

14.5 孟子曰：“梓匠轮舆能与人规矩，不能使人巧。”

14.5 Mencius said, "A carpenter or a carriage-maker may give a man the circle and square, but cannot make him skilful *in the use of them*."

14.6 孟子曰：“舜之饭糗茹草也，若将终身焉；及其为天子也，被袗衣，鼓琴，二女果，若固有之。”

14.6 Mencius said, "Shun's manner of eating his parched grain and herbs was as if he were to be doing so all his life. When he became emperor, and had the embroidered robes to wear, the lute to play, and the two daughters *of Yao* to wait on him, he was as if those things belonged to him as a matter of course."

14.7 孟子曰：“吾今而后知杀人亲之重也：杀人之父，人亦杀其父；杀人之兄，人亦杀其兄。然则非自杀之也，一间耳。”

14.7   Mencius said, "From this time forth I know the heavy consequences of killing a man's near relations. When a man kills another's father, that other will kill his father; when a man kills another's elder brother, that other will kill his elder brother. So he does not himself indeed do the act, but there is only an interval *between him and it.*"

14.8   孟子曰："古之为关也，将以御暴；今之为关也，将以为暴。"

14.8   Mencius said, "Anciently the establishment of the frontier-gates was to guard against violence. Nowadays, it is to exercise violence."

14.9   孟子曰："身不行道，不行于妻子；使人不以道，不能行于妻子。"

14.9   Mencius said, "If a man himself do not walk in the *right* path, it will not be walked in *even* by his wife and children. If he do not order men according to the *right* way, he will not be able to get the obedience of *even* his wife and children."

14.10   孟子曰："周于利者凶年不能杀，周于德者邪世不能乱。"

14.10   Mencius said, "A bad year cannot prove the cause of death to him, whose stores of gain are large; an age of corruption cannot confound him whose equipment of virtue is complete."

14.11 孟子曰："好名之人，能让千乘之国，苟非其人，箪食豆羹见于色。"

14.11 Mencius said, "A man who loves fame may be able to decline a kingdom of a thousand chariots, but if he be not *really* the man *to do such a thing*, it will appear in his countenance, in the matter of a dish of rice or a platter of soup."

14.12 孟子曰："不信仁贤，则国空虚；无礼义，则上下乱；无政事，则财用不足。"

14.12 Mencius said, "If men of virtue and ability be not confided in, a state will become empty and void. Without the rules of propriety and distinctions of right, the high and the low will be thrown into confusion. Without *the great principles of* government and their various business, there will not be wealth sufficient for the expenditure."

14.13 孟子曰："不仁而得国者，有之矣；不仁而得天下者，未之有也。"

14.13 Mencius said, "There are instances of individuals without benevolence, who have got possession of a *single* state, but there has been no instance of the whole empire's being got possession of by one without benevolence."

14.14 孟子曰："民为贵，社稷次之，君为轻。是故得乎丘民而为天子，得乎天子为诸侯，得乎诸侯为大夫。诸侯危社稷，则变置。牺牲既成，粢盛既洁，祭祀以时，然而旱乾水溢，则变置社稷。"

14.14 Mencius said, "The people are the most important element *in a nation*; the spirits of the land and grain are the next; the sovereign is the lightest. Therefore to gain the peasantry is the way to become emperor; to gain the emperor is the way to become a prince of a state; to gain the prince of a state is the way to become a great officer. When a prince endangers the altars of the spirits of the land and grain, he is changed, and another appointed in his place. When the sacrificial victims have been perfect, the millet in its vessels all pure, and the sacrifices offered at their proper seasons, if yet there ensue drought, or the waters overflow, the spirits of the land and grain are changed, and others appointed in their place."

14.15 孟子曰："圣人，百世之师也，伯夷、柳下惠是也。故闻伯夷之风者，顽夫廉，懦夫有立志；闻柳下惠之风者，薄夫敦，鄙夫宽。奋乎百世之上，百世之下，闻者莫不兴起也。非圣人而能若是乎？而况于亲炙之者乎？"

14.15 Mencius said, "A sage is the teacher of a hundred generations: — this is true of Boyi and Hui of Liuxia. Therefore when men now hear the character of Boyi, the corrupt become pure, and the weak acquire determination. When they hear the character of Hui of Liuxia, the mean become generous, and the niggardly become liberal. *Those two* made themselves distinguished a hundred generations ago, and after a hundred generations, those who hear of them, are all aroused *in this manner.* Could such effects be produced by them, if they had not been sages? And how much more did they affect those who were in contiguity with them, and were warmed by them!"

14.16　孟子曰：“仁也者，人也。合而言之，道也。”

14.16　Mencius said, "Benevolence is *the distinguishing characteristic of* man. As embodied in man's conduct, it is called the path *of duty.*"

14.17　孟子曰：“孔子之去鲁，曰：‘迟迟吾行也，去父母国之道也。’去齐，接淅而行，去他国之道也。”

14.17　Mencius said, "When Confucius was leaving Lu, he said, 'I will set out by-and-by;' — this was the way for him to leave the state of his parents. When he was leaving Qi, he strained off with his hand the water in which his rice was being rinsed, *took the rice,* and went away; — this was the way for him to leave a strange state."

14.18　孟子曰：“君子之厄于陈蔡之间，无上下之交也。”

14.18　Mencius said, "The reason why the superior man was reduced to straits between Chen and Cai was because neither the princes *of the time* nor their ministers communicated with him."

14.19　貉稽曰：“稽大不理于口。”孟子曰：“无伤也。士憎兹多口。诗云：'忧心悄悄，愠于群小。'孔子也。'肆不殄厥愠，亦不殒厥问。'文王也。"

14.19　Mo Ji said, "Greatly am I from anything to depend upon from the mouths *of men*." Mencius observed, "There is no harm in that. Scholars are more exposed than others to suffer from the mouths *of men*. It is said, in the *Book of Poetry*, 'My heart is disquieted and grieved, I am hated by the crowd of mean creatures.' *This might have been said by* Confucius. And again, 'Though he did not remove their wrath, he did not let fall his own fame.' *This might be said of* King Wen."

14.20　孟子曰："贤者以其昭昭使人昭昭，今以其昏昏使人昭昭。"

14.20　Mencius said, "*Anciently*, men of virtue and talents by means of their own enlightenment made others enlightened. Nowadays, it is tried, *while they are themselves in darkness*, and by means of that darkness, to make others enlightened."

14.21　孟子谓高子曰："山径之蹊，间介然用之而成路；为间不用，则茅塞之矣。今茅塞子之心矣。"

14.21　Mencius said to the disciple Gao, "There are the foot-paths along the hills; — if suddenly they be used, they become roads; and if as suddenly they are not used, the wild grass fills them up. Now, the wild grass fills up your mind."

14.22 高子曰："禹之声尚文王之声。" 孟子曰："何以言之?"
曰："以追蠡。" 曰："是奚足哉? 城门之轨，两马之力与?"

14.22 The disciple Gao said, "The music of Yu was better than
that of King Wen." Mencius observed, "On what ground do you
say so?" and the other replied, "Because at the pivot the knob of
Yu's bells is nearly worn through." *Mencius* said, "How can that
be a sufficient proof? Are the ruts at the gate of a city made by a
single two-horsed chariot?"

14.23 齐饥。陈臻曰："国人皆以夫子将复为发棠,殆不可复。"
孟子曰："是为冯妇也。晋人有冯妇者，善搏虎，卒为善士。
则之野，有众逐虎。虎负嵎，莫之敢撄。望见冯妇，趋而迎之。
冯妇攘臂下车。众皆悦之，其为士者笑之。"

14.23 When Qi was suffering from famine, Chen Zhen said to
Mencius, "The people are all thinking that you, Master, will again
ask that the granary of Tang be opened for them. I apprehend you
will not do so a second time." *Mencius* said, "To do it would be
to act like Feng Fu. There was a man of that name in Jin, famous
for his skill in seizing tigers. Afterwards, he became a scholar of
reputation, and going once out to the wild country, he found the
people all in pursuit of a tiger. The tiger took refuge in a corner of
a hill, where no one dared to attack him, but when they saw Feng
Fu, they ran and met him. Feng Fu *immediately* bared his arms,
and descended from the carriage. The multitude were pleased
with him, but those who were scholars laughed at him."

14.24　孟子曰："口之于味也，目之于色也，耳之于声也，鼻
之于臭也，四肢之于安佚也，性也，有命焉，君子不谓性也。
仁之于父子也，义之于君臣也，礼之于宾主也，知之于贤者也，
圣人之于天道也，命也，有性焉，君子不谓命也。"

14.24　Mencius said, "For the mouth to desire *sweet* tastes, the
eye to desire *beautiful* colors, the ear to desire *pleasant* sounds,
the nose to desire *fragrant* odors, and the four limbs to desire ease
and rest; — these things are natural. But there is the appointment
of Heaven in connection with them, and the superior man does
not say *of his pursuit of them*, 'It is my nature.' *The exercise of* love
between father and son, *the observance of* righteousness between
sovereign and minister, the rules of ceremony between guest and
host, *the display* of knowledge in recognizing the talented, and
the *fulfilling* the heavenly course by the sage; — these are the
appointment of *Heaven*. But there is *an adaptation of our* nature
for them. The superior man does not say, *in reference to them*, 'It is
the appointment of Heaven.' "

14.25　浩生不害问曰："乐正子何人也？"孟子曰："善人也，
信人也。""何谓善？何谓信？"曰："可欲之谓善，有诸己之谓信，
充实之谓美，充实而有光辉之谓大，大而化之之谓圣，圣而不
可知之之谓神。乐正子，二之中，四之下也。"

14.25　Haosheng Buhai asked, saying, "What sort of man is
Yuezheng?" Mencius replied, "He is a good man, a real man."
"What do you mean by 'a good man', 'a real man'?" The reply was,

"A man who commands our liking, is what is called a good man. He whose *goodness* is part of himself, is what is called a real man. He whose *goodness* has been filled up, is what is called a beautiful man. He whose completed goodness is brightly displayed, is what is called a great man. When this great man exercises a transforming influence, he is what is called a sage. When the sage is beyond our knowledge, he is what is called a spirit-man. Yuezheng is between the two *first* characters, and below the four last."

14.26　孟子曰："逃墨必归于杨，逃杨必归于儒。归，斯受之而已矣。今之与杨、墨辩者，如追放豚，既入其苙，又从而招之。"

14.26　Mencius said, "Those who are fleeing from *the errors of* Mo naturally turn to Yang, and those who are fleeing from *the errors of* Yang naturally turn to orthodoxy. When they so turn, they should at once and simply be received. Those who nowadays dispute with the followers of Yang and Mo, do so as if they were pursuing a stray pig, the leg of which after they have got it to enter the pen, they proceed to tie."

14.27　孟子曰："有布缕之征，粟米之征，力役之征。君子用其一，缓其二。用其二而民有殍，用其三而父子离。"

14.27　Mencius said, "There are the exactions of hempen-cloth and silk, of grain, and of personal service. The prince requires but one of these *at once*, deferring the other two. If he require two of them *at once*, then the people die of hunger. If he require the three *at once*, then fathers and sons are separated."

14.28　孟子曰："诸侯之宝三：土地，人民，政事。宝珠玉者，殃必及身。"

14.28　Mencius said, "The precious things of a prince are three; — the territory, the people, the government and its business. If one value as most precious pearls and stones, calamity is sure to befall him."

14.29　盆成括仕于齐，孟子曰："死矣，盆成括！"盆成括见杀，门人问曰："夫子何以知其将见杀？"曰："其为人也小有才，未闻君子之大道也，则足以杀其躯而已矣。"

14.29　Pencheng Kuo having obtained an official situation in Qi, Mencius said, "He is a dead man — Pencheng Kuo!" Pencheng Kuo being put to death, the disciples asked, saying, "How did you know, Master, that he would meet with death?" Mencius replied, "He was a man who had a little ability, but had not learned the great doctrines of the superior man. — He was just qualified to bring death upon himself, but for nothing more."

14.30　孟子之滕，馆于上宫。有业屦于牖上，馆人求之弗得。或问之曰："若是乎从者之廋也？"曰："子以是为窃屦来与？"曰："殆非也。夫子之设科也，往者不追，来者不拒。苟以是心至，斯受之而已矣。"

14.30　When Mencius went to Teng, he was lodged in the upper palace. A sandal in the process of making had been placed there in a window, and when the keeper of the place *came to* look for it, he could not find it. *On this*, some one asked *Mencius*, saying, "Is it thus that your followers pilfer?" Mencius replied, "Do you think that they came here to pilfer the sandal?" The man said, "I apprehend not. But you, Master, having arranged to give lessons, do not go back to inquire into the past, and you do not reject those who come to you. If they come with the mind to learn, you receive them without any more to do."

14.31　孟子曰："人皆有所不忍，达之于其所忍，仁也；人皆有所不为，达之于其所为，义也。人能充无欲害人之心，而仁不可胜用也；人能充无穿逾之心，而义不可胜用也；人能充无受尔汝之实，无所往而不为义也。士未可以言而言，是以言餂之也；可以言而不言，是以不言餂之也，是皆穿逾之类也。"

14.31　Mencius said, "All men have some things which they cannot bear; — extend that feeling to what they can bear, and benevolence will be the result. All men have some things which they will not do; — extend that feeling to the things which they do, and righteousness will be the result. If a man can give full development to the feeling which makes him shrink from injuring others, his benevolence will be more than can be called into practice. If he can give full development to the feeling which refuses to break through, or jump over, *a wall*, his righteousness will be more than can be called into practice. If he can give full development to the real feeling of dislike with which he receives the salutation, 'Thou,' 'Thou,' he will act righteously in all places and circumstances. When a scholar speaks what he ought not to speak, by *guile of* speech seeking to gain some end; and when he does not speak what he ought to speak, by *guile of* silence seeking to gain some end; — both these cases are of a piece with breaking through a *neighbor's wall*."

14.32　孟子曰："言近而指远者，善言也；守约而施博者，善道也。君子之言也，不下带而道存焉；君子之守，修其身而天下平。人病舍其田而芸人之田——所求于人者重，而所以自任者轻。"

14.32　Mencius said, "Words which are simple, while their meaning is far-reaching, are good words. Principles which, as held, are compendious, while their application is extensive, are good principles. The words of the superior man do not go below the girdle, but *great* principles are contained in them. The principle which the superior man holds is that of personal cultivation, but the empire is thereby tranquillized. The disease of men is this; — that they neglect their own fields, and go to weed the fields of others, and that what they require from others is great, while what they lay upon themselves is light."

14.33　孟子曰："尧舜，性者也；汤武，反之也。动容周旋中礼者，盛德之至也。哭死而哀，非为生者也。经德不回，非以干禄也。言语必信，非以正行也。君子行法，以俟命而已矣。"

14.33 Mencius said, "Yao and Shun were what they were by nature; Tang and Wu were so by returning *to natural virtue*. When all the movements, in the countenance and every turn of *the body*, are exactly what is proper, that shows the extreme degree of the complete virtue. Weeping for the dead should be from *real* sorrow, and not because of the living. The regular path of virtue is to be pursued without any bend, and from no view to emolument. The words should all be necessarily sincere, not with any desire to do what is right. The superior man performs the law *of right*, in order that he may wait simply for what has been appointed."

14.34 孟子曰："说大人，则藐之，勿视其巍巍然。堂高数仞，榱题数尺，我得志，弗为也。食前方丈，侍妾数百人，我得志，弗为也。般乐饮酒，驱骋田猎，后车千乘，我得志，弗为也。在彼者，皆我所不为也；在我者，皆古之制也，吾何畏彼哉？"

14.34 Mencius said, "Those who give counsel to the great should despise them, and not look at their pomp and display. Halls several times eight cubits high, with beams projecting several cubits; — these, if my wishes were to be realized, I would not have. Food spread before me over ten cubits square, and attendant girls to the amount of hundreds; — these, though my wishes were realized, I would not have. Pleasure and wine, and the dash of hunting, with thousands of chariots following after me; — these, though my wishes were realized, I would not have.

What they esteem are what I would have nothing to do with; what I esteem are the rules of the ancients — Why should I stand in awe of them?"

14.35　孟子曰："养心莫善于寡欲。其为人也寡欲，虽有不存焉者，寡矣；其为人也多欲，虽有存焉者，寡矣。"

14.35　Mencius said, "To nourish the mind there is nothing better than to make the desires few. Here is a man whose desires are few — in some things he may not be able to keep his heart, but they will be few. Here is a man whose desires are many: — in some things he may be able to keep his heart, but they will be few."

14.36　曾皙嗜羊枣，而曾子不忍食羊枣。公孙丑问曰："脍炙与羊枣孰美？"孟子曰："脍炙哉。"公孙丑曰："然则曾子何为食脍炙而不食羊枣？"曰："脍炙所同也，羊枣所独也。讳名不讳姓，姓所同也，名所独也。"

14.36　Mencius said, "Zeng Zhe was fond of sheep-dates, and *his son*, the philosopher Zeng, could not bear to eat sheep-dates." Gongsun Chou asked, saying, "Which is best, — minced meat and roasted meat, or sheep-dates?" Mencius said, "Minced and roasted meat, to be sure." Gongsun Chou went on, "Then why did the philosopher Zeng eat minced and roasted meat, while he would not eat sheep-dates?" Mencius answered, "For minced and roasted meat there is a common liking, while that for sheep-dates was peculiar. We avoid the name, but do not avoid the surname.

The surname is common; the name is peculiar."

14.37　万章问曰："孔子在陈曰：'盍归乎来！吾党之士狂简，进取，不忘其初。'孔子在陈，何思鲁之狂士？"孟子曰："孔子'不得中道而与之，必也狂狷乎！狂者进取，狷者有所不为也'。孔子岂不欲中道哉？不可必得，故思其次也。""敢问何如斯可谓狂矣？"曰："如琴张、曾晳、牧皮者，孔子之所谓狂矣。""何以谓之狂也？"曰："其志嘐嘐然，曰'古之人，古之人。'夷考其行，而不掩焉者也。狂者又不可得，欲得不屑不洁之士而与之，是獧也，是又其次也。孔子曰：'过我门而不入我室，我不憾焉者，其惟乡原乎！乡原，德之贼也。'"曰："何如斯可谓之乡原矣？"曰："'何以是嘐嘐也？言不顾行，行不顾言，则曰，古之人，古之人。行何为踽踽凉凉？生斯世也，为斯世也，善斯可矣。'阉然媚于世也者，是乡原也。"万子曰："一乡皆称原人焉，无所往而不为原人，孔子以为德之贼，何哉？"曰："非之无举也，刺之无刺也，同乎流俗，合乎污世，居之似忠信，行之似廉洁，众皆悦之，自以为是，而不可与入尧舜之道，故曰'德之贼'也。孔子曰：'恶似而非者：恶莠，恐其乱苗也；恶佞，恐其乱义也；恶利口，恐其乱信也。恶郑声，恐其乱乐也。恶紫，恐其乱朱也；恶乡原，恐其乱德也。'君子反经而已矣。经正，则庶民兴，庶民兴，斯无邪慝矣。"

14.37　Wan Zhang asked, saying, "Confucius when he was

in Chen, said, 'Let me return. The scholars of my school are ambitious but hasty. They are for advancing and seizing their object, but cannot forget their early ways.' Why did Confucius, when he was in Chen think of the ambitious scholars of Lu?" Mencius replied, "Confucius not getting men pursuing the true medium, to whom he might communicate *his instructions*, determined to take the ardent and the cautiously-decided. The ardent would advance to seize their object; the cautiously-decided would keep themselves from certain things. It is not to be thought that Confucius did not wish to get men pursuing the true medium but being unable to assure himself of finding such, he therefore thought of the next class." "I venture to ask what sort of men they were who could be styled 'The ambitious?' " "Such," replied Mencius, "as Qin Zhang, Zeng Zhe, and Mu Pi, were those whom Confucius styled 'ambitious'." "Why were they styled 'ambitious'?" The reply was, "Their aim led them to talk magniloquently, saying, 'The ancients! The ancients!' But their actions, compared with *their words*, did not come up to them. When he found also that he could not get such as were thus ambitious, he wanted to get scholars who would consider anything impure as beneath them. Those were the cautiously-decided, — a class next to the former. Confucius said, 'They are only your good careful people of the villages at whom I feel no indignation, when they pass my door without entering my house.' Your good careful people of the villages are the thieves of virtue." *Zhang pursued his questioning*, "What sort of people were they who could be styled 'your good careful people of the villages'?" *Mencius replied*, "They are those who say, 'Why are they so magniloquent? Their words have not respect to their actions, and their actions have not respect to their words, but they say, — *The ancients! The ancients!* Why do they act so peculiarly, and are so cold and distant? Born in this age, we should be of this age, to be good is all that is needed.' Eunuchlike, flattering their generation; — such are your good careful men of the villages." Wan Zhang said, "Their whole village styles those men good and careful. In all their conduct they are so. How was it that Confucius considered them the thieves of virtue?" Mencius replied, "If you would blame them, you find nothing to allege. If you would criticize them, you have nothing to criticize. They agree with the current customs. They consent with an impure age. Their principles have a semblance of right-heartedness and truth. Their conduct has a semblance of disinterestedness and purity. All men are pleased with them, and they think themselves right, so that it is impossible to proceed with them to the principles of Yao and Shun. On this account they are called 'the thieves of virtue'. Confucius said, 'I hate a semblance which is not the reality. I hate the darnel, lest it be confounded with the corn. I hate glib-tonguedness, lest it be confounded with righteousness. I hate sharpness of tongue, lest it be confounded with sincerity. I hate the music of Zheng, lest it be confounded with *the true* music. I hate the reddish blue, lest it be confounded with vermilion. I hate your good careful men of the villages, lest they be confounded with the *truly* virtuous.' The superior man seeks simply to bring back the unchanging standard, and that being rectified, the masses are roused to virtue. When they are so aroused, forthwith perversities and glossed wickedness disappear."

14.38　孟子曰：“由尧舜至于汤，五百有馀岁；若禹、皋陶，则见而知之；若汤，则闻而知之。由汤至于文王，五百有馀岁；若伊尹、莱朱，则见而知之；若文王，则闻而知之。由文王至于孔子，五百有馀岁；若太公望、散宜生则见而知之；若孔子，则闻而知之。由孔子而来至于今，百有馀岁，去圣人之世若此其未远也，近圣人之居若此其甚也，然而无有乎尔，则亦无有乎尔。”

14.38　Mencius said, "From Yao and Shun down to Tang were five hundred years and more. As to Yu and Gaoyao, they saw *those earliest sages* and *so* knew their doctrines, while Tang heard their doctrines *as transmitted*, and *so* knew them. From Tang to King Wen were five hundred years and more. As to Yi Yin and Lai Zhu, they saw *Tang* and knew his doctrines, while King Wen heard them *as transmitted*, and so knew them. From King Wen to Confucius were five hundred years and more. As to Taigong Wang and Sanyi Sheng, they saw *Wen*, and so knew his doctrines, while Confucius heard them *as transmitted*, and so knew them. From Confucius downwards until now, there are *only* one hundred years and *somewhat* more. The distance in time from the sage is so far from being remote, and so very near at hand was the sage's residence. In these circumstances, is there no one *to transmit his doctrines*? Yea, is there no one *to do so*?"

培根论说文集 Essays   培根

乌托邦 Utopia   托马斯·莫尔

忏悔录 The Confessions   卢梭

梦的解析 Interpretation of Dreams   弗洛伊德

人类的故事 The Story of Mankind   房龙

宽容 Tolerance   房龙

理想国 Republic   柏拉图

马可·波罗游记 The Travels of Marco Polo   马可·波罗

君主论 The Prince   马基雅维利

菊与刀 The Chrysanthemum and the Sword:
           Patterns of Japanese Culture   鲁思·贝内迪克特

社会契约论 The Social Contract   卢梭

新工具 The New Organon   培根

马克·吐温自传 The Autobiography of Mark Twain   马克·吐温

沉思录 The Meditations of Marcus Aurelius   马库斯·奥勒留

富兰克林自传 The Autobiography of Benjamin Franklin 本杰明·富兰克林

林肯传 The Unknown Lincoln   戴尔·卡耐基

太平洋的故事 The Story of the Pacific   房龙

房龙地理 Van Loon's Geography   房龙

中国的文艺复兴 The Chinese Renaissance   胡适

中国人的精神 The Spirit of the Chinese People   辜鸿铭

论语 The Analects   孔子

道德经 Tao Te Ching   老子

孙子兵法 The Art of War   孙子

孟子 The Works of Mencius   孟子

中庸 The Doctrine of the Mean   子思

大学 The Great Learning   曾子

诗经 The She King